The EPISTLE to the HEBREWS

A Commentary

Homer A. Kent

BAKER BOOK HOUSE
Grand Rapids, Michigan

ILLUSTRATION CREDITS

Dr. John J. Davis, 115, 236 (top)
Ewing Galloway, 99
Dr. Homer A. Kent, 183, 284
Levant Photo Service, 61, 85, 161, 227, 245
The Matson Photo Service, 69, 125, 149, 270
The Metropolitan Museum of Art, 236 (bottom)
The Oriental Institute, University of Chicago, 238
Dr. John C. Trever, 35
The University of Michigan Library, 20

To BEVERLY
my loyal and loving companion
who fulfils her role of wife and mother
with grace and distinction

Acknowledgments

The assistance of many was utilized in the preparation of this volume. In particular the author expresses his appreciation to the following individuals:

Dr. John C. Whitcomb, Jr., who read the manuscript and made valuable suggestions regarding content and style.

Dr. John J. Davis, who graciously granted to the author the use of his manuscript *Moses and the Gods of Egypt* prior to its publication; who also provided certain photographs from his personal files, and made many helpful suggestions.

Mr. Robert D. Ibach, Jr., who as library assistant for Grace Theological Seminary provided much help in locating source materials, and who prepared the drawing of the tabernacle floor plan.

The students at Grace Theological Seminary, who have for many years studied the Epistle to the Hebrews with the author of this volume, and have been of incalculable help in refining the interpretation contained here.

Transliteration Table

Whenever possible, Hebrew and Greek words have been transliterated according to the following form:

Greek	Hebrew Consonants	Hebrew Vocalization
α — a	א — '	◌ָ — ā
ε — e	ב — b, b̲	◌ַ — a
η — ē	ג — g, g̲	◌ֵ — e
ο — o	ד — d, d̲	◌ֶ — ē
ω — ō	ה — h	◌ֵי — ê
ζ — z	ו — w	◌ִ — i
θ — th	ז — z	◌ִי — î
ξ — x	ח — ḥ	◌ֳ — ŏ
υ — u	ט — ṭ	◌ֹ — o
φ — ph	י — y	◌ֹו — û
χ — ch	כ — k, k̲	◌ֻ — u
ψ — ps	ל — l	◌ְ — ( )e
' — h	מ — m	
ῥ — rh	נ — n	
ᾳ — āi	ס — s	
ῃ — ēi	ע — '	
ῳ — ōi	פ — p, p̲	
γγ — ng	צ — ṣ	
γκ — nk	ק — q	
γξ — nx	ר — r	
γχ — nch	שׂ — ś	
	שׁ — s	
	ת — t, t̲	

8

Preface

The Epistle to the Hebrews holds a special place in the minds of Bible students because of its many distinctive features. The identity of its author has been a puzzle from very early times even though he made no effort to hide himself from his readers, for he asked them to pray for him and for his prospective visit to them (13:18, 19). The location of the first readers, the date of the writing, and the particular circumstances which prompted the letter are all greater problems for the serious student than is the case for most other New Testament books.

This remarkable letter contains the only full discussion in the New Testament of Christ as the believers' high priest. Melchizedek is mentioned in only two exceedingly brief passages in the Old Testament, but is made a key point in the argument in Hebrews, forming the basis for a discussion extending over three chapters. The masterful and systematic demonstration of Christ's superiorities is unmatched by any other New Testament writer; and the relentless logic by which the argument is pursued reveals the author's ordered mind, whose grasp of the very essence of Christian truth leaves every Bible student in his debt. The application of the Old Testament to the points at issue is striking, and some of the typological insights are most remarkable. In addition, the sober warnings that appear at various places throughout the epistle are severe enough to tax the best of interpreters.

It is strange, therefore, that knowledge of the message of Hebrews is so little understood. Too many Christians know only the "heroes of faith" passage (chap. 11) and a few other easily memorized texts (e.g., 4:16; 13:8). The grand argument of the book and its stirring challenge to "go out to him outside the camp" need to be recognized and heeded.

It is my sincere hope that this study of the Epistle to the Hebrews may assist the reader to a clearer understanding of its important issues. The use of a literal translation at the beginning of each discussion is intended as an aid in arriving at the author's thought. By the use of such translation rather than a more popular paraphrase, I have endeavored to keep interpretive elements in that portion to a minimum, reserving interpretation for the commentary.

If God will be pleased to use this effort to deepen the understanding of the readers and increase their faith in the Christ who has "offered one sacrifice for sins for ever" (10:12) and who now lives "to make intercession for them" (7:25), my labors will be amply repaid.

Homer A. Kent
Winona Lake, Indiana

Contents

Illustrations

Introduction

The early history of Jewish Christianity holds a special fascination for Bible students. Part of this fascination must be attributed to the historical fact that the first Christians were Jewish Christians. Hence to know the development of the Christian movement within its Jewish constituency is to come to grips with the very beginnings of the Christian church. The opening chapters of Acts record this dramatic story for Palestine. The Epistle of James reflects the way that the gospel was understood and applied by the churches in the Jewish Diaspora.

No small part of the interest that centers upon early Jewish Christianity is caused, however, by the meagerness of our knowledge, particularly as it concerns Jewish Christians during the first century. The Book of Acts devotes most of its latter portion to a delineation of Paul's missionary endeavors as the apostle to the uncircumcised. Only a few tantalizing glimpses are given of the Christian attitudes of Jewish churches (Acts 15:1-29; 21:17-26). Although the New Testament contains many epistles written to local Gentile churches (and from them much is revealed about the strengths, the weaknesses, and the problems which characterized them), not one letter can be confidently assigned to a Jewish congregation in Palestine. Even the Epistles of James and Peter[1] are not addressed to one congregation, but to Jewish readers over a wide area of the Diaspora. Hence any light that can be shed upon the nature and character of first century Jewish churches, especially if

---

1. The Petrine epistles are today less commonly regarded as Hebrew-Christian than formerly, although there are still good reasons for assigning them to a Jewish audience, particularly in the case of I Peter.

it is specific enough to depict an actual congregation, its thinking and its problems, is indeed to be welcomed.

Jewish Christianity is significant also because of the very nature of the Christian movement. Jesus was the Messiah foretold by Old Testament prophets, the son of David whose coming fulfilled specific promises made to that dynastic head. He came "not to destroy [the law], but to fulfil" (Matt. 5:17). He taught that His death was to serve as a ransom, fulfilling the typology of the Old Testament sacrificial system (Matt. 20:28). Christianity was thus deeply rooted in Old Testament revelation, and its first followers so understood it. On the Day of Pentecost a few weeks after Christ's resurrection, Peter explained the phenomena which the believers had just experienced by saying, "This is that which was spoken by the prophet Joel" (Acts 2:16). Yet it was not many years until the whole character of the Christian movement took on a different coloration. The influx of Gentiles into the church, a circumstance which began in earnest with Paul's missionary journeys, eventually transformed an essentially Jewish church into one in which Jews were an ever decreasing segment.

It is scarcely conceivable that such a transformation could be effected without considerable tension. Evidences of this tension are reflected in Acts 11, 15, Galatians 2, and other passages. But there are many questions that still pique our curiosity, especially those which have to do with Jewish Christian thinking and attitudes. Among the problems with which Jewish Christians must have grappled, the following were surely included: (1) How Christ was to be understood in relation to the teaching of many Old Testament passages. (2) The religious, cultural, and ancestral attractions of the Old Testament system, particularly the visible features of that worship in contrast to the largely spiritual nature of Christian worship. (3) The relationship of the Christian movement to the new covenant prophesied by Jeremiah. (4) The persecution from their own Jewish brethren, and the temptation to avoid it by abandoning the Christian faith. (5) The efficacy of Old Testament sacrifices. (6) The relation of Gentile converts to Jewish religious practices. (7) The relation of Jewish Christians to Gentiles socially.

The Epistle to the Hebrews presents priceless information on many of these problems. Its Jewish flavor is obvious to all but a few. Its early date is well attested. And the grandeur of its style, as well as its message, has made it one of the most sparkling gems of the New

Testament canon. It is surprising, therefore, to realize that knowledge of some of the basic features of this epistle is mystifyingly absent. The author is unknown. The original readers can no longer be settled upon with certainty. A brief look at these matters is therefore in order.

CANONICITY

In the earliest extant Christian letter outside the New Testament, the First Epistle of Clement of Rome, there are clear references to the Epistle to the Hebrews. To take just one example, in chapter 36, after referring to "Jesus Christ, the high priest of our offerings," Clement proceeds to quote Hebrews 1:3, 4, 7, 5, and 13.[2] Here is unmistakable evidence from Rome in the last decade of the first century pointing to the honored use of this epistle by Christians in the West. Strange as it may seem, the Western church, which was the first (apparently) to have the epistle, was the last to give general recognition to its canonicity.

Other early writers who knew Hebrews included Polycarp,[3] Justin Martyr,[4] Theophilus,[5] Pantaenus and Clement of Alexandria,[6] and Origen.[7] Eusebius (ca. 260-340), whose *Ecclesiastical History* is the source of much of our knowledge of the opening centuries of the Christian era, listed Hebrews among the acknowledged epistles of Paul as the prevailing view of the church, even though he explained that some rejected it from the canon on the ground that the church at Rome did not think it was by Paul.[8] It did not appear in the Muratorian Canon, although the fragmentary character of this late second century document makes the omission difficult to evaluate. In the third century Papyrus 46, Hebrews appears among the Pauline epistles after Romans. Athanasius of Alexandria (298-373) applied the term *canonical* to a list

---

2. "The First Epistle of Clement to the Corinthians," in *The Apostolic Fathers*, I. 71, trans. A. Kirsopp Lake.

3. "Polycarp to the Philippians" (chap. 12), in *The Apostolic Fathers*, p. 299.

4. Saint Justin Martyr "First Apology" (chaps. 12, 63), in *The Fathers of the Church*, VI.

5. Alexander Roberts and James Donaldson (eds.), *The Ante-Nicene Fathers*, II, 107.

6. Eusebius *Ecclesiastical History* 6. 14, trans. Roy J. Deferrari, p. 26.

7. Eusebius 6. 25, p. 50.

8. Eusebius 3. 3, p. 140.

issued in 367 coinciding exactly with our twenty-seven books, thus including Hebrews as fully recognized.[9] Augustine in North Africa (354-430) accepted Hebrews as canonical,[10] as did Jerome (346-420).[11]

The Third Council of Carthage (A.D. 397) provided the first official decision on the limits of the canon, although of course it merely ratified prevailing opinion. Its listing was the same as our twenty-seven books. It mentions "thirteen epistles of the Apostle Paul" and then adds "one Epistle of the same writer to the Hebrews."[12] The Council of Hippo (A.D. 419, also called by some the Sixth Council of Carthage) lists the same twenty-seven books, but merely says "fourteen Epistles of Paul."[13]

In summary, the canonicity of Hebrews was recognized from the earliest times, even though some especially in the West questioned Pauline authorship.[14] Alexandrine tradition, at least as early as Pantaenus and Clement, accepted Hebrews as canonical on the assumption that Paul wrote it.[15] In the Greek and Syrian church Hebrews was accepted as a canonical epistle of Paul since at least the third century.[16] By the fourth century, the West as well added its assent to the consensus, as reflected by the statements and practice of such leaders as Augustine and Jerome.

9. Archibald Robertson (ed.), "Select Writings and Letters of Athanasius," in Nicene and Post-Nicene Fathers, IV, 552.

10. Philip Schaff (ed.), "St. Augustine's Christian Doctrine," in Nicene and Post-Nicene Fathers, II, 538, 539.

11. W. H. Fremantle (ed.), "The Principal Works of Jerome," in Nicene and Post-Nicene Fathers, VI, 101, 102. The hesitancy expressed regarding Hebrews is due to the question of authorship, not canonicity.

12. Charles Joseph Hefele, A History of the Councils of the Church, II, 36. These canons were actually first passed at the previous council at Hippo in 393, but those records have been lost. They were renewed at Carthage in 397.

13. B. F. Westcott, A General Survey of the History of the Canon of the New Testament, p. 437, fn. 9.

14. Roy J. Deferrari, translator of the Roman Catholic edition of Eusebius' Ecclesiastical History, makes this observation: "The canonicity of this Epistle has never been questioned, but its authorship has been disputed from the early Fathers to our own day." The Fathers of the Church: Eusebius Pamphili, Ecclesiastical History, Books 1-5, p. 140, fn.

15. Eusebius 6. 14.

16. Paul Feine, Johannes Behm, and Werner G. Kümmel, Introduction to the New Testament, trans. A. J. Mattill, Jr., p. 275.

AUTHORSHIP

The search for the author of Hebrews has been going on for centuries, and is no nearer solution than when it began. There is no scarcity of candidates, but conclusive evidence for any one candidate is lacking, and problems exist no matter who is suggested. No name is attached to the epistle, nor are any recipients greeted at the outset, even though the letter was written to a specific group of readers. The most plausible suggestions are listed below.

Paul

By far the most prominent candidate is the apostle Paul. In ancient times it was the belief that Paul was the author which caused its early acceptance in the Eastern portion of the church. In modern times, the editors of the Scofield Reference Bible gave Hebrews the heading "The Epistle of Paul the Apostle to the Hebrews,"[17] and a similar caption occurs in other English Bibles.

The earliest reference to Paul as the author is found in the writings of Clement of Alexandria (ca. 150-215). Eusebius says of him:

> And he says that the Epistle to the Hebrews is Paul's but that it was written for Hebrews in the Hebrew language, and that Luke, after carefully translating it, published it for the Greeks, and that for this reason the same complexion is found in the expression of this Epistle and the Acts; but that "Paul an Apostle" was naturally not prefixed. "For," he says, "when writing to Hebrews who had taken a prejudice against him and were suspicious of him, he wisely did not repel them at the beginning by placing his name [there]."[18]

Origen of Alexandria (ca. 185-253) was also aware of difference of opinion regarding the authorship of Hebrews. He wrote:

> The account that has reached us from some is that Clement, who was Bishop of the Romans, wrote the Epistle; from others, that Luke, who wrote the Gospel and the Acts, is the author.[19]

---

17. The Scofield Reference Bible, ed. C. I. Scofield, p. 1291. This ascription of authorship to Paul has been removed in the New Scofield Reference Bible, p. 1311.
18. Eusebius 6. 14.
19. Eusebius 6. 25.

Origen himself was cognizant of certain stylistic differences in Hebrews as compared to the accepted Pauline epistles, even while recognizing that the content was entirely consistent with Paul. His comment was:

> That the character of the diction of the Epistle entitled "To the Hebrews" does not possess the Apostle's rudeness of speech, who acknowledged that he was rude in speech, that is, in style, but the Epistle is better Greek in the composition of its diction, as anyone who knows how to distinguish differences of phraseology would admit. And yet again, that the thoughts of the Epistle are admirable, this also anyone would agree to be true who gives attention to reading the text of the Apostles.[20]

His final conclusion on the matter was:

> But I would say, if giving my opinion, that the thoughts are those of the Apostle, but the phraseology and the composition are those of someone who recalled to mind the teachings of the Apostle and who, as it were, had made notes on what was said by the teacher. If any church, then, holds this Epistle to be Paul's let it be commended for this, for not without reason have the men of old handed it down as Paul's. Who the author of the Epistle is God truly knows. . . .[21]

In addition to the inconclusive testimony of early history, there are internal considerations that bear upon the problem of authorship. In favor of Paul as the author is the characteristic closing of the epistle (13:25; cf. II Thess. 3:17, 18), the association with "brother Timothy" (13:23), the general pattern of the letter with its doctrinal portion first followed by exhortations to duty, and the occurrence of certain distinctively Pauline concepts in the letter.[22] The reference to Italy can be understood from a Pauline viewpoint (13:24). A statement of Peter has been interpreted to mean that Paul had written a letter to the Jews of the Diaspora, and this has been urged as a reference to Hebrews (II Peter 3:15, 16; I Peter 1:1; II Peter 3:1). It must be admitted, however, that these factors, although consistent with Paul's authorship, are by no means sufficient to settle the case for Paul.[23]

---

20. Eusebius 6. 25.

21. Eusebius 6. 25.

22. For example, the use of "milk" in a somewhat disparaging way in Hebrews 5:12-14 is similar to Paul's usage in I Corinthians 3:2, but different from I Peter 2:2.

23. Although the modern trend is clearly to deny authorship to Paul, some contemporary writers do favor Paul, among them William Leonard, *The Authorship of the Epistle to the Hebrews;* Herman A. Hoyt, *The Epistle to the Hebrews;* Arthur W. Pink, *An Exposition of Hebrews.*

Certain problems have also been pointed out with the traditional identification. No name is given in the epistle, a feature contrary to Paul's otherwise invariable custom. The writer places himself among those to whom the message of Christ was confirmed by others (2:3), whereas Paul always insisted that he received his gospel not from men (Gal. 1:12). This objection is not insuperable (see commentary section), and did not seem to be significant to the early Fathers; but it is considered serious by many. The style of writing, as well as the author's preference for the Septuagint, differs somewhat from that of Paul, whose writing was often more bold than polished and whose use of the Septuagint was not as consistent as is found in Hebrews.

Barnabas

The suggestion of Barnabas was made first (in our literature) by Tertullian of Carthage (ca. 150-222),[24] and is favored by others in recent times.[25] Among the reasons supporting this identification are the following: (1) As a Levite Barnabas would have had a more-than-passing interest in Jewish ritual and would have been intimately acquainted with its procedures. (2) There may be a play on the expression "word of encouragement" (13:22) and the name given to Barnabas, "son of encouragement" (Acts 4:36). (3) As a Jew from Cyprus, he possibly had close contact with Alexandrian or at least Hellenistic thought, such as is reflected in the typology of the epistle and certain philosophical concepts. (4) Barnabas was converted shortly after Pentecost and could have been influenced by Stephen's teaching, reflections of which may appear in the epistle. (5) Barnabas acted as the mediator between Jewish Christians and Paul in Acts 9, and could be understood as doing the same in this epistle where Pauline concepts are being explained to Jewish believers.

Again, however, we confront a situation in which Barnabas could conceivably fit, but is by no means proved to have been the only one who qualifies. The ritual described in Hebrews was not primarily that of the temple but of the tabernacle. And surely there were other Chris-

---

24. Tertullian "On Modesty" (chap. 20), Alexander Roberts and James Donaldson, eds., IV, 97.

25. J. Vernon Bartlet, "Barnabas and His Genuine Epistle," in *The Expositor,* ed. W. Robertson Nicoll, Sixth series V, 421-427.

ΚΑΙ ΚΟΥΑΡΤΟΣ Ο ΑΔΕΛΦΟΣ

ΠΡΟΣ ΕΒΡΑΙΟΥΣ

ΠΟΛΥ ΜΕΡΩΣ ΚΑΙ ΠΟΛΥΤΡΟΠΩΣ
ΠΑΛΑΙ Ο ΘΣ ΛΑΛΗΣΑΣ ΤΟΙΣ ΠΑΤΡΑΣΙΝ ΗΜΩΝ ΕΝ
ΤΟΙΣ ΠΡΟΦΗΤΑΙΣ ΕΠ ΕΣΧΑΤΟΥ ΤΩΝ ΗΜΕ
ΡΩΝ ΤΟΥΤΩΝ ΕΛΑΛΗΣΕΝ ΗΜΕΙΝ ΕΝ
ΥΙΩ ΟΝ ΕΘΗΚΕΝ ΚΛΗΡΟΝΟΜΟΝ ΠΑΝΤΩ
ΔΙ ΟΥ ΕΠΟΙΗΣΕΝ ΤΟΥΣ ΑΙΩΝΑΣ ΟΣ ΩΝ
ΑΠΑΥΓΑΣΜΑ ΤΗΣ ΔΟΞΗΣ ΚΑΙ ΧΑΡΑ
ΚΤΗΡ ΤΗΣ ΥΠΟΣΤΑΣΕΩΣ ΑΥΤΟΥ ΦΕΡΩΝ ΤΕ
ΤΑ ΠΑΝΤΑ ΤΩ ΡΗΜΑΤΙ ΤΗΣ ΔΥΝΑΜΕΩΣ
ΔΙ ΑΥΤΟΥ ΚΑΘΑΡΙΣΜΟΝ ΤΩΝ ΑΜΑΡΤΙΩ
ΠΟΙΗΣΑΜΕΝΟΣ ΕΚΑΘΙΣΕΝ ΕΝ ΔΕΞΙΑ ΤΗΣ
ΜΕΓΑΛΩΣΥΝΗΣ ΕΝ ΥΨΗΛΟΙΣ ΤΟΣΟΥΤΩΝ
ΚΡΙΤΤΩΝ ΤΕΝΟΜΕΝΟΣ ΤΩΝ ΑΓΓΕΛΩΝ ΟΣ
ΩΙ ΔΙΑΦΟΡΩΤΕΡΟΝ ΠΑΡ ΑΥΤΟΥΣ ΚΕΚΛΗ
ΡΟΝΟΜΗΚΕΝ ΟΝΟΜΑ ΤΙΝΙ ΓΑΡ ΕΙΠΕΝ
ΠΟΤΕ ΤΩΝ ΑΓΓΕΛΩΝ ΥΙΟΣ ΜΟΥ ΕΙ ΣΥ
ΕΓΩ ΣΗΜΕΡΟΝ ΓΕΓΕΝΝΗΚΑ ΣΕ ΚΑΙ ΠΑΛΙ
ΕΓΩ ΕΣΟΜΑΙ ΑΥΤΩ ΕΙΣ ΠΑΤΕΡΑ Κ[
ΤΑΙ ΜΟΙ ΕΙΣ ΥΝ ΟΤΑΝ ΔΕ ΠΑ[
ΤΟΝ ΠΡΩΤΟΤΟΚΟΝ ΕΙΣ ΤΑΙ ΤΗΝ ΟΙΚΟΥ
[ ]Ν ΚΑΙ ΠΡΟΣΚΥΝΗΣ[

tians who also shared Stephen's and Paul's viewpoints and would have been capable of writing them. The fact that the name of the prominent Barnabas should have been so thoroughly lost from an epistle he actually wrote (when it was falsely attached to an apocryphal one) also argues against assigning the authorship to him.

Apollos

The name of Apollos, commonly suggested as originating with Luther, is supported by many since his time.[26] Reasons given usually include the following: (1) Apollos was acquainted with Paul, and would have been familiar with Pauline concepts. (2) He was from Alexandria, thus accounting for some of the philosophical overtones of the epistle, as well as for the preference for the Septuagint. (3) He was thoroughly versed in the Old Testament, as the author of Hebrews obviously was. (4) He had contacts with Timothy through the church at Corinth. (5) His eloquence may be reflected in the attractive presentation of the material in the epistle.

The greatest weakness of this hypothesis is its complete lack of any early historical testimony. It is surprising that there is no hint from Alexandria, a great center of Christian learning since Pantaenus, Clement, and Origen, that one of its sons had penned this outstanding epistle.

Other Suggestions

Many other proposals have been made, although most have not aroused the continuing interest as the three mentioned above. *Clement of Rome* was mentioned by Origen, but Clement's own Epistle to the Corinthians makes no such claim, and actually adopts an argument which is opposed to the central thesis of Hebrews. *Luke,* suggested by Clement of Alexandria as the translator of Paul's original Hebrew

---

26. Theodor Zahn, *Introduction to the New Testament,* II, 356; R. C. H. Lenski, *Interpretation of the Epistle to the Hebrews,* p. 22; C. Spicq. *L'Epître aux Hebreux,* I, 209-219.

Papyrus 46 (third century), the oldest extant copy of Hebrews, with the title Pros Hebraious **clearly visible.**

edition, runs afoul of the objection that the Greek Hebrews gives no evidence of being translated material. *Silas* has been suggested on the grounds that he was known at Rome (based on interpreting "Babylon" as Rome in I Peter 5:13), was a companion of Paul and Timothy, had been in the Jerusalem church, and would be aware of the temple operations. Recently this hypothesis has been urged on the grounds of supposed grammatical affinities between Hebrews and I Peter (assuming Silas to have been Peter's amanuensis).[27] The fact that many other names have been offered, including *Philip, Priscilla* with or without *Aquila, John Mark,* and *Aristion,* indicates the inability of present scholarship to achieve any real consensus. Origen said it well for us all, "Who the author of the Epistle is, God truly knows." We, alas, do not.

READERS

The identity of the original readers is lost as completely as that of the author. Neither their nationality nor their geographic location is agreed upon by scholars. The title "To the Hebrews"[28] goes back to the second century, but the letter itself does not mention the readers as being either Jews or Gentiles. Consequently there are many scholars who deny any particular Jewishness to the first readers. Feine-Behm-Kümmel state that it

> is not possibly intended for Jewish Christians. The warning against "falling away from the living God" (3:12) points rather to Gentile-Christian than to Jewish-Christian readers. Hebrews does not know the contrast between Jews and Gentiles at all, and does not even have the words *Ioudaios* and *ethnē.* The author writes to Christians as Christians.[29]

The significance of the ancient title, however, and the prevailing view of the church for centuries are not factors this easily set aside. Furthermore, the contents are considerably more Jewish than the objectors suggest. The epistle makes no reference to Gentile society. Everything in the letter is explained against the backdrop of Jewish history and religion. No Gnostic or pagan ideas or practices are refuted.

---

27. E. G. Selwyn, *The First Epistle of St. Peter,* pp. 463-466.
28. Greek: *Pros Hebraious.* It is found used first by Pantaenus, as recorded in Eusebius *Ecclesiastical History* 6. 14.
29. Feine, Behm, Kümmel, *Introduction to the NT,* p. 280.

William Manson has written:

> The only erroneous teaching which is commented upon in Hebrews concerns food-laws, and this is a point in curious agreement with St. Paul's Romans, where the same or similar doctrines are attributed to a section of the Roman community, and form the only subject on which the Apostle takes the community seriously to task. Again, the call 'not to forsake the gathering of yourselves together' in Hebrews (x.24-25) has a very close inverse parallel in St. Paul's injunction to the Roman brethren to 'accept' or 'welcome' one another.[30]

He also states:

> The only plausible explanation is that doctrines of a Jewish kind regarding food and drink constituted a danger to the community (xiii.9). and were being propagated on the ground of their sanction in the Jewish cultus.
>
> All of these features, as we have seen, acquire a real explanation and point the moment it is assumed that the group had sentimental leanings towards the old religion of Judaism with its worship, sanctions, sacraments, holy prerogatives and means of grace. None of them has equal point and intelligibility if we place the group against an Ethnic-Christian background.[31]

Most conservatives would agree that the Hebrew-Christian character of Hebrews is self-evident, although the precise geographic location of the readers may not yet be settled.

Where did these Jewish Christian readers reside? The list of suggestions is almost endless. Among them are Jerusalem, Caesarea, Samaria, Antioch, Palestine generally, the Lycus Valley (perhaps Colosse), Ephesus, Galatia, Cyprus, Corinth, Berea, Alexandria, and Rome. An excellent résumé is given by F. F. Bruce.[32] With such diversity it should be obvious that the arguments for any one of these have been incapable of producing a consensus. Two of these, however, deserve special mention because they are more widely held than the others.

In spite of the immediate attractions of Jerusalem as the destination of the Epistle to the Hebrews, there are problems attendant upon this identification. It is difficult to see how 2:3 could apply to first century Jerusalem readers, inasmuch as it implies that they had not personally heard Christ. Furthermore, these readers were known for their charity (6:10; 10:34), whereas the Jerusalem Christians were noted for their

---

30. William Manson, *The Epistle to the Hebrews,* p. 13.

31. Manson, p. 158.

32. F. F. Bruce, *The Epistle to the Hebrews,* in *The New International Commentary on the New Testament,* pp. xxxi-xxxv; see also Donald Guthrie, *New Testament Introduction: Hebrews to Revelation,* pp. 37-41.

poverty (except for the very beginning days before persecution of them started). In addition, the readers had not yet suffered any martyrdom (12:4), but the Jerusalem church had already lost Stephen (Acts 7:59, 60), James the brother of John (Acts 12:2), possibly James the Lord's brother (who may have perished by the time of Hebrews), and perhaps others (Acts 26:10). Finally, absence of any mention of the temple when discussing Jewish ritual is harder to understand if the writer was thinking of Jerusalemites (all references in Hebrews are to the tabernacle).

A more plausible case can be made for Rome. The expression "those from Italy greet you"[33] would then refer to Roman Christians who were away from home and send their greetings along with the author to their home church. (The phrase "from Italy" could, however, be interpreted as marking the present location of the writer and these greeters.) The earliest quotations of Hebrews are found in the epistle written by Clement of Rome (however, he also quotes from Ephesians and I Corinthians, which were obviously not sent to Rome). The persecution which brought loss of goods but no loss of life (10:32-34; 12:4) has been explained either as Nero's persecution in A.D. 64, or as the result of the edict of Claudius in A.D. 49.

Lenski concludes that Paul's arrival in Rome and his meeting with Jewish leaders resulted in the conversion of half of the chief men (Acts 28:17-24) and thus enabled their synagogue itself to be transformed into a Christian congregation without any need for the converts to join the Gentile Christians who were already in the city. When Nero's persecution began after the fire in A.D. 64, it was directed against the Christian congregation; but Jewish Christians who had remained in their synagogues escaped the main blow. Lenski concludes that Hebrews was written by Apollos to the body of Jewish Christians at Rome shortly after Paul's death. He sees the problem as involving a movement forming to give up Christianity and go back to their former Judaism. [34]

William Manson, on the other hand, although agreeing that Rome offers the best location, explains the reference to persecution in terms of the edict of Claudius in A.D. 49. He regards the reference in Suetonius to "Chrestus" as denoting disputes in the Jewish community at the preaching of the Christian gospel, and concludes that all Jews—

---

33. Greek: *aspazontai humas hoi apo tēs Italias* (13:24).
34. Lenski, *Interpretation of Hebrews*, pp. 14-21, 22, 23.

Christian and non-Christian—suffered economic loss but not martyrdom (see Acts 18:2). He views the problem among the readers, not as a possible reverting to Judaism but of remaining too closely tied to their Jewish culture and failing to see the world mission of Christianity. [35] They had not grasped the wider view of the messiahship of Jesus as had Stephen.

Nevertheless the identification of the destination as Rome is not without its problems. Guthrie reminds us that there would have been few in Rome who had been evangelized by eyewitnesses (2:3, 4), unless we also assume that most of them had emigrated to Rome from Palestine. He also points out that the type of Judaism reflected in Hebrews (apparently more influenced by Hellenism) differs considerably from the Judaism seen in the Epistle to the Romans.[36] This point, however, would be disputed by Manson.[37] Another question for the Roman hypothesis is the absence of any reference to Gentiles in Hebrews. Only if it be supposed that the epistle was written to a Jewish Christian group exclusively, and not to the whole church at Rome, can this difficulty be explained.

To this writer it seems clear that the original readers to whom the epistle was addressed were Hebrew Christians, probably at Rome, but possibly somewhere else (although not likely in Palestine). A careful study of the five warning passages shows their problem to have been the very serious one of wavering before the temptation to leave the Christian movement and retire to the safer haven of Judaism. By such a move, they could avoid persecution from their Jewish kinsmen, and also enjoy the legal protection which Judaism had from the government—a boon which Christians at this time did not possess. Such passages as 6:4-6; 10:26-29; and 10:38-39 appear to be inadequately handled when one sees in them merely an encouragement to the readers to free themselves from peripheral Jewish customs.

DATE

The problem of date is dependent upon the matters of authorship and destination. Since both of these have resisted complete solution,

---

35. Manson, *Epistle to the Hebrews,* pp. 40, 41, 71, 163, 24.
36. Guthrie, *Hebrews to Revelation,* p. 40.
37. Manson, *Epistle to the Hebrews,* p. 13.

the date of Hebrews must also remain a somewhat open question. However, there are some guidelines available.

Inasmuch as the epistle was utilized by Clement of Rome in his Epistle to the Corinthians, no date for Hebrews can be fixed later than A.D. 96. Internal considerations from the letter give some additional light. Timothy was still alive at the time of writing (13:23). Assuming that he was around twenty years old when Paul chose him in A.D. 50 (Acts 16:1-3), we have no reason from this reference to find conflict with any date within the second half of the first century. We cannot date Hebrews too early, however, because the readers had been believers for some time. They were apparently second generation Christians (2:3), and had been believers long enough for spiritual maturity to have developed, although unfortunately in some cases it had not (5:12). Their conversion had occurred long enough ago that they could look back upon persecutions which they had suffered (10:32-34; 12:4). If the persecution involved the edict of Claudius in A.D. 49, then a date somewhere in the 60s (but probably before A.D. 64 when under Nero some did shed their blood[38]) would allow a sufficient interval. Furthermore, some of their original leaders had died (13:7).

There are also indications that the Jewish sacrifical system was still operating, and this would demand a date prior to A.D. 70. We note the following passages:

And here, on the one hand, dying men take tithes (7:8).

. . . there are those who are offering the gifts according to law (8:4).

. . . never able yearly with the same sacrifices which they offer continually to bring to completion those who draw near; for otherwise would they not have ceased being offered. . ? (10:1, 2).

. . . which are being offered according to the law (10:8).

And every priest stands daily ministering and offering many times the same sacrifices. . . (10:11).

---

38. Lenski, however, has argued that the letter was sent to a Hebrew Christian group in Rome which escaped Nero's persecution against primarily Gentile Christians, and thus he suggests a date of A.D. 68 or 69. *Interpretation of Hebrews,* pp. 21, 22.

It is sometimes argued that the present tenses employed in the above passages are no more than literary or historical presents. Reference is made to other writers subsequent to A.D. 70 who describe the Jewish ritual with present tenses.[39] The fact that it is the tabernacle ritual that is described, not the Herodian temple, is urged as rendering any argument based on tenses irrelevant.[40] Nevertheless, this argument cannot this readily be dismissed in view of the thesis of the author of Hebrews. Surely it must be understood that in Jewish worship the tabernacle and the temple were essentially one (although of course the latter was historically subsequent to the former). Furthermore, it is hardly possible that the author would have spoken as he did about sacrifices being offered, if as a matter of fact they had ceased because of the temple's destruction. Would not this feature have affected his wording in 10:2? One of his major points was the insistence that the Mosaic economy was temporary and would be superseded. To show this, the author referred to a statement in Jeremiah which implied that the Mosaic covenant was "old," and he argued that this also implied obsolescence and eventual replacement (8:13). If he could have pointed to the divine judgment upon Jerusalem which brought the sacrificial system to a decisive end and thus could have corroborated his thesis, it is virtually inconceivable that he would not have done so. In the light of these circumstances, the present tenses do make a positive contribution to the problem of date.

A date therefore in the sixties accords well with the data available.

---

39. See Guthrie, *Hebrews to Revelation*, p. 42.
40. Feine, Behm, and Kümmel, *Introduction to the NT*, p. 282.

Outline

I. **Doctrinal discussion. 1:1—10:18**

A. **Christ is superior to the prophets. 1:1-4**

1. God's revelation in the prophets. 1:1

2. God's revelation in His Son. 1:2-4

B. **Christ is superior to the angels. 1:5—2:18**

1. Christ's superiority to angels asserted by the Old Testament. 1:5-14

FIRST WARNING PASSAGE. 2:1-4

a. Exhortation. 2:1

b. Old Testament analogy. 2:2

c. Present obligation. 2:3, 4

2. Christ's superiority to angels not contradicted by His humanity. 2:5-9

3. Christ's superiority to angels not contradicted by His suffering. 2:10-18

a. Suffering was necessary to complete His identification with humanity. 2:10-13

b. Suffering (even to death) was necessary to destroy the devil and deliver believing men. 2:14-16

c. Suffering was necessary to qualify Him as a merciful high priest. 2:17, 18

C. **Christ is superior to Moses. 3:1—4:16**

1. Both Christ and Moses were faithful to God. 3:1, 2

2. Christ is the builder of the house, but Moses was a part of the house. 3:3, 4

3. Christ is the Son over the house, but Moses was only a servant in the house. 3:5, 6

   SECOND WARNING PASSAGE. 3:7–4:13

   a. Israel's wilderness experience. 3:7-11

   b. Warning against unbelief. 3:12-19

   c. Warning against missing God's rest. 4:1-13

4. Christians should therefore make use of Christ, their superior mediator. 4:14-16

D. Christ is superior to Aaron. 5:1–7:28

   1. The priesthood of Aaron. 5:1-4

   2. The priesthood of Christ. 5:5-10

      THIRD WARNING PASSAGE. 5:11–6:20

      a. Rebuke for spiritual immaturity. 5:11-14

      b. Encouragement toward spiritual maturity. 6:1-3

      c. Warning against the consequences of apostasy. 6:4-8
         (1) The case envisioned. 6:4b-6a
         (2) The consequence. 6:4a, 6b
         (3) The reason. 6:6c
         (4) The illustration. 6:7, 8

      d. Reminder of the certainty of God's promises. 6:9-20

   3. The priesthood of Melchizedek. 7:1-28

E. Christ's ministry is superior to the Old Testament ministry. 8:1–10:18

   1. Introduction. 8:1-6

   2. The two covenants. 8:7-13

PART I

Doctrinal Discussion

1:1 - 10:18

A. CHRIST IS SUPERIOR TO THE PROPHETS. (1:1-4)

1. God's revelation in the prophets. (1:1)

*God, after speaking long ago to the fathers in the prophets
by many portions and many ways. . . . (1:1)*

The epistle begins without any sort of address or greeting. Nothing is allowed by the writer to detract from the tremendous theme which he sets forth in unparalleled beauty of literary form.

Although **God** is the subject of the sentence, and it is less awkward to have it as the first word in the English translation, it is actually the sixth word in the original text. The author really began his treatise with the words **by many portions and many ways.** He was referring, of course, to divine revelation in the Old Testament era. This was granted to men in **many portions.** It came piecemeal, bit by bit. Various persons made their contributions; no one prophet or prophecy delivered it all. Abraham was the recipient of some basic revelation. David received some more. Isaiah, Jeremiah, Ezekiel, and Daniel provided still more as God revealed His truth to them.

Old Testament revelation came also in many ways. God employed dreams, visions, and events, as well as direct communication to announce His truth. These two descriptions are by no means to be understood as a disparagement of Old Testament revelation, as though it were unworthy. The many fragments and varied ways point to the graciousness and versatility of God in matching His revelation to the capability of men to understand it. At the same time, however, the implication is certainly here that this revelation was long ago, with perhaps the suggestion that anything that long ago *(palai)* was due for renovation or at least a fresh restatement (see 8:13).

To the ancestors of the Jewish people being addressed in this epistle God had spoken. He did this in *(en)* the prophets. Even though *en* has an instrumental use, there is a good likelihood that more is involved in verse 1 than passive instrumentality. This phrase must be considered in the light of the parallel construction in verse 2, "in a Son." As God was "in" Christ, using Him to confront men with His saving message, not as a passive instrument but as a person through whom God spoke by word, deed, and by His very presence, so in a generally analogous way God was in the prophets.[1] They were not automatons, but God's Spirit was in them, empowering their minds and using their bodies to bring His message to Israel and the world. These Old Testament prophets need not be limited to those who were popularly regarded as prophets in Israel, but must also include all spokesmen who conveyed God's revelation to men. Such men as Abraham and Moses, as well as many others, would certainly be in the scope of the author's thinking in verse 1.

2. God's revelation in His Son. (1:2-4)

> .. in these last days [God] *has spoken to us in a Son,*
> *whom he appointed heir of all things, through whom also*
> *he made the ages; who being the radiance of the Glory and*
> *the exact representation of his essence, and carrying all*
> *things by the word of his power, after making purification*
> *for the sins, sat down at the right hand of the Majesty on*
> *high. . . .* (1:2, 3)

---

1. The analogy, of course, does not extend to the theanthropic person of Christ.

Dead Sea Scroll of Isaiah "a" (1Q1s[a]). Dated about 100 B.C., it is the oldest complete Biblical manuscript known to exist. By such prophets God spoke long ago "to the fathers" of the Jewish people.

A literal rendering of the Greek time expression here translated in these last days would be "at the last of these days," and it is tempting to interpret it as meaning "recently." Thus the author would be calling attention to the recent occurrence of the revelation in Christ, coming at the end of the Old Testament period previously mentioned.[2] However, it must be recognized that this is precisely the Septuagint rendering of the frequent Old Testament expression *be'aherith hayyāmim* ("in the end of the days"), which usually denoted messianic times in some way (see Num. 24:14, et al.). Hence the author should be understood to say that the last days have been inaugurated with the coming of Messiah.[3]

---

2. This appears to be the view of R. C. H. Lenski, *Interpretation of the Epistle to the Hebrews*, p. 31.

3. So B. F. Westcott, *The Epistle to the Hebrews*, p. 6; Gleason L. Archer, Jr., *The Epistle to the Hebrews*, p. 15; F. F. Bruce, *The Epistle to the Hebrews*, p. 3; Marcus Dods, "The Epistle to the Hebrews," in *Expositor's Greek Testament*, IV, 248.

This concept of the "last days" is shared by New Testament writers generally (e.g., Acts 2:16, 17; James 5:3; I Peter 1:20; II Peter 3:3; I John 2:18; Jude 18).

In these momentous times God has spoken in a Son. The absence of the Greek article (thus not "the Son" nor "his Son") throws the emphasis upon the nature or quality of the noun itself. It is the "son-ness" that is being stressed. In contrast to the Old Testament prophets, great as they were, God has now spoken in one who is a Son. Thus the very person of the revealer is on a higher plane generically from all others. This emphasis is all the more striking, as Westcott has observed,[4] because the article does appear with "prophets," the other member of the comparison. The prophets were referred to as a definite group, but the Son is referred to not simply as a particular person but by the nature of His relationship to God.

A sevenfold description of God's Son is next given, which elaborates the incomparable superiority of the Son to any prophet or other agent.

First, the Son was appointed by God as heir of all things. This is language reminiscent of Psalm 2, to which the author makes specific reference in verse 5. In that psalm, God places His Anointed One (i.e., Messiah) upon the messianic throne, and grants Him the earth and its people for His inheritance (Ps. 2:2-8). The Son's messianic office is thus fully assured, although Christ has not fully entered into the possession of His inheritance. That must await the messianic kingdom which is yet to be established. Many other passages indicate the same truth, such as Daniel 7:13, 14; Matthew 11:27; 28:18.

Second, the Son was the one through whom God made the ages (*aiōnas*). To speak of Christ as creator stresses a divine activity quite apart from the ability of any prophet. Here is a function of deity. Although the term "ages" commonly meant periods of time, such as the "present age," it was also used in a way very similar to "world" (*kosmos*), as the usage by the same author in 11:3 clearly attests. It apparently refers in our passage to the vast periods of time along with all that transpires within them. It denotes this world not only as a physical entity, but also its time extent. It was by the creative agency of Christ the Son that the universe and its temporal development came into being.

---

4. Westcott, *Epistle to the Hebrews*, p. 7.

Third, the Son is the possessor of deity as the radiance of the Glory. In this description radiance (*apaugasma*) is used in the sense of a shining forth or effulgence. The term occurs only here in the New Testament. Another usage conveys the idea of "reflection," but that meaning does not seem as appropriate here. Patristic interpretation of this passage favored the sense of "effulgence."[5] As the rays of light are related to the sun, and neither exists without the other, so Christ is the effulgence of the divine glory. They are essentially one; that is, both are God.

Fourth, the Son is the exact representation of his [God's] essence, and thus is the perfect revealer. *Charaktēr* was the impress made by the engraving tool. This is its only occurrence in the New Testament, although the cognate *charagma* ("imprint," "image") appears eight times. As the imprint of the die perfectly represents the original design, so in Christ there is the display for those who have eyes to see of God's very essence. In a similar assertion in Colossians 1:15, Christ is set forth as the timeless image (*eikōn*) of God. Jesus Himself said, "He that hath seen me hath seen the Father" (John 14:9).

Fifth, the Son is the carrier of all things. Carrying (*pherōn*) suggests more than just sustaining or maintaining. The durative form of the participle, as well as the meaning of the word itself as "bring" or "carry," indicates that the sense involves both upholding and movement toward some goal. It is one of Christ's functions to sustain this universe in its existence and operation, and to carry it forward to reach the consummation which God has planned. This thought is expressed also in Colossians 1:16, 17: "all things were created . . . for him . . . and by him all things consist." Dods notes an interesting use of *pherein* in the Septuagint rendering of Numbers 11:14, where Moses said, "I am not able to bear all this people alone."[6] Thus *pherein* may also connote the idea of being responsible for governing and guidance.

By the word *(rhēmati)* of his [Christ's] power is the universe sustained and carried forward. This term emphasizes utterance, in contrast to *logos* which stresses the concept. Christ's creative word brought the universe into being (so Heb. 11:3; John 1:3; Col. 1:16). The Gospels record other utterances of Christ by which the world was modified as to its operation in carrying out the will of the creator. The stilling of

---

5. Gerhard Kittel, "Apaugasma," in *Theological Dictionary of the New Testament,* ed. Gerhard Kittel, trans. Geoffrey W. Bromiley, I, 508.

6. Dods, *Expositor's Greek Testament,* IV, 251.

the storm, healing of the sick, and raising of the dead were a few instances where Christ's "word of power" was in obvious operation.

Sixth, the Son is the producer of purification from sins. This refers to Christ's redemptive work at the cross, where by one perfect offering, He secured eternal salvation for men (a point to be discussed at greater length later in the epistle). This purification was obtained objectively by Christ at Calvary, and is entered into subjectively by believers individually on the basis of faith. Although the documentary support for the King James Version phrase "by himself" is probably insufficient, the idea may well be included in the middle voice of the participle *poiēsamenos*, "having made of himself."

The seventh and final assertion about the Son is that He is seated at God's right hand. Following His redemptive work there came the exaltation to the place of honor and authority. This present exaltation of the Son conveys several important truths. The fact that He sat after making purification indicates that His atoning work was finished. No Old Testament priest ever sat while performing his duties because the task was never finally accomplished. There were no chairs in the tabernacle. Christ, however, wrought full satisfaction for sin, and is now described as seated.

The place of Christ's sitting was at the right hand of the Majesty on high. Although some insist on construing "on high" with the verb "sat," word order favors leaving it with "Majesty." Thus it is clear that the majesty here in view is no earthly pomp but is the very majesty of God Himself. The Majesty on high is thus another way of saying "God" (cf. 8:1), and at the same time it connotes the awesome greatness of God. Old Testament prophecy of this exaltation was made in Psalm 110:1, a passage to be cited explicitly in verse 13 of this chapter. Jesus Himself quoted it during His last week of public teaching (Matt. 22:43, 44).

The position at the right hand indicates honor and authority. It was the place of special favor, as well as the place of the sovereign's prime minister. Even in our society we speak of someone's "right-hand man." God, of course, is spirit and has no physical right hand. We understand such expressions as anthropomorphisms in which God reveals Himself to human understanding through the use of descriptions in human terms. As Bruce reminds us, Paul expressed the same thought in different language in Ephesians 4:10 and Philippians 2:9, by saying that

Christ "has ascended far above all heavens," and that "God highly exalted him."[7] Verse 4 provides such a perfect transition that some place it with the previous section, and others with what follows. Grammatically it is part of the preceding sentence; therefore it will be treated here as concluding the opening section and preparing the reader for the next.

> ... *having become as much better than the angels as he has inherited a more excellent name than they.* (1:4)

Better (*kreittōn*), a term occurring thirteen times in the epistle, is one of the characteristic words of Hebrews as the author sets forth the superiorities of Christ to any other person, group, or institution. He is better than the prophets because He is God's Son, the messianic King, and He is Himself deity. His exaltation to heaven demonstrated this as it lifted Him far above any mere prophet. However, angels too are in heaven, so the author must make it clear that Christ is not merely their equal but is their superior.

Having become (*genomenos*) so much better indicates that it is the incarnate Christ in view, for in His preexistent deity there was no development involved. Our author is about to explain, however, that by incarnation Christ became for a time lower than angels (2:9). Nevertheless, His subsequent exaltation elevated Him to the highest place, far above every angelic being. The word inherited also confirms the view that the exaltation following His earthly task is what the author means (cf. Phil. 2:9).

Christ's name is more excellent than that of angels. This could hardly mean a proper name, such as "Jesus" (as though this name per se were more euphonious or pedigreed than Gabriel or Michael, or all the other angels whose names are totally unknown to us). The name is thought by some to mean "Lord" or "Jehovah," based upon a comparison with Philippians 2:9-11.[8] Many adopt the explanation that "name" is used in the sense of character, dignity, position, or as Westcott put it, "all that Christ was found to be by believers, Son, Sovereign, and

---

7. F. F. Bruce, *The Epistle to the Hebrews*, p. 8.
8. E.g., Herman A. Hoyt, "The Epistle to the Hebrews," unpublished course notes, p. 10.

Creator, the Lord of the Old Covenant."[9] Most commonly "name" is understood here as the title "Son of God," in view of verse 5 and the remaining context.[10] He was always the divine Son, but Paul asserts that the resurrection (first phase of the exaltation) was the public declaration of His sonship and the Father's authentication of it (Rom. 1:4). Thus the exaltation of Christ by the Father when He raised Him from the dead and seated Him at His right hand was the divine acknowledgment that Jesus, in spite of His time of earthly humiliation, was truly the unique Son, with all the prerogatives that belong to such a Son.

B. CHRIST IS SUPERIOR TO THE ANGELS. (1:5–2:18)

1. Christ's superiority to angels asserted by the Old Testament. (1:5-14)

In a series of seven quotations, probably all but one from the Psalms, the author shows how the Old Testament itself ascribes to Messiah a superiority above any angel. Basing his argument squarely on Scripture, he should surely have won his Hebrew Christian hearers.

> *For to which of the angels did he ever say,*
>   *"You are my Son; today I have begotten you"?*
> *And again,*
>   *"I will be a Father to him,*
>   *And he will be a Son to me"?* (1:5)

The answer to these rhetorical questions is: "Not even one angel was ever so addressed by God." The first quotation is the messianic Psalm 2:7, a psalm which is attributed by Peter to David (Acts 4:25-26). Even though angels are called "sons of God" in the wider sense of direct creations of God, it was always as a group. No individual angel is ever addressed as "son of God" in all of Scripture, and certainly not in the unique sense indicated by Psalm 2:7.

Elsewhere in the New Testament Paul uses the same quotation and applies it to the resurrection of Christ (Acts 13:33). Thus we must

---

9. Westcott, *Epistle to the Hebrews,* p. 17.

10. So F. F. Bruce, *The Epistle to the Hebrews*, p. 4; Dods, *Expositor's Greek Testament,* IV, 253; Lenski, *Interpretation of Hebrews,* p. 44.

abandon any notions of origination or birth in the term "begotten." Rather, the expression has to do with public declaration, acknowledgment, or inauguration. In conjunction with Romans 1:4, the idea seems clear that the one who was always the divine Son was openly declared or demonstrated to be such by the culminating events of resurrection and subsequent exaltation. Of course, Christ was previously acknowledged as Son by the Father at the baptism (Matt. 3:17) and transfiguration (Matt. 17:5), but the crowning event was the resurrection and its aftermath. The psalmist clearly depicts God as directly addressing the Anointed One (i.e., Messiah, or Christ) and calling Him **my Son.**

The second quotation comes also from the career of David. In II Samuel 7:14, the prophet Nathan conveyed God's message to David, denying him the privilege of building the temple but promising to establish David's dynasty after him. In the prophecy were the words regarding David's seed, "I will be his father and he shall be my son." The original reference involved specific information regarding David's son Solomon, but there were overtones of a more distant future also in the prophecy (e.g., II Sam. 7:13, 16). Some of these words found only a limited fulfilment in Solomon, but he in turn became typical of that greater Son of David, Jesus Christ. It was in this typological sense that our author has applied the words of II Samuel 7:14 to Jesus. The point being made in both quotations is that Jesus the Messiah is acknowledged by God as **Son,** a relationship far superior to that enjoyed by any individual angel.

> *And whenever he again brings in the Firstborn into the world he says, "And let all angels of God worship him."* (1:6)

Not only is Christ superior to angels because He is God's unique Son, but also because angels are commanded to render worship to Him. The interpreter is confronted with a number of problems in this third quotation. The first has to do with the introduction of this citation. Does **again** (*palin*) merely introduce this additional passage (as for example the *kai palin* of 1:5b and 2:13)? This understanding is reflected by the King James Version, Revised Standard Version, and New English Bible, and is urged by F. F. Bruce.[11] Or does it modify the verb

---

11. F. F. Bruce, *The Epistle to the Hebrews,* p. 15.

"brings in" and thus refer to the second advent of Christ? This explanation is adopted by Westcott,[12] Dods,[13] Lenski,[14] and Hewitt,[15] and is reflected in the American Standard Version and the New American Standard Bible.

In favor of the latter interpretation is the position of again in the sentence. It would normally be understood as going with the verb rather than as introducing the clause, inasmuch as it follows the subordinate conjunction whenever (hotan) and is thus part of the clause. Furthermore, the use of the subjunctive mood for the verb brings in (eisagagēi) argues strongly for an event still future, rather than for the past act of incarnation. Hence the statement refers to angelic worship of Christ at His second coming. Many other Scripture references also point to this feature of Christ's return (see Matt. 13:41; 16:27; 25:31; II Thess. 1:7).

Christ is here called the Firstborn (ton prōtotokon), a term which may have either temporal or positional emphasis, or both. In Jewish culture, the oldest son (i.e., "firstborn") received a double portion of the inheritance and certain other prerogatives. Thus he had a higher rank than his brothers. At times this emphasis on rank overshadowed considerations of age, so that a younger son might be elevated to the place of firstborn (e.g., Gen. 48:17-20; Exod. 4:22). The term was sometimes used in the sense of "chief," without any thought of age at all (Job 18:13, "firstborn of death"; Isa. 14:30, "firstborn of the poor"). In Psalm 89:27, "firstborn" is a title given to Messiah, with the emphasis clearly being upon primacy of position and dignity. It is also used of Christ in Colossians 1:15, 18, again with the emphasis on rank or position. To call Christ the Firstborn is to assert His superiority in position in the eyes of God.

Another problem in this passage is the source of the Old Testament quotation. The wording is exactly that of the Septuagint at Deuteronomy 32:43, but the clause does not appear at that point in the Hebrew Scripture (Massoretic text) at all. A similar statement occurs, however, in Psalm 97:7, so that there is no question that God made

---

12. Westcott, Epistle to the Hebrews, pp. 21-23.
13. Dods, Expositor's Greek Testament, IV, 254.
14. Lenski, Interpretation of Hebrews, p. 48.
15. T. Hewitt, The Epistle to the Hebrews, in Tyndale New Testament Commentaries, pp. 55, 56.

such a statement. In Psalm 97:7 the wording is, "Worship him, all ye gods" (*'elohîm*, Hebrew text). The Septuagint has translated "gods" as "angels." The point of our author in his usage is clear: Christ is superior to angels because God specifically commanded them to worship Him.

> *And concerning the angels, he says,*
> *"He who makes his angels winds,*
> *And his ministers a flame of fire."* (1:7)

This fourth quotation is from Psalm 104:4, and asserts that angels are created beings (who makes his angels) who serve God. The next quotation will show how Christ is infinitely above such a position. The context in Psalm 104, as well as the parallelism in the statement, makes it almost certain that winds is the proper rendering of *pneumata* here. This is one of the few times when this word should not be translated "spirits" (John 3:8 is another).

Winds are one of the striking phenomena in the psalmist's country. They ranged from the refreshing breezes off the Mediterranean Sea that make the largely arid land of Israel a climatically pleasant place to live, to the searing blasts from Arabia that burn and wither everything in their path. Winds, particularly in the evening, pour down over the mountain slopes and whip the waters of the Sea of Galilee into dangerous turbulence. Psalm 104 does not picture nature in her violent moods, however, but in her prevailing condition. Some would translate the psalm passage this way, "Who maketh winds his messengers," and thus rule out any specific reference to angels as separate entities. However, the writer of Hebrews obviously understood the reference to be to angels. Thus the verse means that God uses angels as His instruments to carry out His will, just as the winds and flaming fire (lightning?) are the agents of swift destruction. In fact, there are times when these physical elements are placed under angelic control (see Rev. 7:1 for an instance where angels are described as controlling the winds). Here the point of emphasis is that angels, although the most exalted of creatures, are nevertheless subordinates, servants to do the divine will.

> *But to the Son* [he says]:
> *"Your throne, O God,* [is] *forever and ever,*
> *And the sceptre of uprightness* [is] *the sceptre of your kingdom.*

> *You have loved righteousness and hated lawlessness;*
> *For this reason God, your God, has anointed you with*
> *the oil of gladness above your colleagues."* (1:8, 9)

The fifth quotation is drawn from Psalm 45:7, 8. Although it was written for the marriage of a king, certain portions of the psalm cannot be limited to any earthly king—not to Solomon nor any other. It thus is a messianic psalm, and was properly employed by the writer of Hebrews. In this usage, Messiah is shown to be superior to the angels because, in contrast to them, He is God and has an eternal throne.

In spite of attempts to reword the translation along such lines as "God is your throne" or "Your throne is God,"[16] none of these makes as good sense to most interpreters as the usual rendering, **Your throne, O God.** By treating **God** (*ho theos*) as a vocative, the messianic King is addressed as full deity. He also sits upon a throne which endures forever. Thus He is a sovereign, and no temporary one either. His superiority to subordinate angels is a permanent position. The sceptre symbolizes governing power in operation, and Christ's kingdom will be characterized by absolute righteousness. For this reason God will anoint His divine King with the oil of gladness. It is not the anointing of inauguration in view here, but of festivity and rejoicing. **Above your colleagues** refers in the psalm to the associates of the king in the celebration. In the application to Jesus, it refers not to angels (they are servants, not colleagues) but to believers who will share His reign in the age to come, whom Christ is not ashamed to acknowledge as His brethren (Heb. 2:10, 11).

It is possible that the first "God" in the expression "God, your God" in verse 9 could be a vocative, just as in the preceding verse. If so, then Christ is again addressed directly as God, and the sense of the statement would be this: "O God, your God has anointed you. . . ." One cannot be certain about this point, however, and the more common rendering poses no problems. Either way, the messianic King is the recipient of joyous blessings from God. Christ Himself acknowledged the Father as "my God" in John 20:17.

And,

> *"You at the beginning, Lord, laid the foundation of the*
> *earth,*

16. Westcott, *Epistle to the Hebrews*, p. 25.

> *And the heavens are works of your hands.*
> > *They will perish, but you remain;*
> > > *And they all will become old as a garment,*
> > *And as a cloak you will roll them up,*
> > > *As a garment they will also be changed;*
> > *But you are the same,*
> > > *And your years will not end."* (1:10-12)

Psalm 102:25-27 provides the sixth quotation. The author of Hebrews uses it to demonstrate that Messiah is creator, and thus is prior to creation, and also that He will outlast creation. The psalm is addressed to Jehovah, but in His messianic function as the Coming One who will show mercy on Zion (Ps. 102:13, 16). Thus the author properly understood these verses as referring to Christ. Furthermore, he has already asserted that Christ was the creator (Heb. 1:2), and thus related the statements in Psalm 102:25 quite naturally to Christ. He has quoted the Septuagint form of the verse in which "Lord" (*kurie*) occurs, although it does not appear in the Hebrew text at this point. Apparently the Septuagint inserted it for clarification, having drawn it from earlier occurrences in the psalm (e.g., Ps. 102:1, 12).

By this passage, the readers are reminded that the divine Messiah was the creator of the earth and the heavens. He also is the one who will bring the universe to its consummation ("will roll them up"). Christ, however, because He is God, will endure forever. No angel shares such a position.

> *But to which of the angels has he ever said,*
> > *"Sit at my right hand until I make your enemies a footstool for your feet"?*
> *Are they not all ministering spirits sent out for service for the sake of those who are about to inherit salvation?* (1:13, 14)

The seventh and final quotation is Psalm 110:1, a passage already alluded to in Hebrews 1:3. The messianic character of Psalm 110 was recognized in Old Testament times, and the usage by Jesus of it (Matt. 22:43-45) assumes an awareness of this fact by His contemporaries. Jesus said that David was the author of this psalm, and in it he has pictured Messiah as exalted to the Father's side and ruling over all foes.

No angel was ever so pictured in Scripture. Treating one's enemies as a footstool is a metaphor drawn from the Old Testament practice of a conquering king placing his foot upon the neck of a vanquished king to emphasize his triumph. The psalm depicts the future reign of Christ, when He will reign over the messianic kingdom and all enemies will be finally brought into submission.

Now, of course, this function is never asserted of angels. On the contrary, they are agents and servants, not rulers. From the human standpoint, it may appear at times as if they were rulers (e.g., "prince of Persia," "prince of Grecia," Dan. 10:13, 20). However, when we see the whole teaching of Scripture, it is clear that they are not independent sovereigns, but are agents only, and that God is still in final control.

By the author's rhetorical question, he expects full agreement from his readers that angels are ministering spirits. Furthermore, this is true of all of them, regardless of what rank they may hold. Ministering (*leitourgika*) does not convey the idea of slavery, but of official functioning. They have been duly commissioned and sent forth (*apostellomena*) with the responsibility of aiding believers. So far from angels being above Christ, they have actually been appointed as ministrants to those humans who will someday share in Christ's rule. About to inherit (*tous mellontas klēronomein*) looks to the final phase of salvation (*sōtērian*). Salvation is the present possession of every believer; yet there is still the promise of an inheritance in which the final consummation of our deliverance will occur. It was salvation in this sense that Paul spoke of in Romans 13:11, "Now is our salvation nearer than when we believed."

The point has been amply proved. Christ is superior to angels by the unimpeachable witness of Scripture. Sometimes it is asked why the author devotes so much time to proving Christ's superiority to angels in contrast to just a few sentences comparing Christ and the prophets. The answer may be that he is dealing with his readers in the areas where their problems were. As Hebrew Christians, they had already trusted Christ as the Son of God, one who was obviously higher than ordinary men. Therefore, they may not have been particularly troubled by comparisons between Jesus and the prophets. Such suggestions would probably have been rejected immediately. But lifting Christ above the realm of ordinary mortals did not necessarily prove that He was God.

Angels too were above mortals, and were highly respected in the Old Testament and by Jews generally. Thus the point needed to be clearly established that Christ as the Son of God was superior to every angel, because He existed on an even higher plane.

FIRST WARNING PASSAGE (2:1-4)

At this point in the argument, the author injects an exhortation and warning into the discussion. This is the first of five such occurrences in the book—each of which is pertinent to the discussion at that point, but is also something of a digression for purposes of applying the truth under discussion to the readers' lives.

a. Exhortation. (2:1)

Because of this, it is necessary for us to give much closer attention to things which have been heard, lest we drift on by [them]. (2:1)

An exhortation is first given to the readers to pay careful attention to the Christian truths they have been taught. The warning has its basis (because of this) in the fact just elaborated—that Christ as the Son of God is superior to angels. The verb **give attention to** (*prosechō*) occurs numerous times in the New Testament in this sense, but was also commonly used elsewhere of bringing a ship to land. This may have suggested the use of *pararuōmen* (drift) in the next clause. The **things which have been heard** were the teachings of Christ and the gospel which these readers had previously heard and acknowledged. The danger was that they might **drift on by**. The meaning of the word ("drift," "slip away") and its personal subject ("we") indicate not that something might drift away from us, but that "we" might drift away from something. The author's point is: If men reject the truth of God's revelation in Christ, there is no other haven before the catastrophe. He says "we," not because he has any doubts about himself, but because he follows the very common practice of identifying himself with his readers in the exhortation.[17] Further, even though he writes to pro-

---

17. Another clear example is found in James 3:9.

fessed Christians, he is wise enough not to take for granted that all profession is genuine. Not all the seed sown by the sower reached the full cycle of maturation, not even some that showed a bit of initial activity (Matt. 13:18-23). Thus warnings to examine ourselves are always in order.

b. Old Testament Analogy. (2:2)

For if the word which was spoken through angels became valid, and every transgression and disobedience received a just retribution. . . . (2:2)

An Old Testament analogy demonstrates the author's point. The word referred to here is the Mosaic law (including the entire Old Testament probably). In some way not fully elaborated in Scripture, the law was given by angels. This point was surely not a new idea to the first readers, for the writer assumes that his readers know it to be true and makes no effort to prove it. Furthermore, both Stephen (Acts 7:53) and Paul (Gal. 3:19) say the same thing, so that we understand that this identification was quite general in the first century. Probably the nearest we can come to an Old Testament assertion is Deuteronomy 33:2: "And he said, The Lord came from Sinai, and rose up from Seir unto them; he shined forth from mount Paran, and he came with ten thousands of saints [ASV "holy ones"]; from his right hand went a fiery law for them." The Septuagint has for the last clause, "at his right hand were angels with him," apparently as an interpretive parallel to the "holy ones" in the previous clause. Psalm 68:17 says, "The chariots of God are twenty thousand, even thousands of angels: the Lord is among them, as in Sinai, in the holy place." Thus Hebrews does not contradict the Old Testament, and is in agreement with both ancient and contemporary opinion as to the events at Sinai.

The validity (*bebaios*) of the angel mediated law was fully acknowledged by every Jew, as his national history amply testified. Every breaking of the law's commands (transgression) and every failure to carry out what the law specified (disobedience) brought its appropriate penalty. The Old Testament thus contained ample illustration that the law mediated by angels could not be ignored with impunity.

c. Present obligation (2:3, 4)

> *... how shall we escape if we disregard so great a salvation,*
> *which, after it had its beginning in being spoken through*
> *the Lord, was confirmed to us by those who heard, God*
> *testifying at the same time by signs and wonders and*
> *various miracles, and distributions of the Holy Spirit ac-*
> *cording to his will.* (2:3, 4)

The present obligation resting upon the readers is now emphasized. The question **how shall we escape?** has as its obvious answer: "We shall not escape." The "we," of course, is the customary way of including an author among his readers as a matter of courtesy. It takes us back to 1:2, where God is said to have spoken to "us" (which included the writer, Christian readers, and in a general way all men). Thus the obligation rests upon men (and particularly those who have heard the gospel) to give it their utmost attention. **If we disregard** treats the circumstantial participle as conditional. The word was used of men who rudely and wilfully ignored a gracious invitation to a feast (Matt. 22:5), and of Timothy's obligation not to neglect the exercise of his spiritual gift (I Tim. 4:14).

Men are warned against failure to appropriate to themselves the saving message of the gospel which is their only escape from certain judgment. This spiritual deliverance is characterized as so great (*tēlikautēs*) in the light of the person of the Savior previously explained. In particular, three things are mentioned to illustrate the greatness of this **salvation**: (1) it was proclaimed by Christ Himself; (2) it was confirmed by eyewitnesses; (3) it was authenticated by God through various signs.

The Lord Jesus Christ gave this salvation its **beginning** (*archēn*). Of course, God's message had been previously announced by the prophets (1:1), but it was Christ who initiated the announcement of a finished salvation. Previous announcements had been somewhat partial and predictive. With Christ's coming, fulfilment occurred and full expiation for sin was made. Thus Jesus proclaimed, "The Son of man is come to seek and to save that which was lost" (Luke 19:10) and "to give his life a ransom for many" (Matt. 20:28). Jesus also said, "The Spirit of the Lord is upon me, because he hath anointed me to preach the gospel to the poor. . . . This day is this scripture fulfilled in your ears" (Luke 4:18-21).

In addition to this incomparable beginning, the message of salvation in Christ was confirmed by eyewitnesses. Those who had been present when He spoke and who had seen His works were able to corroborate what had happened by their own testimony. Such testimony was a confirmation to us, the implication being that the writer and his readers were not companions of Christ during His ministry. Many see in this statement a strong indication that the writer of Hebrews was not Paul, inasmuch as Paul claims in Galatians 1:12 to have received his gospel not from eyewitnesses but from Christ Himself. This would not appear conclusive, however, for all will readily admit that Paul had not been an eyewitness of the miracles or of the preaching of Jesus, and thus had the confirming testimony of others for these things. The statement does not speak of initial impartation of the message but of confirmation. Thus even Paul could have said, "The Lord Jesus brought God's final word of salvation to men, and there are many eyewitnesses still living who have amply confirmed what he said and did."

There was also divine confirmation of the message of salvation. By **signs** (supernatural occurrences which acted as proofs or indicators) and **wonders** (supernatural acts which produced awe among the beholders) and **various miracles** (a variety of displays of divine power), God indicated His involvement in the message of salvation. Many of these are recorded in Acts (e.g., 3:6-8; 5:12, 18-20; 6:8; 8:6; 9:33-34, 40-41, et al.).

Distributions of the Holy Spirit may be understood as God's bestowal of the Spirit upon each believer (treating "Holy Spirit" as an objective genitive). A supporting passage would be Galatians 3:5, "He that ministereth to you the Spirit, and worketh miracles among you. . . ." With this understanding, **according to his will** would clearly refer to the Father, and perhaps should be construed not only with "distributions of the Holy Spirit," but also with "signs and wonders and various miracles." On the whole it seems more likely that **Holy Spirit** is a subjective genitive, and that the reference is to those Spirit produced evidences in men's lives which offer living proof of salvation. This truth is stated in I Corinthians 12:11, "But all these worketh that one and the selfsame Spirit, dividing to every man severally as he will." **According to his will** would then probably refer to the Spirit, although it could conceivably refer to the Father, with whose will all Persons of the godhead are always in perfect harmony. Pink notes that the act of distributing spiritual gifts is attributed in Scripture to the Father (I Cor. 7:17), the Son (Eph. 4:7), and the Spirit (I Cor. 12:11).[18] Such a salvation, provided with strong authentication like this, leaves man without excuse for his neglect.

2. Christ's superiority to angels not contradicted by His humanity. (2:5-9)

After the warning in which the implications of Christ's superiority to angels were made the basis of a strong exhortation to heed the Christian message, the author resumes the discussion by considering two possible objections. The first has to do with Christ's superiority to angels as it relates to the incarnation. Even if one accepted the Old Testament assertions given previously that the Son of God is above angels, he might still question whether this superiority was retained when the Son became man. It is to that question that the following discussion is addressed.

> *For not to angels did he subject the world which is coming,*
> *concerning which we are speaking.* (2:5)

Angelic position in the present order is certainly superior to humanity. They were involved in the giving of the Mosaic law to which men were subject (2:2). Angelic beings have certain governmental functions over the earth today, as is clearly stated by Daniel (10:13, "prince of the kingdom of Persia"; 10:20, "prince of Grecia"; 10:13, 21, "Michael, one of the chief princes"). They are also God's emissaries at times in the natural world (Heb. 1:7). In the Book of Revelation, angels are frequently described as bringing divine judgments upon the present world (chaps. 8, 9). However, this is not an eternal arrangement, for Scripture uses no such terminology of angels regarding the coming age. The world to come (*tēn oikoumenēn tēn mellousan*) refers to the coming age, when Christ at His return (same word is used for "world" as in 1:6) shall establish His rule as the promised Davidic King

---

18. A. W. Pink, *An Exposition of Hebrews*, I, 92.

(*oikoumenē* means "inhabited earth"). Angels are not described as sovereigns in that world, but believers are depicted as reigning with Christ for a thousand years (Rev. 20:6). In fact, believers are even declared as ultimately being judges of angels (I Cor. 6:1-3). Hence whatever angelic superiority may now exist is temporary in relation to man.

> But one testified somewhere saying:
> > "What is man that you are mindful of him,
> > Or the son of man that you are looking after him?
> > You made him for a little [time] lower than angels,
> > You crowned him with glory and honor,
> > And you set him over the works of your hands.[19]
> > You subjected all things underneath his feet." (2:6-8a)

The somewhat indefinite introduction of Psalm 8 was not a lapse of memory as to the source (since the Septuagint is quoted verbatim), but was a fairly common rhetorical device used by Philo and others. The passage was well known and to identify the source would perhaps divert attention from the point he wished to draw from the quotation. Our author ordinarily does not name the source of his quotations (for example, none of the seven quotations in chapter 1 are identified; however, in 4:7 he does give the source). In his view, God was the speaker of all Scripture, and the human spokesman was incidental (e.g., 1:6; 3:7).

Psalm 8 is the psalmist's reflection upon man in the light of creation around him and of God's dealings with him. When viewed in relation to the starry universe, man seems to be but a speck. Yet when man is considered in the light of what God has done for him and what prerogatives God has given him, the answer to the psalmist's question can only be: Man must possess from his creator an essential greatness in view of God's actions toward him. For man has been made as the crown of God's creation and was to exercise dominion over all the rest of creation. The psalmist was sensitive not only to the natural world

---

19. This clause is omitted by Nestle (Greek NT edited by G. D. Kilpatrick, 1958), and the omission is given a "C" rating by the Bible Societies text (Greek NT published by the United Bible Societies, 1966). However, it was in the Hebrew of Psalm 8, and is found in Aleph, A, C, and D.

around him but was also aware of the divine mandate to Adam (Gen. 1:26, 28).

No distinction should be made by the interpreter between man and son of man in the psalm, because they are a clear example of the very common synonymous parallelism in Hebrew poetry. Hence this passage was not regarded as a messianic prediction by Jewish teachers, but as a description of what God intended man to be.

The Hebrew text has *'elohîm* ("God," "gods") in Psalm 8:5, where the Septuagint has *angelous* ("angels"). If *'elohîm* means "God" in Psalm 8:5, then the Septuagint has misinterpreted it, and the writer of Hebrews has merely quoted the well-known version without alteration because that particular word was not his emphasis. (His point was that Psalm 8 was not addressed to angels but to man.) However, *'elohîm* many times was used in a lesser sense of angels and even of men (Ps. 97:7; cf. Heb. 1:6; Ps. 82:6, quoted by Jesus in John 10:34-35). Hence it is better to conclude that the Septuagint has properly interpreted the sense of the Hebrew, and that the author of Hebrews has quoted the Septuagint with approval. The meaning then is "lower than angels," rather than "lower than God." Man is presently lower than angels because he is subject to mortality (Luke 20:36) and other frailties. But this is not a permanent condition for man, nor was it God's original intention.

A little (*brachu ti*) can refer to space, time, or degree. The Hebrew expression allows the same latitude, although "a little lower" may be the more probable. If the meaning is "for a little time lower," then the temporary nature of the lowness is asserted. If "a little lower" is the sense, then the temporary nature of this humiliation must be gotten from the ensuing context: **crowned with glory and honor.**

> *For in subjecting all things to him, he left nothing unsubjected to him. But now we do not yet see all things subjected to him. But we see Jesus. . . . (2:8b)*

These words are not part of the psalm, but are the author's comment. He draws the conclusion that God's plan was to subject all things to man. However, he hastens to add that the realities of life force us to admit that such complete subjection has not yet occurred. Man seems to be more often victim than victor. The problem was that the Fall of man had intervened and prevented man from reaching the goal which

God desired. Sin with its curse held man back from reaching the ideal set forth in Psalm 8. Now did that mean that all was hopeless? Our author's view is that what man lost by the Fall, the man Christ Jesus has achieved. Thus all believing men will ultimately reach the goal of Psalm 8 by virtue of being in union with Christ.

> *But we see Jesus, who was made for a little* [time] *lower than angels, on account of the suffering of death crowned with glory and honor, in order that by the grace of God he might taste death for everyone.* (2:9)

In contrast to sinful man's failure, we may contemplate the man Jesus (note the use of the human name) who fulfilled the description of Psalm 8. The Greek word order would seem to separate the phrase **on account of the suffering of death** from **lower than the angels.** Hence it is best to regard it as going with what follows and naming the grounds for the crowning: "on account of the suffering of death crowned with glory and honor." As the divine Son, our Lord became man that He might die for sinners and thus provide the redemption that the Father in His matchless grace desired. The successful accomplishment of this plan brought the exaltation which Christ now enjoys.

That he might taste death is the purpose of the incarnation, death, and its aftermath. At first reading, one might think that the crowning must precede the tasting of death because of the order of the clauses. However, the difficulties of such an interpretation make this explanation unlikely. As Bruce points out, the general approach of the epistle presents the glory as the sequel to the passion, as in 12:2, not as some prior event.[20] It is better to see the author as regarding the humiliation, suffering, death, and subsequent glory as the progressive unfolding of the one grand event whose purpose was to provide the Savior's death for sinners.

Taste was a common metaphor which meant "to experience." It did not suggest a mere sip or sampling, but the full experience of eating (see the use of this word in Acts 10:10, translated "eaten" in the King James Version). **Everyone** (*pantos*) indicates that in some sense the atonement was made for every person. Of course, not all will avail

---

20. F. F. Bruce, *The Epistle to the Hebrews*, pp. 38, 39.

themselves of the gift on their behalf. Thus the man Christ Jesus, by dying for sinners, has made it possible for men yet to reach the heights described in Psalm 8. One Man has already done so, and believers have the prospect of reigning with Him in the age to come (Rev. 20:6).

3. Christ's superiority to angels not contradicted by His suffering. (2:10-18)

Even if one would agree with the author's previous assertions—that Scripture itself places Christ superior to angels, and that the assuming of true humanity was no denial of this inherent superiority—he might still have an objection. Does not Christ's human suffering pose a dilemma? Surely the humiliating sufferings which our Lord endured make His superiority to angels difficult to accept. To this problem the next section is devoted.

a. Suffering was necessary to complete His identification with humanity. (2:10-13)

For it was fitting for him, on account of whom are all things and through whom are all things, in bringing many sons into glory to make the originator of their salvation complete through sufferings. (2:10)

So far from suffering being humiliating to God and unworthy of His position, our author says it was fitting for him. Because of God's holy nature He could not overlook sin. At the same time, because of His love He desired to save sinners. By providing His unique Son as Savior, God was true to His own righteousness and still was able to save men. On account of whom are all things refers here to the Father (although similar terms are used elsewhere of the Son, Col. 1:16, 17), and reminds us of the transcendence and sovereignty of God whose plan of redemption is consistent with and in harmony with all His operations in the universe.

Bringing many sons into glory is in contrast to the suffering and death of the one Son. Thus the grand purpose and accomplishment of Christ's suffering and death fully warranted the drastic action that was taken. To suffer needlessly is foolishness; to suffer in a noble cause is heroic. In the case of sinners, Christ's death was their only hope. The aorist participle *agagonta* (bringing) appears to be timeless here, and merely states the event. It should not be restricted to a past occurrence, as though it referred only to Old Testament saints, or New Testament saints who had died by this time.

To call Christ the *archēgos* of salvation was to employ a term which sometimes meant originator (Heb. 12:2) and sometimes leader or pioneer (Acts 5:31). At times these meanings may coalesce, and this may be the case here. Christ is the one who by His death obtained our salvation, and He has also led the way as our forerunner into heaven (Heb. 6:20). Through sufferings, God made Christ complete (*teleiōsai*). In order to become the Savior, He had to die in man's place, and this necessitated the acquiring of humanity. Although Christ did not partake of fallen humanity, He did become a genuine man in a fallen world, and He lived on the earth which had been cursed at the Fall. Suffering is the common lot of all men in such a world. The particular sufferings in view here are the ones which brought Him to the goal for which He had been born. He accomplished the purpose of His coming when He suffered death for every man (2:9).

> *For both the One sanctifying and those being sanctified are all of one; for which cause he is not ashamed to call them brothers, saying:*
> *"I will declare your name to my brothers; in the midst of the congregation I will sing praise to you."* (2:11, 12)

The One sanctifying is, of course, Christ, and those being sanctified are believers. Both are said to be of one (*ex henos*). The usual interpretation explains the "one" as God or the Father. God is the origin of the human nature of both Jesus and believers (Luke 3:23, 38), and both are conceived by the Holy Spirit in their spiritual nature (Luke 1:35; John 3:5).[21] This interpretation offers a satisfying explanation of the spiritual oneness involved between Christ and those being sanctified, since it is obvious that only believers are in view, not all humanity; and surely it is believers alone that Christ regards as His brothers.

Another possibility is to explain of one as referring to the common

---

21. H. A. Hoyt, *The Epistle to the Hebrews*, p. 20.

source of their humanity.[22] This is precisely the meaning of the same phrase which Paul used at Athens, "He made of one [*ex henos*] every nation of men to dwell upon all the face of the earth" (Acts 17:26). In the Acts passage "one" refers to Adam, and that could well be the meaning here. This fits well into the argument of the passage, in which Christ's humanity is set forth as honorable. It also provides an easier relation to the context regarding angels, for angels can also claim to be of God, and thus Christ's difference and superiority would not be clearly demonstrated. But to say that Christ and believers share a common descent from Adam is to set Christ apart from angels, and the author has already shown that man is not inherently nor ultimately inferior to angels.

Since Christ and believers share both a common spiritual life and a common humanity, He is not ashamed to call them His brothers. Believers are not "poor relations." When Christ became man, it was no patronizing condescension.

Three Old Testament quotations are cited to demonstrate the identification of Christ with men whom He came to save. The first is drawn from the messianic Psalm 22:22. The psalm contained the prediction that Messiah would faithfully reveal the Father to men whom He acknowledges as "brothers." The Gospels are saturated with instances of such activity (John 17:6; 5:17-23). The following clause of the quotation emphasizes the thought that Messiah's testimony would be given in the midst of the congregation. It was not a message sent from some distant Olympus, but was delivered by one who partook of flesh and blood and gave His witness in the very midst of men. While on earth Jesus attended synagogue and temple worship with His fellow Jews, and identified Himself with them in every way except in sinning.

> *And again,*
> *"I will put my trust in him."*
> *And again,*
> *"Behold, I and the children whom God has given me."*
>   (2:13)

The second quotation is taken from Isaiah 8:17 (Septuagint). A similar statement occurs in II Samuel 22:3, but the fact that the next

---

22. So Lenski, *Interpretation of Hebrews*, pp. 84, 85, and O. Procksch, "Hagiazō," in *Theological Dictionary of the NT,* I, 112.

quotation is from Isaiah 8:18 makes it extremely probable that the former is also drawn from Isaiah. The words were spoken originally by the prophet Isaiah, as he contemplated himself as part of the faithful remnant which looked to Jehovah for salvation in the midst of a rebellious nation. The author of Hebrews regards Isaiah as typifying Christ in these words.

The third quotation—introduced by the formula **and again,** *kai palin*—is actually a continuation of the previous one in Isaiah. Our author has cited it separately because he wished to emphasize an additional point. The prophet identifies himself with his children, both of whom trust in God in spite of unbelief all around them. Once again Hebrews interprets the passage typologically of Christ, and uses it because of its associating the **children** with the typified Messiah. A look at the context in Isaiah may give some clue as to the validity of such an interpretation. The rest of the statement says: "I and the children whom the Lord hath given me are for signs and wonders." Hence to see in Isaiah and his children more than one family unit is not out of harmony with Isaiah's own words. F. F. Bruce has also pointed out that Isaiah 8:17, which speaks of Jehovah hiding His face from Jacob, provides a link with the messianic Psalm 22 (source of the first quotation), which describes Jehovah as temporarily hiding His face from the righteous sufferer of the seed of Jacob (note especially vv. 1, 2, 23, 24).[23] Thus the Isaiah and Psalm passages are tied together in thought, and the writer of Hebrews so uses them.

b. Suffering (even to death) was necessary to destroy the devil and deliver believing men. (2:14-16)

Since, therefore, the children are sharers of blood and flesh, he himself also similarly participated in the same, in order that through death he might render powerless him who had the power of death, that is, the devil, and might release these, as many as by fear of death through all their lifetime were subject to slavery. (2:14, 15)

Inasmuch as men are related to one another by a common sharing of humanity, Christ needed to participate also in genuine manhood if He

---

23. Bruce, *The Epistle to the Hebrews,* pp. 46, 47.

as the substitute was to suffer the penalty which men had incurred. The expression "flesh and blood" occurs three times in the New Testament (Matt. 16:17; I Cor. 15:50; Gal. 1:16) and the phrase "blood and flesh" occurs twice (Eph. 6:12; Heb. 2:14). Perhaps the order of terms was a matter of indifference, but some have seen in the former a reference to weakness and fallen humanity, and in the latter merely the physical substance. Such a distinction is difficult to see from the words themselves, but would tend to be supported by the various New Testament uses. If it is valid, the point is even more clearly made that our author is talking about the common physical humanity which Christ shares with believers.

Christ did this in order that through death He might accomplish His purpose. Sin had been committed in the realm of human life and its penalty was imposed in that realm. Since God could not die, He sent the Son to become man that He might pay the penalty of death for men.

The devil is termed the one who had the power of death. This, of course, does not mean that Satan is an independent sovereign who inflicts death upon men at his whim. Scripture does teach, however, that in opposition to the kingdom of light where God rules there is a realm of darkness in which men are enslaved to Satan, sin, and death (Eph. 6:12; I John 2:9-11; 3:12, 14; Col. 1:13). It was Satan's activity that introduced sin, and death followed from it as its penalty. Further, he functions as the slanderer of men, calling for their death from God (Job 1–2). Thus Satan exercises the power of death in that he promotes sin and rebellion against God, slanders God's people, and calls for their death from God. But Christ destroyed the devil at the cross. The verb is *katargēsēi*, "to bring to nought," "render inoperative," "make ineffective." He did this by satisfying fully the claims of God's outraged righteousness. By paying the penalty in full, the very grounds of death and of Satan's accusations were removed. No more could Satan slander a believer before God and impugn God's righteousness because the sinner had not paid with his life. The penalty was paid in full by Christ.

As a consequence, believers have been released from the bondage of dread regarding death which once had enslaved them. They have been removed from the kingdom of darkness into the jurisdiction of Christ's kingdom (Col. 1:13). Death has always enslaved men in fear because of the Satan instigated Fall (whether men realize the reason or not), in which the connection was made between death and the penalty for sin. Now Christ's death has borne the penalty, and thus the fear-producing cause has been removed for those who appropriate the benefits of Christ's death. Although physical death still remains, even that will be cared for by resurrection, and at present death is for believers the gateway to God's presence. As Paul put it in I Corinthians 15:54-56, its sting has been removed.

> *For surely not of angels does he take hold, but of Abraham's seed he takes hold.* (2:16)

Take hold (*epilambanomai*) does not mean "take on the nature of" as in the King James Version, but "to take hold in order to help." The word was used of Jesus when He "caught" Peter as he began to sink while attempting to walk on the water (Matt. 14:31), when He "took" the blind man by the hand in order to heal him (Mark 8:23), and when He "took" the man with dropsy so as to heal him (Luke 14:4). This also provides a better understanding in the present passage, since to translate as "took on the nature of" would be a repetition of verse 14. The point here is that Christ became a man, even to the point of suffering and death, because it was men, not angels, whom He planned to save.

Seed of Abraham would normally be understood as the physical descendants of Abraham, especially in a letter written to Jewish Christians. It is possible, of course, to regard the expression as referring to the spiritual seed of Abraham, including Gentiles as well as Jews (e.g., Gal. 3:29). Westcott, for instance, stresses the absence of the article with "seed" here as emphasizing the character of these men rather than their racial identity.[24] However, the same expression appears without the article in John 8:33, where the sense is certainly racial, so that this argument has little weight. To this writer, there appears no strong reason to insist upon any meaning other than the simplest. Our author tells us that Christ came in fulfilment of the ancient promise to Abraham and of other prophecies given subsequently to the Jewish people. The fact that Gentiles also would be helped is not denied, but is not the point here.

---

24. Westcott, *Epistle to the Hebrews,* p. 55.

    c. Suffering was necessary to qualify Him as a merciful high priest. (2:17, 18)

Therefore, he ought in all things to be made like his brothers, in order that he might become a merciful and faithful high priest in things pertaining to God, in order to expiate the sins of the people. For whereby he himself has suffered by having been tempted, he is able to help those who are being tempted. (2:17, 18)

Since it was men He would help, and particularly for Abraham's seed He would become the high priest to fulfil the Old Testament sacrificial system, it was proper for Him to become a man in all things. No mere pretense of humanity would do. Therefore, in all respects He became a man (apart from those explicit exceptions indicated in Scripture—such

The traditional Mount of Temptation, near Jericho, where Jesus faced Satan (Heb. 2:18).

as sinlessness). Suffering is part of human life in the present world, and therefore Jesus experienced this as well. Such genuine involvement in human life qualified Christ as a merciful and faithful high priest. By His own sufferings, Christ knew human needs from the standpoint of personal experience, and thus can be expected to be merciful toward those in need. By remaining unswerving in His performance of His task, even when it meant suffering and death, Christ showed Himself to be faithful to His purpose. Hence the sinner can confidently entrust himself to this high priest to care for his relations with God.

This is the first mention in Hebrews of Christ as high priest, but this theme will be expanded greatly in succeeding chapters. To Jewish Christian readers, this mention would cause remembrance of the Day of Atonement, and the Aaronic priesthood. As the believer's high priest, it was Christ's purpose to expiate the sins of the people. Expiation refers to the actual taking away of sins so that God's wrath does not fall upon the sinner. In the Old Testament, animal sacrifices atoned for sin, but the New Testament avers that the blood of bulls and goats could not actually take away sins (Heb. 10:4). Only Christ could finally and actually expiate sins. Those for whom Christ is their high priest have one who is qualified to deal once and for all with the problem of their sin.

As the high priest, Christ not only made expiation but also is able to assist believers as they undergo temptation. This may have been one of the immediate problems faced by the original readers. As Jewish Christians they were continually confronted by pressure from their fellow Jews to repudiate Christ or face persecution. There was also the hostility of Gentiles. To such Christ ministers as a merciful and faithful priest because He is fully conversant with human suffering. Being a true man who experienced the attacks of Satan, He is able to render sympathy to the distressed person and function as a spiritual guide and faithful priest to him. He knew from experience what Satan's approaches were like as He faced the suggestion that He should turn aside from the Father's will. He knew by personal involvement what it meant to choose the way of suffering instead of yielding to sidestep the hard places. Thus through identification with humanity even in suffering, Christ fitted Himself superbly so as to be worthy of the confidence of each believer. No angel is so qualified.

C. CHRIST IS SUPERIOR TO MOSES. (3:1–4:16)

The author now moves to a comparison between Christ and Moses, interrupted by a second warning passage. In this discussion he is careful to avoid offending the Jews whose regard for Moses was genuine and deep, and yet he sets forth Christ's superiorities in unmistakable fashion.

1. Both Christ and Moses were faithful to God. (3:1, 2)

Wherefore, holy brothers, sharers of a heavenly calling, consider the Apostle and High Priest of our confession— Jesus, as being faithful to him who appointed him as Moses also [was] *in all his house.* (3:1, 2)

By addressing his readers as **holy brothers,** the author is speaking spiritually rather than racially. He means "holy fellow Christians," not "fellow Jews." Both these designations are familiar terminology within the Christian community, although the combination is not found precisely like this in the New Testament (unless the variant at I Thessalonians 5:27 is accepted). Believers were often called "brothers" (Gal. 1:11) and "holy ones" (i.e., "saints," I Cor. 1:2), and both terms occur together in Colossians 1:2.

They were **sharers of a heavenly calling** in that they had received the effective call of God to salvation, which was heavenly both in its origin from God and in its ultimate goal (Phil. 3:14). Until this point the author had included himself among his readers ("us," "we," etc.); now he is about to address them directly by saying, "You consider." Yet this separating of himself from them had no holier-than-thou implication, for he had described their spiritual status in the most respectful of terms.

Consider Jesus, says the writer. The word (*katanoēsate*) indicates serious attention, careful study. The readers have already made their confession of faith in Christ (*homologias*). Yet as Dods reminds us, "A 'confession' does not always involve that its significance is seen." [25] Every believer needs to examine continually the content of his Christian confession in order that the implications of that confession may be

---

more clearly understood in the light of his increasing spiritual understanding.

Jesus is termed **the Apostle and High Priest**. The fact of Christ's priesthood was introduced at 2:17, and will be elaborated much more in succeeding chapters. Nowhere else is the title apostle ascribed to Christ in Scripture. However, there is no problem in recognizing the appropriateness of this designation. He was God's highest messenger to men. John's Gospel speaks of Him as "he whom God hath sent" (John 3:34). Jesus spoke regarding Himself that "the Father hath sent me" (John 5:36, 37), and to the apostles whom He had chosen He said, "As my Father hath sent me, even so send I you" (John 20:21).

As being faithful is a more accurate rendering of the predicate adjective *piston* than the King James Version "who was faithful." The readers are urged to consider Jesus as to His faithfulness as an apostle and high priest. He was faithful to God His Father, even as Moses was. The sense of *poiēsanti* (appointed) seems certainly to refer to Christ's office as apostle and high priest. Hence to translate it as "made" and use it in the interest of Arianism as asserting that Christ was a created being is unwarranted. What is stated is that He was "made apostle and high priest." The background of the statement may be I Samuel 12:6 American Standard Version, where it is stated that Jehovah "appointed [Septuagint, *poiēsas*] Moses and Aaron," and the reference is clearly to their official appointment, not their physical creation.

Moses is also declared by the author to have been faithful to God. He is not disparaged in this statement, for this would have alienated the readers. At no point in this discussion is any suggestion made that Jesus was *more* faithful than Moses (although such a point might well have been established had he wished to make it, for Moses did have some lapses). The author is rather contending with those who were so enamored with Moses that they were about to forsake the Christian society and return to Judaism. At this point in the discussion, our author is content to make the observation that Jesus is not to be disparaged, for great as Moses was, a careful consideration of Jesus will reveal no deficiencies either. In fact, he will go on to show that each was faithful, but Jesus is on an entirely different and vastly higher plane.

The attributing of faithfulness to Moses was not just a deduction by the author, but was based upon God's statement in Numbers 12:7, "My servant Moses is not so, who is faithful in all mine house." The his house of Hebrews 3:2 is thus "God's house" (not Moses' house), and refers to the people of God in the Old Testament economy.

2. Christ is the builder of the house, but Moses was a part of the house. (3:3, 4)

For this one was counted worthy of more glory than Moses inasmuch as the one who built it has more honor than the house. For every house is built by someone, but he who built all things is God. (3:3, 4)

The reason for the superior glory of Jesus is explained on the basis of rank, not faithfulness. The first illustration used is a builder and the edifice he constructs. The one who built (*ho kataskeuasas*) refers not only to the person who constructs, but also involves the work of planning and furnishing. One may marvel at a beautiful and well-equipped building, but it is self-evident that the real credit belongs to the architect and builder. The author does not imply by his illustration that Moses was the house, but that Moses must be considered as part of the house or household (in conformity with the concepts expressed in verses 2 and 5, where Moses was "in" God's house). In spite of the greatness of Moses, whose responsibilities in Israel made him unquestionably the leader of God's people, he was still an integral part of those people, on the same plane with them as far as their relationship to God was concerned. Christ stands on a higher plane and deserves to be considered as the builder of the house, rather than a mere part of it.

The self-evident truth is stated in verse 4 that the existence of any building testifies to the fact of a builder. This is true whether *oikos* be regarded as a "house" or a "family" (household). No matter how highly the Jews may regard Moses, all would admit that God stood above him. Thus he who built all things is God. The argument in this passage becomes clear only when it is recognized that the author is attributing deity to Jesus. God is the ultimate builder, and Christ has been stated to be the builder of the house in verse 3. It should be evident that in the author's mind Jesus is God's unique Son, and thus possesses the divine nature. This point has been made so clearly in chapter 1, that it is assumed every reader will recognize that it is Christ in His deity that is meant by God in verse 4.

3. Christ is the Son over the house, but Moses was only a servant in the house. (3:5, 6)

And Moses was faithful in all his house as a servant for a testimony to the things which were to be spoken, but Christ [was faithful] as a Son over his house, whose house are we if we hold fast the confidence and the glorying in the hope. (3:5, 6)

Again the faithfulness of Moses is not impugned. Whatever lapses we may find in the life of Moses were more personal than official. As God's appointed messenger to His people, Moses always delivered God's word, and thus was faithful to his authorization. Furthermore, his faithfulness was specifically stated in Numbers 12:7. However, that very passage also indicated the status of Moses as a servant (Septuagint, *therapōn*), and the author of Hebrews picks out this term for emphasis. This is the only New Testament occurrence of *therapōn*, although it is common in the Septuagint, and is used of Moses in Exodus 4:10; Numbers 12:7; and the apocryphal Wisdom of Solomon 10:16. In distinction from other terms denoting servants, *therapōn* connotes such ideas as willingness to serve,[26] personal service freely rendered,[27] and an honorable position.[28] Thus the status of Moses was not without dignity, but he was nevertheless a servant.

The things which were to be spoken is regarded by some as based also upon the quotation from Numbers (12:8, "with him will I speak mouth to mouth"), and is referred by these interpreters to later revelations which God gave to Moses in contrast to Miriam and Aaron.[29] However, the wording is not at all close to the Septuagint at this point, and it is better to regard the statement as referring to subsequent revelation regarding Christ which has now seen its fulfilment in the present dispensation. One example of how Moses' ministry gave testimony to the present economy is the prophecy of Christ in Deuteronomy 18:15.

Christ, however, occupies a vastly different position in God's house

---

26. H. W. Beyer, "Therapon," in *Theological Dictionary of the NT,* III, 128 ff.

27. Westcott, *Epistle to the Hebrews,* p. 77.

28. Dods, *Expositor's Greek Testament,* IV, 273.

29. So Dods, IV, 273, 274; Lenski, *Interpretation of Hebrews,* pp. 106, 107.

of believers. He is the Son, the heir of God, possessing an authority which is inherently superior to any mere servant. Thus He is not merely "in" the house as Moses was (although Moses did have special responsibilities in the house) but is over the house as the lord and master. Even though during Christ's earthly sojourn He appeared to be a servant (Phil. 2:7), He was actually equal to the founder, a position never enjoyed by Moses.

"His own house" (King James Version) can be misleading. There is no word "own" in the text. It was probably the translators' intention to bring out the idea that Christ bears a relation to His people like that of a son over his own house. Sometimes, however, the conclusion is drawn that "his own house" was meant to designate a different house from Moses' house, and thus two houses were in view. This is hardly possible in view of the relation of Christ to Moses stated in verse 3, and in view of the quotation of Numbers 12:7 where the house in view is "my house" (i.e., God's). Whose house are we makes it clear that Christian believers are also involved in this house of God. The best understanding sees one house throughout this passage. It is God's house, the household of faith, including true believers from the Old Testament period as well as the Christian era. In the old economy Moses had a special responsibility, and in the discharge of it he testified of the Christ who would come (Deut. 18:15). Now that Christ has come, the Son has displaced the servant (the annulment of the old system will be explained in chapter 7), and believers enjoy the direct lordship of the Son. In addition, we learn by revelation that the preexistent Son was also the builder even in the Old Testament era.

If we hold fast reminds the readers of their responsibility to the faith they have espoused. Abandonment in favor of Judaism would demonstrate that they had never really become new creatures in Christ. Bruce puts the matter clearly: "The doctrine of the final perseverance of the saints has as its corollary the salutary teaching that the saints are the people who persevere to the end."[30] These Jewish Christian readers (and Gentile Christians as well) must maintain resolutely their confident assurance of the truth they have heard and confessed, and must keep alive their joy in the blessed hope which is the prospect of each believer. This hope looks ahead to the consummation of salvation when

30. F. F. Bruce, *The Epistle to the Hebrews*, p. 59.

the promises of Scripture become fully realized in the believer's experience. ("Firm unto the end," although appearing in the King James Version, is textually doubtful, and perhaps was interpolated from verse 14.)

SECOND WARNING PASSAGE (3:7—4:13)

a. Israel's wilderness experience. (3:7-11)

Having shown that Christ was superior to Moses, the writer pauses to warn against a similar lapse of faith from Christ as was demonstrated in the days of Moses. The implication is that since Christ is superior, such a lapse would be all the more reprehensible. If this illustration is a telling one to us, how effective must it have been to those Jewish Christians to be reminded of their own ancestors.

> *Wherefore, just as the Holy Spirit says,*
> *"Today if you hear his voice,*
> *Harden not your hearts as in the embitterment,*
> *At the day of the temptation in the wilderness." (3:7, 8)*

The basis of this paragraph is Psalm 95:7-11. It is attributed here to the Holy Spirit's inspiration, although in 4:7 the human author is noted as David. The obligatory nature of this exhortation is therefore heightened. Although it is possible to regard only verse 7b as the quotation, so that the main clause introduced by "Wherefore" (v. 7a) is resumed with "Harden not" in verse 8, this would mean that the remaining words of the psalm are made the author's own, rather than being part of the quotation, and this is extremely doubtful. It is much more likely that the quoted material is to be understood as including verses 7b through 11, and that "Wherefore" is resumed with "Take care" (*blepete*) in verse 12.

The emphasis upon the today of Psalm 95:7 will be noted throughout this discussion. The psalmist, in giving his warning to his own generation by the Spirit's inspiration, regarded it as still a possibility for

The possible site of Kadesh-barnea, one of the places where Israel tempted God in the wilderness.

men to come to a place of pleasing God and of enjoying the salvation He provides. The author of Hebrews shares this view, and will demonstrate its truth by careful deduction in his discussion.

The terms embitterment and temptation are drawn from the Septuagint (Ps. 94:8). The Hebrew has "Meribah" and "Massah." The Septuagint has translated these proper names by their etymological meaning, and Hebrews does the same. This was surely the divine intent in bestowing them since they are not geographic place names but were epithets assigned to characterize certain events that happened. Actually, we find these same names assigned at different times and to different places. The first occurrence was at Rephidim near the start of the Exodus (Exod. 17:1-7). At that time Israel complained over the lack of water, and God authorized Moses to smite the rock. As a result "he called the name of the place Massah and Meribah because of the chiding of the children of Israel, and because they tempted the Lord" (Exod. 17:7).

However, this was not the only instance where these designations were used of events in Israel's wilderness experience. Hence we should not restrict the day of the temptation to one twenty-four-hour day, but must regard it as probably covering the whole forty-year period. At any rate, near the end of the wilderness wanderings, Israel provoked God at Kadesh in the incident where even Moses disobeyed God by smiting the rock instead of speaking to it. On that occasion God said, "This is the water of Meribah, because the children of Israel strove with the Lord" (Num. 20:13). Even earlier, when the people were persuaded by the ten disheartened spies and refused to enter Canaan, God was provoked with them (Num. 14:11) and accused them of tempting Him ten times (Num. 14:22, 23). Because of this, all the adults were denied entrance to the land except Caleb and Joshua (Num. 14:23, 24).

> "Where your fathers tempted [me] in a testing,
>   And saw my works forty years.
> Wherefore I was disgusted with this generation,
> And I said, 'They always go astray in the heart;
>   And they did not know my ways.'
> As I swore in my wrath,
>   'They shall not enter into my rest.' " (3:9-11)

Where (*hou*, v. 9; not "when," KJV), refers to the wilderness period in which Israel saw numerous miracles and other instances of divine guidance, but still continued to resist. In spite of God's unmistakable presence among them, they frequently acted as if they had been abandoned, and demanded continuing proofs of God's leading. Such testing of God is a demonstration of unbelief, for it says in effect, "We don't believe your promises to provide for us, and we demand new evidence." This went on for a period of forty years, throughout the entire wilderness experience from Rephidim onward. Such action in the face of repeated miracles was clearly inexcusable.

An interesting rearrangement of the phrase forty years has occurred in Hebrews. Both the Hebrew text of Psalm 95:10 and the Septuagint place "forty years" with the following words, thus naming the period of God's anger. The author of Hebrews has placed "forty years" with the preceding words (although he follows the Hebrew in placing it with God's anger in verse 17). The reason for this change of position is not known. One good possibility is that the writer was conscious of a parallel in years between the forty years of Israel's rebellion in the wilderness and approximately the same period that had now elapsed since the rejection of Christ in A.D. 30. It is doubtful that we could place the writing of Hebrews beyond A.D. 70; but if it was written in the 60s, already it was the fourth decade since the crucifixion, and the parallel would provide opportunity for some sober reflection.

The Holy Spirit (through David) assessed Israel's sin as a continual wandering away from God in the attitude of their heart, and a failure to know and experience the ways of God. "Heart" to the Hebrews represented the center of man's being, and included his intellectual faculties as a basic constituent. To the Hebrews, man did his "thinking" with his heart. Thus Israel was here characterized as possessing minds that continually turned aside from God's revelation and wandered down paths of their own choosing. They were wilfully ignorant of God's ways—that is, His purposes and plans for them. They refused to trust Him for their physical needs at Rephidim. They rejected the way He wished to lead them at Kadesh-barnea. It was not that they were intellectually unaware of what God wanted, but they did not know in the sense of "did not acknowledge" (*ouk egnōsan*) what God's ways really were.

Consequently, God gave His solemn oath, They shall not enter into my rest. In the Greek text the statement begins with an "if" (*ei*). This is an elliptical form of the Hebrew negative oath, which regularly was prefaced with some statement calling upon God. For example, "The Lord do so to me and more also, *if* aught but death part thee and me" (Ruth 1:17). The meaning was, "Nothing but death shall part us." Here the full expression would have been something like this: "If they shall enter into my rest, then my name is not Jehovah." The meaning obviously was, "They shall not enter."

Our author has quoted Psalm 95:11, which in turn was based upon the statement in Numbers 14:28-30: "Say unto them, As truly as I live, saith the Lord, as ye have spoken in mine ears, so will I do to you: Your carcases shall fall in this wilderness; and all that were numbered of you, according to your whole number, from twenty years old and upward, which have murmured against me, doubtless ye shall not come into the land, concerning which I sware to make you dwell therein, save Caleb the son of Jephunneh, and Joshua the son of Nun."

The word "rest" did not appear in that passage. Nevertheless it is clear that entrance into the promised land of Canaan was what God was denying to Israel (note Num. 14:23, 30, 35). This understanding of "rest" is corroborated by Deuteronomy 12:9, 10: "For ye are not as yet come to the rest and to the inheritance, which the Lord your God giveth you. But when ye go over Jordan, and dwell in the land which the Lord your God giveth you to inherit, and when he giveth you rest from all your enemies round about, so that ye dwell in safety. . . ."

Further substantiation is found in three passages in Joshua, after Israel had entered the land.

> And the Lord gave them rest round about, according to all that he sware unto their fathers: and there stood not a man of all their enemies before them; the Lord delivered all their enemies into their hand (21:44).

> And now the Lord your God hath given rest unto your brethren, as he promised them: therefore now return ye, and get you unto your tents, and unto the land of your possession, which Moses the servant of the Lord gave you on the other side Jordan (22:4).

> And it came to pass a long time after that the Lord had given rest unto Israel from all their enemies round about, that Joshua waxed old and stricken in age (23:1).

"Rest" denoted more than just entrance into Canaan, however, as the succeeding discussion will show. The original occasion which drew God's oath had specific reference to the rest in Canaan, but there was an underlying meaning, whose depth was seen by David in Psalm 95, and will be examined carefully by the author of Hebrews.

b. Warning against unbelief. (3:12-19)

Take care, brothers, lest there be in any of you an evil heart of unbelief in departing from the living God, but keep encouraging one another daily, while it is called "Today," in order that no one of you be hardened by the deceit of sin. (3:12, 13)

Take care resumes the discussion begun at verse 7 ("Wherefore"). What follows is a searching warning for each believer to examine his own spiritual condition. The author views the danger to his readers as unbelief, similar to that which characterized their forefathers in the wilderness. Any problem of wrong deeds is the result of a wrong heart, for "out of it are the issues of life" (Prov. 4:23).

In particular, the unbelief in view is a **departing from the living God.** This "departing" (*apostēnai*) gives us the word *apostasy.* It refers to a departure from and repudiation of one's position. In the case before us, it was a departure from the Christian faith, an act which the author regards as apostasy from God. One can imagine the readers protesting. They were not about to become atheists. Yet for a Jewish Christian to abandon Christ and return to Judaism is here called apostasy from the living God. In the author's mind, it was impossible for one to turn his back upon the highest revelation of God (i.e., the Son, 1:2) and yet possess a true faith in God. The true spiritual remnant of the Old Testament religious system was sensitive to the message of God spoken in Christ (John 8:47; 10:27). To reject Christ was to demonstrate an unbelieving heart that did not know God at all.

To counteract the tragic possibilities, the author urges that the readers **exhort one another daily.** Exhort (*parakaleite*) denotes encouragement, rather than criticism or castigation. What is urged is a spirit of mutual helpfulness which regards the Christian society as a spiritual unity. Thus it is important that the whole be in a strong and prosperous state. Christian faith is not merely a matter between a man and his God, but has also its corporate implications. Believers have not fulfilled the intent of this admonition until they are engaging in a helpful concern for their fellow Christians, and are active in strengthening their brethren in the faith. Such an attitude is required daily because the problem exists daily. The bracing effect of faithful Christians upon one another is one of the great values of the local church. Through regular and frequent gatherings, believers can share one another's burdens and provide spiritual encouragement to the weak and the disheartened.

While it is called 'today' picks up the today of Psalm 95:7. The use of the article (*to sēmeron*) indicates that the reference means "the term 'today' " (since *sēmeron* is actually a Greek adverb, not a noun). Today as used by the author here refers to the present opportunity afforded his readers to strengthen their faith. This opportunity would be gone when they reached the end of their lives, or when Christ would return. Inasmuch as the precise time of either event was not known, the logical time to care for this responsibility was *now*.

The problem was that one of their group (or more than one—the pronoun *tis* is indefinite) might be hardened by the deceit of sin. Sin deceives because its dire effects are not usually seen at once. The human heart is then fooled into thinking that there is no penalty at all, and it becomes dulled and insensitive to the heinousness of sin. The blinding and dulling effects of sin might cause some weak Christians to think that reverting to Judaism was not really much of a step, and certainly not a backward one. The temporary advantages (easing of social pressures from the Jewish community, and so forth) would be made to seem of much more practical importance than the theological implications of such a move. Sin is a master at deception, and believers as well as others need to recognize its character.

> For we have become sharers of Christ, if indeed we hold
> fast the beginning of the confidence firm until [the] end.
> (3:14)

This is not a future promise, but a statement of a present fact. The perfect tense we have become (*gegonamen*) names the present state that is resultant from a past action. At regeneration all true believers become sharers of the very life of Christ. Sharers is the same term used in 3:1, describing believers as sharers of a heavenly calling. Believers are participants in a vital union with Christ, and this fact should provide the greatest incentive to loyalty and firm faith.

There is also a human responsibility resting upon believers: if indeed we hold fast the beginning of the confidence. This is not a warning that a true "sharer of Christ" will ever have that status withdrawn, but a solemn reminder that a true "sharer" will continue in the first faith, and will not apostatize to Judaism. The beginning of the confidence is the original faith which the believers had placed in Jesus Christ for salvation. A real "believer" by definition is one who is believing. He never ceases to believe. He is not one who "believed" something once in the past, and never needs to believe again. Rather, he is one who reposes his trust completely in Christ; and even though this had a moment of beginning, it was the start of a continuing state. The "if" clause, then, does not tell us that we will become sharers of Christ ultimately if we hold fast long enough; but it tells us how we can recognize the true sharers of Christ.

> In saying,
>   "Today if you hear his voice,
>   Harden not your hearts as in the embitterment,"
> who, indeed, after they heard, made God embittered?
> Yea, [was it] not all who came out of Egypt through Moses?
>   (3:15,16)

It is not agreed by all whether verse 15 should be attached to the preceding verses or connected with what follows. If it is construed with the preceding, the thought is that we should hold fast our confidence in light of the saying, "Today . . . harden not your hearts." If it is regarded as introducing what follows, the thought is that in the psalm certain ones provoked God, and it must be clearly understood who those were. Many object to the latter explanation because of the use of *gar* at the beginning of verse 16. This fails to take into account the exclamatory use of *gar* ("indeed"), and thus does not pose an insurmountable obstacle. The choice is not easy, and fortunately the argument is not materially affected. The present writer has chosen the second alternative, placing it with verse 16.

Once again referring to Psalm 95, the author focuses this time upon the word embitterment. God was provoked by certain ones, and the reason for it was of particular interest. The psalm, of course, had reference to the wilderness experience of Israel, as explained in Exodus 17 and Numbers 14—20 (note the discussion above, vv. 7-11).

The King James Version translates *tines* as the indefinite "some," and regards the second clause as an assertion that takes cognizance of Caleb and Joshua as not causing God's embitterment. Against this rendering are several factors. It is a bit strange to call six hundred thousand men merely "some," when the defection was complete with only two exceptions. Also, the thrust of the discussion was not to emphasize that some were not guilty, but that the provocation was wholesale. Furthermore, there appears to be a parallelism running through the remaining verses of the chapter, and to treat verse 16 as a declaration rather than as a question destroys this.

For these reasons it is better to regard *tines* as the interrogative "who," along with the American Standard Version, Revised Standard Version, New American Standard Bible, New English Bible, and the editors of Nestle and the Bible Societies Greek text. The verse then asks: **Who made God embittered?**, and the answer is given in the rhetorical question, **Was it not all who came out of Egypt?** The "howbeit" of the King James Version is more properly the confirmatory use of *alla*, and should be regarded as yea, indicating that there should be general agreement with the author's answer. In spite of their deliverance in the Exodus, the very ones who had been brought out of Egypt were the ones who rebelled against God and provoked Him into giving His oath that they could not enter the promised land. All (*pantes*) takes no notice of Caleb and Joshua, but these two exceptions hardly weaken the force of the argument. The statement uses all in a general way to indicate that unbelief characterized the nation in the wilderness, and as a result that generation perished under the wrath of God. The point to note is that those who had already experienced the blessing of God to a great degree nevertheless fell victim to unbelief.

And with whom was he disgusted forty years? [Was it] not with those who sinned, whose bodies fell in the wilderness? (3:17)

This second of the three questions emphasizes the fact that God's anger was against those who sinned. It was not a capricious act on

God's part, but was the direct result of sinning on the part of Israel. Their sin was utterly inexcusable for they had been witnesses of God's mighty acts on their behalf at the Exodus, and had personally experienced many of His providences and His special provisions for their care (v. 16). Thus their sin was in spite of the clearest light.

Nor was God's anger caused by just one act of faithlessness. God's displeasure was aroused throughout forty years—from the opening stages of the Exodus until near the end (note discussion on 3:8, 9).

To call the ones who perished those who sinned does not imply that Caleb and Joshua were not sinners (as all men are), but only that they were not guilty of the particular sin which is in view here. The statement must be related to the argument of the passage, which in turn is based upon Psalm 95 and the history of Israel in the wilderness. Those whose bodies fell in the wilderness were those who refused to trust God at the time of the spies' report, and said they preferred death in Egypt to the prospects before them in Canaan (Num. 14). They sinned by repudiating God's leadership and His leader. For this sin God allowed all the adults to perish in the wilderness (Num. 14:23, 29, 32, 33).

> And to whom did he swear that they should not enter into his rest, but to those who disobeyed? And we see that they were unable to enter on account of unbelief. (3:18, 19)

The third question is based upon the concluding part of the psalm quotation, and emphasizes the fact that God's denial of rest was directed against those who had deliberately disobeyed. The fact that they had gone astray in their hearts and did not know God's ways (Ps. 95:10) was not due to lack of information, but is explained by the author as disobedience. They had participated in the deliverance from Egypt. They had the continuing presence of God leading them. They had God's faithful spokesman Moses to tell them God's will. At the sending of the spies, they had also the witness of Caleb and Joshua. Their refusal to go forward was a clear case of disobedience to the revealed will of God. No excuses for them should be attempted. They knew God's will and disobeyed it. As a result they missed the blessing of God's rest in Canaan. The blame lay entirely with them.

Verse 19 draws the conclusion that unbelief was what kept the first generation from the promised land. It was not the fault of circumstances nor of God's intransigence. It was due to the unbelief of Israel in refusing to trust the promises of God to give them the land. The application to the readers is clear: professed Christians who through lack of trust in Christ would revert to Judaism are exhibiting the same faithlessness toward God's revelation as their fathers had done, and the consequences could be equally disastrous. (And perhaps in some cases more so. We need not conclude that all the Jews who perished in the wilderness were eternally lost. Moses himself, as a result of a later incident, did not attain the "rest" of the promised land, but he was spiritually saved, as his presence at Christ's transfiguration attests. In most cases, however, the temporal judgment of physical death no doubt implied spiritual death as well.)

c. Warning against missing God's rest. (4:1-13)

The warning section now proceeds to its second emphasis, the danger of missing the rest which God provides.

> *Let us therefore fear lest, a promise being left to enter into his rest, anyone of you should think he has come short.* (4:1)

The fear (*phobēthomen*) that is expected is not the terror of the ungodly who still carry the guilt of sin, but the godly fear which produces soberness and solemn recognition of God's awesomeness. The exhortation is built upon the premise that God's promise to enter into his rest is still valid. The failure in the wilderness did not nullify it, nor did the next generation which actually entered Canaan complete it. The absence of the article with promise (*epangelias*) is significant in that reference is not just to that specific promise to Israel during the Exodus (i.e., "the" promise), but to something which partakes of the same character but may not be absolutely identical. It needs to be demonstrated, however, that the promise is still left for us, and this will be done masterfully in the succeeding discussion. It will take careful explanation, in view of the fact that rest can hardly mean entrance to Canaan in this passage, as it did in chapter 3.

In challenging his readers to treat with reverential respect the issues that confront them, the author reminds them of what might occur. The concluding words of verse 1 may be understood a number of ways. The

King James Version has "should seem [*dokei*] to come short of it."
This appears to be a delicate way of saying "should come short,"
although the colorless "seem" is surely a weakening of the expression.
However, the problem was not in "seeming" to come short, but was the
danger of actually coming short. The Revised Standard Version and the
New English Bible treat the puzzling verb as "be judged" or "be found"
in the judicial sense. The implication may be that God will be the judge.
Arndt-Gingrich do not list such a usage, and the present tense of *dokei*
would suggest more of a continuing process than of a judicial pronouncement.

The best explanation regards the verb in its common usage as
meaning "think." The thought is: No one should be misled into
thinking that he has come short of God's rest by following Christ alone
apart from the Old Testament ritual. The problem was that some of the
readers were contemplating a return to Judaism on the false assumption
that Christianity was not itself sufficient. They thought they had fallen
short unless they resumed all the rites and ceremonies of the Old
Testament system. The writer wants to make it clear that this is not so.

> For even we have had good news announced [to us], *just as*
> those also, but the word of hearing did not profit those, not
> having been mixed with faith in the ones who heard. (4:2)

This explains why no one should think that adopting the Christian
faith was to come short of God's rest, and that reverting to Judaism
would be to recover it. It is pointed out that present believers have had
the good news of God's rest proclaimed to them, just as those in the
Old Testament system. The good news was not absolutely the same, for
the promise of physical rest in Canaan did not apply to Christians (as a
matter of fact, it did not apply to the Jews in David's day either [Ps.
95], for the promise then was offered to those who were already in
Canaan). Yet in its essential character as a participation in God's rest
for His people, apart from local and temporal aspects, the good news
was proclaimed to both groups. (Cf. Matt. 11:28, "Come unto me . . . I
will give you rest.")

The promise of God's rest in the Old Testament did not find
fulfilment in those who heard the message, because the hearing of it
was not met with faith. An interesting variant occurs at this point in the
text, and the sense of the statement is considerably affected. The

reading adopted by Nestle, and followed by the King James Version, American Standard Version, Revised Standard Version, and New English Bible is *sunkekerasmenos* (having been mixed), in which the participle is nominative, agreeing with *logos* (word). This reading has the support of Aleph, some of the Old Latin, Syriac, and Coptic evidence, as well as Ephraem, Cyril, and Theodoret. To adopt this reading is to understand that the word which was heard by Israel was not mixed with faith in the hearers.

An alternative is adopted by the Bible Societies text (with a C rating denoting a considerable degree of doubt), and found in the English Revised Version. The reading is *sunkekerasmenous*, an accusative form agreeing with *ekeinous* (those). This reading has the more impressive support of papyri 13 and 46, uncials A, B, C, and D, as well as certain minuscules. The meaning would be that "those in the wilderness were not united in faith with those who heard." "Those who heard" would presumably be Moses, Caleb, and Joshua. In spite of the early and substantial documentary evidence for the latter, intrinsic probability would seem to favor the former, and this reading has been employed for the translation given above. Whichever reading is followed, the main point remains that Israel's lack of faith lay at the root of the problem.

> *For we who believed are entering into the rest, just as he*
> *   has said,*
> *"As I swore in my wrath,*
> *They shall not enter into my rest,"*
> *although the works were finished from the foundation of*
> *   the world.* (4:3)

The author must now prove that God's plan of providing rest is still in effect. He has just shown that refusal to believe was what prevented Israel from enjoying rest. Now he asserts that Christians are ones who have believed, and as a consequence are entering God's rest. He must, of course, deal with the implications of God's oath. Why was it given? What did it imply as to God's ultimate purpose? Did it mean that God's rest was no longer available?

The truth insisted upon by the author is that Israel's failure to believe, and the subsequent oath of God which prevented their participation in His rest did not annul the fact that God's plan for believers to enter this rest would still be carried out. Indeed, Christians (both Jew and Gentile) are entering it now. Entering (*eiserchometha*) is a present indicative form, and this asserts that the action was going on currently. It is true that a past tense is not used, which would have stated that entrance had already been accomplished. On the other hand, neither is the tense future, which would point to an event still to be accomplished. Hence it should be regarded as a statement of present experience in which true believers presently enjoy God's rest to a certain extent, while at the same time looking forward to a glorious consummation in the life to come. It was the message of rest announced in recent years by Jesus Himself that these Christian readers had received: "Come unto me, all ye that labor and are heavy laden, and I will give you rest. Take my yoke upon you, and learn of me; for I am meek and lowly in heart: and ye shall find rest unto your souls. For my yoke is easy, and my burden is light" (Matt. 11:28-30).

The promise to enter God's rest was unfulfilled by Israel. This was certain because God said so and confirmed His statement by an oath, as Psalm 95:11 asserts. Now if Israel did not fulfil it, does that mean that God's rest was no longer available? The author answers this question with two facts. The first was that the rest of God has been available ever since creation. **Although** introduces a clause which prevents the false conclusion that God refused His rest to Israel because the rest no longer existed. On the contrary, God's rest has existed since the six days of creation when the world was founded. His creative works were finished, and there has been no resumption of such work that would terminate God's rest.

> *For he has said somewhere concerning the seventh* [day] *thus, "And God rested on the seventh day from all his works." And in this* [psalm] *again, "They shall not enter into my rest."* (4:4, 5)

These two quotations are the author's proof texts for his propositions laid down in verse 3. The indefinite way in which the first one is introduced is characteristic of Hebrews. Perhaps here it is partly caused by the fact that the statement occurs in three places in the Old Testament (Gen. 2:2; Exod. 20:11; 31:17). It must also be remembered that exact citation of Scripture references was much less common in a day when versification was not practiced and when the manuscripts were in scroll form. Westcott cites examples from Philo and Clement of Rome to illustrate this indefinite introducing of quotations.[31]

The first quotation gives the Biblical support for the contention that God does have a rest prepared. Each of the six days of creation had its beginning and ending marked by the words "the evening and the morning," but the seventh day had no mention made of its terminus. [32] Thus God's rest is viewed as still occurring (i.e., God did not resume creating on the eighth day). This understanding is supported also by the statement of Jesus in the course of His argument with the Jews in John 5. When accused of sabbath breaking, Jesus defended Himself by referring to the Father's present activity as justifying His action, "My Father worketh hitherto, and I work" (John 5:17). The argument depends for its validity upon the fact that God's rest was still in effect and yet was not broken by the circumstance that He "worketh."

What is this rest of God? Certainly it did not connote the cessation of all activity, for that is contradicted by the Biblical teaching of miracles and providence, as well as by the statement of Jesus cited above (John 5:17). Inasmuch as the author takes us to God's rest after creation, the prominent thought would seem to lie in the concept of the rest which comes with accomplishment, completion, and satisfaction. At the conclusion of creation, God "rested" from His project because it was accomplished; and because His work was good, His rest was also one of satisfaction and enjoyment. This rest of eternal blessedness and fulfilment is what God wants to share with His children.

The second quotation is the Biblical basis for the conclusion that Israel did not enter God's rest. The author returns to Psalm 95, the passage providing the basis for the major part of the discussion in this section, and again cites God's oath, **They shall not enter into my rest.** Hence the exclusion is not a matter of questionable interpretation, but was unequivocally stated by God, and supported with His oath.

Since therefore it remains for some to enter into it, and those who formerly had the good news proclaimed [to them] *did not enter on account of disobedience. . . .* (4:6)

---

31. Westcott, *Epistle to the Hebrews,* p. 96.

32. This does not imply that the seventh day was not a literal day with an evening and a morning, just as the previous six days of creation. However, the author has used the silence of Scripture on this point to illustrate his argument that God's sabbath rest has never ended. The same method of argument is used in 7:3 regarding Melchizedek's absence of recorded birth, parentage, or death.

The argument is here summarized before it is taken to the next step. Because God's rest still exists and the generation under Moses did not fulfil it, the author concludes that the promise still remains to be fulfilled. A number of other assumptions seem to be in the background of this conclusion. It is assumed that God's word is sure, and that His promises will ultimately be fulfilled, if not by one generation, then by another. Perhaps it is also concluded that God's oath to rebellious Israel was sworn in His wrath (a fact mentioned in 3:11 and 4:3, and implicit in 3:8, 15, 16, 17), and this was not His calm, deliberate, or original intention, and thus was not the ultimate conclusion of the matter. At any rate, to recognize that God's rest has existed since creation, that He wants to share it with men, and then to suppose that such a desire would be forever unrequited because Israel under Moses failed is hardly tenable. However, the author does not base his conclusion on such reasoning alone (though it would appear to be a logical deduction), but demonstrates its validity by again appealing to Scripture.

> ... *again he fixes a certain day, "today," saying in David*
> *after so long a time, even as has been said before,*
>   *"Today if you will hear his voice,*
>   *Harden not your hearts." (4:7)*

Psalm 95:7, a psalm attributed here to God speaking in David, repeats God's invitation to rest, and offers it today. Our author notes that this was after so long a time. The psalm was penned over four hundred years after God's oath to the wilderness generation. Yet the clear implication is that Israel's earlier failure did not mean that the promise was dropped, but only that the particular generation involved was excluded. It was still valid for David's generation centuries later. (As has been said before is the author's recognition that he has already mentioned this passage in 3:7, 13, and 15.) Inasmuch as the good news of God's rest was still available in David's day, and there has been no indication of any withdrawal of God's offer, we must regard the invitation as still in force. It is still today, just as in David's time. These first century readers, whose Scripture for the most part was the Old Testament, would not have thought of relegating the Old Testament to an entirely different era which had no relevance to them. They would have had no reason to suppose that the "today" of Psalm 95:7 was not just as applicable to them one thousand years after David, as it was to David's generation four hundred years after Moses.

> *For if Joshua had given them rest, he would not be speaking about another [day] after these days. There remains then a sabbath rest for the people of God. (4:8, 9)*

A reader might object that even though the Exodus generation perished under the wrath of God, certainly the next generation did enter Canaan. Could it not then be concluded that the promise has been fulfilled because some Israelites did enter the rest in Canaan?

The names Jesus and Joshua are spelled exactly the same in Hebrew and in Greek, and Greek readers had to determine from the context whether *Iēsous* the Christ or *Iēsous* the son of Nun was intended. There can be little doubt that it was the latter referred to here, and English versions should render the name as Joshua. The author's contention is that **Joshua** did not provide Israel with rest in the fullest sense of Psalm 95:11, even though he did lead the people into the promised land. In fact, the Old Testament asserts that he did lead them into rest of a limited sort (Josh. 21:44; 22:4; 23:1). However, the rest in Canaan was only one very limited aspect of that blessed rest which God had planned for His people; and the far more important spiritual rest in salvation which is the possession as well as the prospect of believers was beyond Joshua's capability to bestow. The proof is the fact that long after the days of Joshua God would not have spoken in Psalm 95 about a need today to enter into rest if it had been previously accomplished. Grammatically, it is a condition contrary to fact: "If Joshua had given them rest [but he didn't], he would not be speaking about another day [but God did in Psalm 95]."

Verse 9 summarizes the conclusion which has been so carefully explained. God's rest for believers still remains. One does not need to despair of having come short (4:1). What was needed was care that faith did not falter, and that the readers were truly the people of God. The term "rest" employed here (*sabbatismos*) occurs only this once in the New Testament, and is thus different from the word used for "rest" elsewhere in the discussion (*katapausin,* 3:11, 18; 4:1, 3, 5, 10, 11; *katepausen,* 4:8, 10). The change to sabbath rest was doubtless made because the author wants his readers to think in terms of God's own rest, which was just explained in its connection with creation (v. 4).

Qattara Hills, near Gilgal, traditional place of Israel's entry into Canaan under Joshua (Heb. 4:8).

The rest in Canaan is not what remains to be entered, but the sharing of God's presence and the blessedness which that affords.

> *For he who entered into his rest also himself rested from his works, even as God* [rested] *from his own* [works].
> (4:10)

Considerable disagreement exists in the interpretation of this verse. Three views merit special comment. One interpretation explains he as the believer who has experienced spiritual rest in salvation, and thus has ceased from his own worthless works.[33] Somewhat similar is the explanation which interprets it of a deeper consecration in which the believer comes to rest his soul more fully in the Lord and ceases from legalistic efforts at greater sanctification. Both of these share a common weakness in that they interpret the believer's works as something bad. This, in turn, injects a jarring note into the analogy with God and His works. In the analogy, the one who has entered rest has ceased from something, just as God did. The analogy is certainly awkward if the sense is that just as God ceased from His good works of creation, so we are to cease (or have ceased) from bad works.

The second interpretation refers it to the believer at death. The aorist participle lends itself well to the concept that this entry has been completed.[34] Furthermore, the thought and terminology is similar to that expressed in Revelation 14:13: "Blessed are the dead which die in the Lord from henceforth: yea, saith the Spirit, that they may rest from their labors; and their works do follow them." This view preserves the analogy in that the believer's "works" are regarded as his Christian labors on earth, and thus are good, just as God's works were good. Interest in the believer's death is one of the concerns of the author, as 13:7 indicates.

A third interpretation refers the verse to Christ, who has finished His earthly work and has entered the rest of heaven.[35] This view regards

---

33. So Archer, *Epistle to the Hebrews,* p. 32.

34. So F. F. Bruce, *The Epistle to the Hebrews,* pp. 77, 78; Hewitt, *Epistle to the Hebrews,* pp. 88, 89; Lenski, *Interpretation of Hebrews,* pp. 137, 138.

35. So Henry Alford, *The New Testament for English Readers,* pp. 1480, 1481; Hoyt, *Epistle to the Hebrews,* pp. 26, 27; Pink, *Exposition of Hebrews,* pp. 210, 211. A variation of this view is given by Owen, who views the "rest" as Christ's resurrection. John Owen, *Exposition of the Epistle to the Hebrews,* pp. 800-804.

the "works" in the same way as the previous interpretation. To cite Christ's example as an incentive for believers to follow (v. 11) is fully consistent with the author's practice elsewhere of regarding Christ as the believer's forerunner, opening the way for him to follow (see 6:20). At first glance, it appears to be a weakness that Christ is not mentioned in the immediate context. However, He has been in view since the beginning of the discussion (3:1), and at the end of this section it is clear that the author has had Christ in mind all along. In verse 14, he mentions the fact that Jesus our high priest has entered heaven, and the manner in which the reference is made ("Therefore, since. . . .") suggests that it is a conclusion or summation of what has just been said. One notices also that when believers have been referred to in the discussion, the reference was a plural "us" or "we." Hence the singular "he" in verse 10 is noteworthy and may suggest a change to Christ. Either of the last two views seems preferable to the first, and with either one it is the final rest that is emphasized.

> *Let us therefore be diligent to enter into that rest, lest someone might fall in the same example of disobedience.* (4:11)

The exhortation includes the writer as well as his readers. He implores them to give due attention and energy to the goal of entering that rest of which he has been speaking. Because he has already stated that his believing readers "are entering" rest (4:3), there must be a shift of some sort in the concept of "rest" as used in verse 11. As noted in the discussion of verse 10, the matter is clear if the final rest of the believer is in view. Bruce puts it this way, "Our author urges his readers once more to make it their earnest endeavor to attain the eternal home of the people of God. . . ."[36] It is the ultimate rest into which Christ passed at the Ascension, and to which all true believers look as the time of final rest from their labors (Rev. 14:13). Certainly the author is not advocating a morbid longing for death. But to remain spiritually firm until Christ returns, or to die in the faith if that should occur first, was entirely consistent with his general viewpoint. Note 11:13; 12:4; and 13:7 as examples of the author's concern for personal faithfulness until the present life is ended.

---

36. F. F. Bruce, *The Epistle to the Hebrews,* pp. 79, 80.

Diligence must be given to this pursuit lest someone might fall in the same example of disobedience. The reference, of course, is to Israel's experience in the wilderness. The analogy was hardly obscure. Even though an entire nation had been delivered from Egypt through the intervention of God, and had actually begun their trek through the wilderness, the vast majority of them failed to enter the rest in Canaan which God had offered. The reason was **disobedience** (*apeitheias*) to the good news of God's promise. So the readers of this epistle had likewise made a beginning. All of them had heard the gospel and had responded to it sufficiently so as to be recognized as Christians, at least outwardly on the basis of their profession of faith. To revert now to Judaism would be disobedience to the one who promised rest (Matt. 11:28-30) and who said, "No one cometh unto the Father but by me" (John 14:6b), and would thus be a departure from God (Heb. 3:12). This had already happened in Israel's history when a whole nation which supposedly trusted the God of Abraham, Isaac, and Jacob, was exposed as having no real faith at all. It must not be allowed to happen again. Holding fast their confidence in Christ would demonstrate that they were not like their fathers (Heb. 3:14).

To summarize the idea of rest in these two chapters, it can be seen that the concept may have as many as four aspects:

1. God's rest (or, creation rest): 4:4
2. Canaan rest: 3:7-19
3. Salvation rest: 4:1, 3a, 8, 9
4. Heaven rest: 4:10, 11

Basic to the entire discussion is God's rest, begun at the conclusion of creation. It is this present blissful condition of God which He longs to share with men. From this beginning the author develops the theme from one step to another. The physical rest in Canaan was merely one limited aspect, and is used as a type or picture of a deeper spiritual concept. That spiritual reality is the spiritual rest which the true believer may have even in this life, but it does not bring the fullest satisfaction until the future day when believers actually enter God's presence in heaven and "rest from their labors." God's salvation for man thus is covered in broad strokes, and is shown to involve physical as well as spiritual blessings, both in time and in eternity.

For the word of God is living and active and sharper than
any two-edged sword, and piercing even to the dividing of
soul and spirit, and of joints and marrow, and is a discerner
of thoughts and intents of [the] *heart.* (4:12)

For indicates this verse to be a further reason for believers to give
proper attention to their spiritual condition. True faith is absolutely
essential for pleasing God, and God cannot be fooled by sham or
halfhearted faith. He is fully able to discern, and someday all must
render an account to Him. The **word of God** is not a reference to the
personal Logos, but describes the revelation of God enshrined as Scripture. The argument in the context has been based on certain Old
Testament passages, particularly ones showing that God opens His rest
to believers but denies it to unbelievers. Now the author reminds his
readers that God's Word continues to distinguish believers and unbelievers. It is **living and active**, filled with the vitality of God Himself
and energetic in its operation. The statement reminds us of Stephen's
reference to "living oracles" (Acts 7:38) and Peter's "word of God
which liveth and abideth for ever" (I Peter 1:23).

God's Word is **sharper than any two-edged sword**. Emphasis here is
not upon its destructive work (such as upon unbelievers) but upon its
dividing, discriminating function. A two-edged instrument was much
better fitted for this sort of task than a single-edged knife would be.
Further description of the Word's discriminating activity is expressed as
**piercing even to the dividing of soul and spirit, and of joints and
marrow.** God's Word with its clear and convicting insights can distinguish between the person who lives only in the realm of the soul (i.e.,
mere physical life, aesthetic pursuits), and the one whose spirit has been
made alive to the things of God by regeneration. Although this verse
clearly makes a distinction between soul and spirit, it hardly settles the
long-debated issue of dichotomy versus trichotomy. Whether the spirit
is a completely separate entity from the soul, or resides in the soul as
one part of it, cannot be resolved by this verse. **Joints and marrow** is
probably metaphorical here, illustrative of the most precise and inner-
most discriminating. Inasmuch as joints and marrow are not contiguous,
the thought is not that of dividing joints *from* marrow, but of separating joints from the bones which meet at that point, and laying bare
the marrow which is inside the bones. As a **discerner of thoughts and**

intents of the heart, God's Word probes the deepest recesses of the human heart and provides spiritual light for those who will accept its truth. If allowed to do its probing work, the Word leaves nothing hidden. It will reveal completely what a man is.

> *And no creature is invisible in his sight, but all things are naked and laid bare to his eyes, with whom we have to reckon.* (4:13)

A slight shift is now made from the "word" as the discerning instrument (v. 12) to the person of God Himself. In His sight no man can hide himself or his deeds. Under the discerning gaze of God, everyone appears fully exposed (*gumna*, naked). Laid bare (*tetrachēlismena*) translates a word used only this once in the New Testament. It is related to the word *trachēlos*, meaning "neck" or "throat." Whether the metaphorical use here is based upon the act of the victorious wrestler grasping his opponent's throat to render him helpless, or derives from the exposing of the sacrificial victim's throat just before the knife is thrust, is not certain. It is clear that the idea of being fully exposed is demanded by the sense of the verse.

With whom we have to reckon is the rendering of a difficult Greek phrase, *pros hon hēmin ho logos*. A literal translation would be "to whom the reckoning [is] for us." Since all men are responsible to one God, and He is one who cannot be deceived by human hearts or hypocritical faith, it is fitting that the warning should end on this solemn note. At the same time there is encouragement here, for God's Word is not only a judge but an instrument to reveal one's condition. Therefore rectification can be accomplished while it is still "today."

4. Christians should therefore make use of Christ, their superior mediator. 4:14-16

> *Therefore, since we have a great high priest having passed through the heavens, Jesus the Son of God, let us hold fast the confession.* (4:14)

The paragraph beginning at this point is a transition leading to the discussion of Christ as high priest. Consequently, the commentator is torn between attaching it to what precedes or placing it with what follows. This writer prefers to view it as summarizing the previous discussion, and resuming the thought of 3:1-6 which was interrupted by the warning passage. Christ had been mentioned as high priest in 3:1, and 4:14 seems to be picking up that thought, since we have a great high priest. (This verse also adds some weight to the view that 4:10 refers to Christ, since He is here implied to have been in view in the previous context.)

Was part of the readers' problem that they missed the Jewish priesthood? Then let them understand that Christians have a great high priest. No priest in the Old Testament was ever called a "great high priest." Furthermore, the Christian's high priest has passed through the heavens. Just as the Aaronic priest passed from the altar through the outer court and then through the holy place to the holy of holies beyond the veil, so Christ also has passed from view. It was not a momentary passing through some earthly chambers, but an ascension through the heavenly regions to the actual throne room of God (v. 16). Hence His present absence from our view is no disadvantage as compared to Aaronic priests, but is due to the fact that He is actually performing for us what Aaron could accomplish only in the most limited and largely symbolic way.

Our high priest is Jesus the Son of God. This designates Him both in His nature as man ("Jesus") and as God, and also clearly distinguishes Him from the *Iēsous* ("Joshua") of 4:8. The readers, therefore, have every reason to hold fast the confession. They had previously confessed their faith in Christ as God's Son who had made expiation for their sin. The exhortation was to stand firm and not let that former position be abandoned.

> *For we do not have a high priest unable to sympathize with*
> *our weaknesses, but one having been tempted in all respects*
> *in likeness* [to us] *apart from sin.* (4:15)

The negative way in which this statement is introduced suggests that rebuttal is being made to an objection. Was it being implied that having a high priest in heaven was no substitute for a priest on earth to whom one could go with his problems? At any rate the author's point is that Christ's presence in heaven, and His identity as the Son of God, did not remove Him from an understanding of humanity. This truth has already been expressed in 2:17, 18. Christ is fully able to sympathize with us in our weaknesses. These weaknesses are not necessarily sins, but may refer to the various frailties which often are the occasions for sin. The proof of Christ's ability to understand human weakness sympathetically is found in His own experiencing of temptation. As a man on earth, Jesus did not live in isolation from human temptation. On the contrary, He was tempted in all respects as ordinary men save one. In fact, one may conclude that He experienced temptation to the full since He never yielded before its full force was spent (as we so frequently do). Furthermore, His was a direct confrontation with Satan himself (Matt. 4:1-11; Luke 4:1-13).

Only in one respect did Christ's temptation differ from ours. Apart from sin (*chōris hamartias*) has been understood by many to describe the result of our Lord's temptation—that He did not sin. However, the point in the passage does not seem to be whether He sinned or not (of course, He did *not*), but whether He was truly tempted and thus could really sympathize. It seems better to regard apart from sin as naming the only exception in the way Christ was tempted as compared to ordinary men. None of His temptations arose out of a sinful disposition, such as all fallen men have since Adam. All of Christ's temptations came to Him from outside Himself (i.e., from Satan). This in no sense violates the truth that Jesus was genuinely tempted, and that He thus understands and sympathizes with men who face such situations.

> *Let us therefore come with confidence to the throne of grace, in order that we may receive mercy and find grace for well-timed help.* (4:16)

Since our great high priest is in the most advantageous place (heaven), and is both Son of God and yet through His human experiences is fully qualified to understand our needs, we have the best of reasons for using the good offices He provides. This verse encourages us to approach confidently the throne of grace. As our high priest, Christ has entered the divine presence in heaven, having made full expiation with His own blood. Thus we can approach without fear of rejection the very throne of God where our priest is seated at His right hand.

The context suggests that the approach to God in view is that made by the believer in times of special need. This obtaining of mercy is not the initial reception of the mercy of God at conversion (e.g., I Tim. 1:16), for these readers are already Christians. Instead it is what believers need when their weaknesses seem overwhelming. **Mercy** speaks of God's relieving of man's miseries. **Grace** is the favor of God which He bestows without regard for merit to those who put their trust in Him. In times of weakness, temptation, and sin, believers find in their access to God through Christ the timely **help** that is tailored to their particular need.

D. CHRIST IS SUPERIOR TO AARON. (5:1—7:28)

1. The priesthood of Aaron. (5:1-4)

For every high priest being taken from men is appointed on behalf of men regarding things pertaining to God, that he might offer both gifts and sacrifices for sins. . . . (5:1)

The subject of Christ's priesthood had been mentioned in 2:17; 3:1; and 4:14, 15, so that the groundwork has been well laid for this next discussion. Although the expression **every high priest** sounds very general, the facts that Jewish readers are addressed and that the description in verses 3 and 4 is clearly Levitical make it certain that the priesthood of Aaron is in view. The author means "every high priest in the Jewish system."

Obviously the priest was a man himself, and was thus properly fitted to act as man's representative. The Old Testament task of priestly mediation was not committed to angels, but to men. The function of priests was to act **on behalf of men**, specifically in regard to those matters having to do with men's relations with God. It was the priest who offered to God the various sacrifices which the worshipers brought. It is probable that **gifts** refer to voluntary gifts in the Old Testament system (i.e., meal offering, peace offering), and **sacrifices for sins** denote the bloody offerings when sins were committed (i.e., sin offering, trespass offering). It is, of course, possible that "for sins" goes with both nouns in a general way.

. . . being able to deal gently with the ignorant and wandering ones, inasmuch as he also is surrounded by weakness,

and on account of it he ought, just as regarding the people
so also regarding himself, to offer [sacrifices] *for sins.* (5:2,
3)

In addition to the appropriateness of the high priest being a man so
as to be man's representative, another important feature was provided
in the Aaronic system. A human priest would be able to deal gently
with sinners. The verb *metriopathein* carried the idea of moderating
one's feelings. The point stressed seems to be that of mental and
emotional balance, neither coldly distant nor uncontrollably excited.
Neither extreme would be helpful in a priest. One article joins ignorant
and wandering ones, thus indicating that only one group is referred to.
They were without proper understanding of God's truth and thus had
sinned by wandering from it. Ignorant points to the Old Testament
distinction between sins of ignorance for which atonement could be
sought, and sins of presumption for which no sacrifices were available
(Num. 15:27-31). A good priest should be able to fulfil his task because
he knew by personal experience the problems of his people. He too was
surrounded by weakness, just as they were. Thus he could invite the
confidence of the sinner and help him because he should have been
fully aware of the avenues along which sin and temptation overtake
men. This does not imply that each priest must have participated in
every type of sin to be the best qualified, but he must have sufficient
experience of human problems to achieve the proper balance between
leniency and severity, encouragement and rebuke.

The Old Testament priest was personally surrounded with weaknesses, and because he was a fallen man like everyone else, he also
needed some provision made for his own sins. Here lay one of the
weaknesses of the Aaronic system. The priest himself needed a priest. A
further weakness was that sinfulness in the priest often prevented him
from being perfectly sensitive or aware of the needs of others. Nevertheless, God took into account the sins of the high priest by establishing the Day of Atonement ritual in such a way that the high priest
made atonement for himself before he did so for the people. Leviticus
16 describes the annual observance. Before killing the goat of the sin
offering on behalf of the people and sprinkling its blood within the veil
in the holy of holies, he first entered the veil with the blood of a
bullock which was a sin offering for himself and his household (Lev.

16:6, 11-14, 17). After caring for his own atonement, the high priest then offered the blood of a goat as a sin offering for the congregation. A second goat was released into the wilderness as the "scape goat," picturing the removal of the iniquities of Israel (Lev. 16:10, 20-22). The ceremonial observances reminded the priest of his own sinfulness, and thus should have helped him to "deal gently" with his wandering brethren.

> *And not to himself does anyone take the honor, but as being called by God, just as also Aaron* [was]. (5:4)

Another basic characteristic of the Old Testament priesthood was its divine authorization. This was not only true of its general origination as a priesthood, but also of its individual occupier of the high priest's office. This principle is valid, both from logical deduction as well as from Biblical statement.

If men need priests because sin has separated them from God, and if the offering of sacrifice is the only way to find acceptance, then the choosing of an acceptable priest is a crucial matter. Furthermore, if men generally cannot be their own priests but must make use of the good offices of another, and if no sinless priest can be found to serve in this capacity, the problem would seem humanly insoluble. One is thus thrown upon the mercy of God, and must depend solely on His instructions as to what priest would be acceptable. It is God whose wrath must be placated, and we must be sure He will accept our representative.

The Bible is clear that God did this precisely. When the priestly system was established under Moses, **God** appointed **Aaron** as the first high priest (Exod. 28, Lev. 8). The problem of sinfulness in the priest was handled by providing for a ceremonial cleansing of the priest on the Day of Atonement prior to the offering for the people. Furthermore, all succeeding priests were to be not only Levites but descendants of Aaron (Num. 16:40; 18:1-7). Any exceptions to this likewise required the explicit command of God, such as in the case of Samuel who was directed by God to offer sacrifice at the house of Jesse (I Sam. 16:1-13). Examples of those who violated this principle are not missing from Scripture. The cases of Korah, a Levite but not of Aaron (Num. 16), and Saul, a Benjamite (I Sam. 13:5-14), are well known. Another instance was Uzziah, king of Judah, who intruded into the temple in spite of the efforts of the priests to dissuade him, and was smitten with leprosy by direct intervention of God and forced to spend his remaining days in isolation (II Chron. 26:16-23).

2. The priesthood of Christ. (5:5-10)

*So also Christ glorified not himself to become high
priest, but he who spoke to him,*
　"You are my Son,
　Today I have begotten you";
even as also in another [psalm] *he says,*
　"You are a priest forever
　According to the order of Melchizedek." (5:5, 6)

Inasmuch as Jesus was of Judah, not of Levi and Aaron, it must be demonstrated that to regard Him as priest is not an illegal intrusion into the priestly office. It needs to be shown that Jesus possessed a call from God to the priesthood. Two passages from the Psalms are cited as proof texts that Christ holds His priesthood by divine appointment.

The first quotation draws upon Psalm 2:7, a passage already used by the author in 1:5 to demonstrate Christ's Sonship (see the discussion in loco). In the passage God addresses Messiah in His capacity as the duly installed messianic King, and acknowledges Him as my Son. It may be questioned why this particular passage is cited, since it seems to have no direct bearing on the priesthood. However, it does state Christ's authority as the messianic King, and the question of authority is a prime consideration here. Furthermore, Christ is acknowledged as my Son by God. No Old Testament priest was so described. Thus there is no question of His acceptability to God. In addition, the author of Hebrews has Melchizedek in mind, and he was a king as well as a priest. Hence the two quotations fully substantiate Christ's qualifications as a Melchizedek-type priest, showing Him to be recognized by God as king as well as priest.

The second quotation employs Psalm 110:4. This psalm likewise has previously been utilized in Hebrews, although not this particular verse. Verse 1 of the psalm was quoted in Hebrews 1:13 and alluded to in 1:3. In the quotation, God addresses Messiah and calls Him a priest forever.

Thus priesthood is asserted as one of the important functions of the messianic King. We conclude, therefore, with our author that Christ's authorization as a priest is fully substantiated. Indeed, certain things about His divine call mark Him as superior to any priest known in Judaism. His identification as my Son and His establishment as a priest forever are both features that are superior to anything known in the Levitical system.

Christ's priesthood was asserted by Psalm 110:4 to be according to the order of Melchizedek. Thus He would not be Levitical at all, even though the Levitical system did provide much symbolism particularly in the offerings which found fulfilment in the person and work of Christ. Rather, His priesthood would be after a different order, that of Melchizedek. Melchizedek is mentioned in the Old Testament only in Genesis 14:18-20, except for the brief reference to him in Psalm 110:4. He is called king of Salem and priest of the most high God, a circumstance impossible in the Levitical system. Hence there is yet another reason for the superiority of Christ to Aaron, for He is a royal priest.

The functions of priesthood and throne were carefully distinguished in Israel, with the offices being allocated to different tribes. The practical advantages lay in the avoidance of concentrated power in the Jewish state. Yet there were certainly benefits to be had with a royal priest, provided that the person possessing the office had the integrity to avoid abuses. There were times when a godly priest in the Old Testament was faced with a wicked monarch.[37] On other occasions the king was more godly than the priest, and had to take the spiritual leadership.[38] God has planned that Messiah should concentrate in Himself the authority of kingly rule, and this will involve also His spiritual ministration as the great high priest. Because He is the Son of God, believers need not fear that abuse of His power will occur, or that either aspect will be ignored. He is presently our high priest in heaven, and when He comes again it will be to reign as King of kings, while continuing His perfect representation of His people to God.

He who in the days of his flesh, after offering both prayers
and supplications with strong crying and tears to the One

---

37. E.g., Jehoiada the priest and the evil Athaliah, II Kings 11; also Azariah the priest and King Uzziah, II Chron. 26.
38. E.g., Josiah and his religious reforms, II Kings 22, 23.

> *able to save him out of death, and after being heard from*
> *his godly fear, although being a Son, learned the obedience*
> *from the things which he suffered.* (5:7, 8)

Not only does Christ as high priest possess a proper authorization from God, but also He is a man who can sympathize with His dependent people. The days of his flesh refer to the earthly career of Jesus, when He became incarnate and was subject to mortality and other frailties of humanity (although, of course, He was sinless and remained so). Flesh is used here in the physical rather than the ethical sense. The particular instance in view is surely the Gethsemane experience in which Christ prayed to His Father on the eve of His crucifixion. The description of our Lord as engaging in **prayers, supplications, strong crying,** and **tears** is more detailed than the Gospels record. The additional information (such as the tears) could have come from oral tradition handed down in the church by the three eyewitnesses. The four terms used here are progressively stronger. **Prayers** (*deēseis*) are expressions of need, and **supplications** (*hiketērias*) denote urgent requests. The latter term and its cognates were used of suppliants carrying an olive branch in their right hands, seeking help or protection. [39] **Strong crying** (*kraugēs ischuras*) describes the loud outcries of one deeply disturbed, and **tears** (*dakruōn*) are the visible manifestation of grief.

These prayers of Christ were directed to the one who was able to save him out of death. For what did Jesus pray in Gethsemane? To answer it, one must consider also the difficult passage in the Gospels, "Let this cup pass from me" (Matt. 26:39, et al.). It can hardly be that Jesus was praying that He might not die on the cross, for this prayer was hearkened to and yet He did die. (To suggest that the prayer was heard, but the answer was no, hardly satisfies the language here.) The suggestion that Christ prayed that Satan not be allowed to take His life prematurely in the Garden[40] seems strange, since Jesus had said regarding His life, "No one taketh it from me, but I lay it down of myself" (John 10:18). Lenski reminds us that the prayer included the qualification, "If it be possible"; and thus the prayer was answered in the larger

---

39. F. Buchsel, "Hiketēria," in *Theological Dictionary of the NT,* III, 296, 297.

40. Hewitt, *Epistle to the Hebrews,* pp. 99-101.

The traditional Garden of Gethsemane on the slopes of the Mount of Olives. Christ prayed here on the eve of His crucifixion (Heb. 5:7).

sense that Jesus asked only for what was possible within the Father's will.[41]

If it is understood that the cup from which Jesus shrank was the "cup" of suffering the wrath of God as the bearer of man's guilt, then to some extent it may be appreciated why He who had never known forsakenness by the Father dreaded the prospect.[42] Yet His will was so completely submissive to the Father that He asked, "Thy will be done" (Matt. 26:42). Out of death (*ek thanatou*) may well suggest that the resurrection is in view.[43] Thus Christ is understood to pray that the separation from God involved in His approaching death for sinners (Matt. 27:46) would not be the end of the experience, but that death might issue in resurrection life. (To object that Christ knew He would rise, and had even predicted it, and thus would not have prayed for it is invalid, for the same objection might be raised to all of Christ's prayers. Prayer does not always involve asking about uncertainties, but may include statements of acquiescence to God's revealed will.) It should also be observed that the text does not actually say that Christ prayed to be saved out of death, but to the One able to save him out of death. Can this not suggest the reposing of perfect trust in the Father, and the acceptance of His will regardless of the cost and without trying to alter it?

Christ's prayer in Gethsemane was heard (*eisakoustheis*, "hearkened to") because of His godly fear. This is apparently a reference to Christ's perfect submission to God's will as He prayed "Thy will be done." This display of absolute reverence for the Father resulted in the granting of the request. From (*apo*) is used here in the sense of source or cause. As a perfect man His prayer was in full harmony with God's will and thus was certain of being answered. How encouraging to have such a priest representing us before the Father.

By submitting to the will of God, even though in His own right He was God's Son, equal in nature to His Father, Christ learned the

---

41. Lenski, *Interpretation of Hebrews,* p. 164.

42. See the similar uses of "cup" as a metaphor of divine judgment in Isaiah 51:17, 22; Jeremiah 25:15, 17; 49:12; Ezekiel 23:33.

43. So Archer, *Epistle to the Hebrews,* p. 36; Westcott, *Epistle to the Hebrews,* p. 126.

בֿ7דֿ6בֿ

obedience. He did not learn to obey, for He had always done that. The particular obedience here in the author's mind was the death of the cross. He learned by experiencing suffering and death the price that full obedience to the will of God can exact. **Obedience** is not theoretical but experiential. Christ endured the suffering demanded in order to secure our redemption.

> *And having been made complete, he became to all who obey him* [the] *source of eternal salvation, designated by God* [as] *high priest according to the order of Melchizedek.* (5:9, 10)

Having been made complete (or "perfect," KJV) has nothing to do with moral perfection. The statement is similar to 2:10, in which God is stated as making Christ "complete" through sufferings. In the preceding verses of chapter 5, the author has discussed the basic qualifications of priesthood, and then shown how Christ fulfils them. He has concluded by saying that Christ learned obedience by what He suffered (v. 8). Thus the point of the statement is that Christ was brought to full qualification as our priest not only by His divine call and genuine humanity, but also by His suffering.

Our Lord now has become the **source of eternal salvation**. His was no atonement one year at a time. In fact, inasmuch as the blood of animals could not really expiate sin (10:4), it was Christ's work which gave validity to the sacrifices offered by the Levitical priests. This salvation, however, is only for **all who obey him**. It is eternal, but it is not universal. To obey Christ is to do what He asks, and the first thing He asks of men is that they believe Him (John 6:29; I John 3:23).

To conclude this segment of the discussion, the author reminds his readers that Christ is their **high priest** who provides the basis for their salvation, not only because He is superbly qualified, but because God actually **designated** Him as such in Psalm 110:4. It is on the authority of God Himself that we look to Christ as the great high priest. His priesthood after the **order of Melchizedek** posits certain differences from the more familiar Aaronic system, and this will be elaborated in chapter 7. First, however, the readers need to give some very serious thought to certain tendencies in their midst.

THIRD WARNING PASSAGE (5:11–6:20)

At this point the writer's third passage of warning occurs, providing an interruption in the main discussion. Included is some of the severest language in Scripture directed against God's people.

a. Rebuke for spiritual immaturity. (5:11-14)

Concerning whom we have much to say and [it is] *hard to explain, inasmuch as you have become dull in the hearing.* (5:11)

Whom refers to Melchizedek, regarding whose priesthood the author wishes to elaborate in relation to Christ. In fact he will proceed to do so at some length, beginning at 7:1. There is much explanation to make to these Hebrew Christian readers, whose primary knowledge of priesthood was restricted to the Levitical order. It must be explained why Christ was of a different order, and what the advantages were. Such would be difficult to explain to them, however, not because the writer was not knowledgeable, nor because the material itself was abstruse, but because of certain faults in the hearers.

They were, he says, **dull in the hearing.** The adjective *nōthroi* denoted them as lazy or sluggish. At the moment they were already this way in their hearing. The danger was that this might soon characterize their very selves. We note also that this condition was an acquired one. They **have become** (*gegonate*) dull in the hearing. Their original eagerness to hear and respond to the Word of God had cooled. Now they were no longer ready listeners. Other interests had captured their attention.

For even though you ought to be teachers on account of the time, you have need again that someone teach you the elements of the beginning of the oracles of God, and you have come to be having a need of milk and not of solid food. (5:12)

A sufficient interval of time had elapsed since their conversion for them to have become well grounded in the faith. They should have been spiritually mature so as to be teachers of others. After all, every believer is expected to give reasonable explanations of his faith to the questionings of unbelievers (I Peter 3:15), even though not every believer may possess the special gift of teaching (Eph. 4:8-11; James 3:1). Yet these readers were spiritually like children. They seemed capable of understanding spiritual truth on only the lowest level.

The elements of the beginning of the oracles of God constituted the extent of their spiritual advancement, and even these things are said to be in need of review. To identify precisely what is meant is not an easy task, at least if a consensus among commentators is the criterion by which one measures success. To this writer it is clear that these elements of the beginning of the oracles of God (5:12) are the same as "the beginning of Christ" (6:1), and that they are described as milk in distinction from solid food (5:12). Hence the elements of the beginning have to do with the simpler matters of doctrine. The same contrast between milk and solid food is used by Paul in I Corinthians 3:2 (in distinction from Peter, who uses "milk" metaphorically without any implication of inferiority, I Peter 2:2). Can we be more specific than merely defining milk and solid food as the simple versus the complex? The next statement gives the explanation.

For everyone partaking of milk is unaccustomed to [the] word of righteousness, for he is a babe. But the solid food is for mature ones, who because of practice have their senses trained for distinguishing between good and evil. (5:13, 14)

The milk user in this illustration is the infant who is confined to milk. He has not grown sufficiently so as to tolerate more solid food. The illustration is applied to the spiritual infant who is incapable of anything except the simplest of spiritual truths. His spiritual perceptions are not yet accustomed to the word of righteousness. It can hardly be that righteousness here means "justification," for these readers are appealed to on the basis that they are babes in Christ and thus have experienced the imputed righteousness of Christ. On the other hand, to treat the phrase *logou dikaiosunēs* as simply "right discussion" as Lenski insists[44] is most unlikely in this passage involving priesthood and expiation of sin. Verse 14 clearly states that discernment of right and wrong is involved, and that this should be the normal

---

44. Lenski, *Interpretation of Hebrews,* pp. 172, 173.

experience of believers who have grown spiritually. Thus the word of righteousness would refer to God's revelation about righteousness of life which is expected of every believer. Christian faith is not an abstraction. It is never divorced from life. The content of doctrine to which the believer assents *must* issue in a transformed life or something is radically wrong. Scripture gives no comfort whatever to the person whose claim to have trusted Christ has not resulted in a life of righteousness.

The problem which was posed by the readers was that they still partook of the characteristics of spiritual babyhood, although they had been converted long ago (v. 12). They needed the solid food that belongs with adulthood. The characteristic of maturity emphasized here is the ability of discernment. This is a basic quality of maturity in ordinary human life. Children are made subject to their parents both legally and by nature itself because of their undeveloped powers of discernment. Good judgment comes with the accumulation of experiences, and this demands the passage of time. Likewise in the spiritual realm, maturity is marked by discerning ability in the realm of righteousness. Through practice (*tēn hexin*), that is, the skill acquired by experience, the believer's spiritual senses (*ta aisthētēria*) are trained like an athlete (*gegumnasmena*). This enables him to distinguish between good and evil in his daily walk, and thus to maintain that righteousness of life which chooses the good and shuns the evil. Just as the mature man does not make the foolish choices that characterize childhood, so the spiritually mature Christian displays a stability in his conduct that should set him apart from the stumblings that so often accompany the new believer.

Maturity is reached by believers through the word of righteousness. Instead of being unaccustomed (*apeiros*) to it, they must feed upon God's Word, including all parts of it. Only as believers saturate their minds with God's standards of righteousness and His differentiation of what is good from what is evil can they hope to develop the spiritual maturity of which this passage speaks. Only then can they consistently choose the good and shun the evil in the decisions they face.

b. Encouragement toward spiritual maturity. (6:1-3)

Wherefore, having left the teaching of the beginning of Christ, let us be moved along to maturity, not again laying a

foundation of repentance from dead works, and of faith
toward God, of instruction about washings, and of laying
on of hands, and of resurrection of the dead, and of eternal
judgment. (6:1, 2)

One might expect the author to restrict his teaching to "milk" in view of his foregoing complaint. However, he is not content to leave his readers in their spiritually infantile state, and knows that the only way to bring them out of it is to insist that they begin a serious consideration of a more mature diet. Of course, they must depend upon God and their great high priest to make it possible.

Let us be moved along (*pherōmetha*) implies that, as Westcott so aptly puts it, "The thought is not primarily of personal effort . . . but of personal surrender to an active influence."[45] The concept is consistent with 1:3 where the same verb is used of Christ who "carries" (*pherōn*) all things forward to their proper end. The believer's responsibility is to stop putting hindrances in the way. By allowing Christ's priesthood to do its work in our lives, we may arrive at that spiritual maturity (*teleiotēta*) that is expected of each believer within a reasonable time.

The readers are assumed to be Christians. Therefore, the problem was one of advancing from babyhood to full growth. To accomplish this they must leave the **teaching of the beginning of Christ**. Of course, the author does not mean "leave" in the sense of "repudiate," but in the sense of advancement beyond the first stage. The identity of the **teaching** (*ton logon*) is disputed. Are these listed items to be explained as Christian doctrines or elements of Judaism viewed as foundational to Christianity? It is admitted that there is little that is distinctively Christian in the list of six doctrines. However, this writer is unconvinced by attempts to restrict the reference to pre-Christian practices for a number of reasons. (1) The use of *tēs archēs* in 6:1 would seem to be related to the same expression in 5:12. The author's complaint there was not that his readers did not know Old Testament doctrine, but that they were content to remain babies in Christian understanding. (2) The expression "the beginning of Christ" (*tēs archēs tou Christou*) is better understood of truly Christian doctrine. (3) The aorist participle "having left" (*aphentes*) must be understood as relative to the leading verb.

---

45. Westcott, *Epistle to the Hebrews,* p. 143.

Thus it names what must be done in order for progress to occur. It does not demand that it has already occurred in the readers' lives. (4) Only those who had actually become Christians could be challenged to "be moved along to maturity."

Six items of Christian foundational truth are named. Each of these items is vitally important (just as milk is absolutely essential for babies), but one must not think that Christianity is merely adoption of a creed. The foundation must be crowned with a superstructure of righteous living. The first two doctrines mentioned involve the believer's conversion. **Repentance from dead works** and **faith toward God** describe the believer's response to the gospel. In the gospel the sinner learns that all his efforts to please God are merely dead works, and his only hope for salvation is a complete reversal of attitude. He must cease trusting his own righteousness (which is no real righteousness at all) and must cast himself upon the mercy of God, receiving by faith the gift of salvation in Christ. It is this that transforms him from one dead in sins to one born again as a babe in Christ.

The second pair involve ordinances or ceremonies. **Instructions about washings** have been one of the reasons why many insist that Jewish doctrine alone is in view, inasmuch as the term "washings" (*baptismōn*) is plural, and is not the term used regularly for Christian baptism (*baptisma*). The problem would appear to be sufficiently answered by seeing a reference to the instruction given, particularly to Jewish converts, about the distinctions among the various washings in Judaism as compared to Christian baptism. The term "washings" needed to be broad enough to cover all ceremonial ablutions. This becomes all the more understandable when we recognize that at least twice in the New Testament there are examples of such distinctions being discussed, once regarding John's baptism as compared to that of Jesus (John 3:25, 26), and once regarding certain Christians who were confused about John's baptism as compared to the Christian rite (Acts 19:1-5). **Laying on of hands** was a practice sometimes associated with the initiatory rite of water baptism among Christians, and seems also to have symbolized the imparting of the Holy Spirit (Acts 8:17; 19:6).

The last pair, **resurrection** and **eternal judgment**, are doctrines involving eschatological truth. Yet they are among the first teachings that a Christian believer learns. Upon receiving Christ as Savior and Lord, the believer acquires eternal life. For him death need hold no terrors, for his new life in Christ has assured him of resurrection. He need not shrink from the prospect of judgment for sin because Christ has borne his judgment and his sins are now eternally forgiven. The importance of these doctrines can hardly be overestimated. They are vital to normal Christian beginnings. They are foundational. For this very reason they are termed "milk," and must not be thought of as the end of the believer's interest and understanding, but as the start. There must be advancement to the solid food which leads to practical righteousness.

And this we will do if God permits. (6:3)

The writer will proceed to discuss the more advanced matters, and thus encourage his readers toward maturity. However, he recognizes the necessity of God's involvement if his task is to be successful. **If God permits** is more than a pious sentiment. It is an acknowledgment that only God can change the course of a man's life when it is going in the opposite direction.

c. Warning against the consequences of apostasy. (6:4-8)

The following paragraph is one of the most disputed in the New Testament. Nearly all schools of interpretation face problems in trying to explain the passage consistently. The interpreter is hard-pressed to treat it forthrightly without letting his explanations be shaded by his particular theological system. The expositor who approaches each text with a completely neutral mind probably does not exist. The present writer certainly could not claim perfect freedom from such influences. Nevertheless, the attempt will be made to deal fairly with the data confronted here, and then interpret in harmony with other Biblical teaching.

> *For it is impossible for those who were once enlightened, and have tasted the heavenly gift, and have become sharers of the Holy Spirit, and have tasted the good word of God and powers of the coming age, and have fallen away....* (6:4-6a)

(1) The case envisioned. (6:4b-6a)

The author constructs a case to teach his readers the seriousness of one's relationship to God through Christ. We note that he shifts from "you" (5:11, 12), "us" (6:1), and "we" (6:3) to those (6:4). He does not suggest that he is actually describing any of his readers (cf. v. 9).

Five participles are employed in a generally parallel construction to describe the persons in this case. They are ones having been enlightened, having tasted the heavenly gift, having become sharers of the Spirit, having tasted the Word of God and powers of the coming age, and having fallen away. Grammatically there is no warrant for treating the last one in the series any differently from the others. If the last one is regarded as conditional, "if they have fallen away," then each of the others should be treated as "if" clauses also.

The first participle, enlightened (*phōtisthentas*), is qualified by *hapax,* which means "once for all" (used also in 9:7, 26, 27, 28; 10:2; 12:26, 27). It is possible to understand *hapax* as governing each participle in the series. Although some of the ancients (e.g., Justin) explained this enlightenment as water baptism, and many today explain it of spiritual exposure or illumination short of regeneration, the use of "once for all" points to something complete, rather than partial or inadequate. The very same participle is used in 10:32, with no hint that there was anything inadequate or tentative about their spiritual enlightenment. Normal understanding of the passage in 10:32 as well as 6:4 would lead us to assume real enlightenment by regeneration.

The expression have tasted the heavenly gift employs the word "tasted" (*geusamenous*) in the common metaphorical sense of "experienced." The verb itself did not mean a mere sampling, but a real experience, as its use in Acts 10:10 attests. The writer of Hebrews has already used "tasted" in the sense of "experienced" in 2:9, where Christ "tasted death." Surely the meaning is that He actually experienced it. Thus the people in this illustration have actually experienced the heavenly gift. Certain identification of this gift (*dōreas*) is difficult. Suggestions include salvation, eternal life, forgiveness of sin, the Holy Spirit, or Christ, to give a sampling. To this writer the likelihood is strong that Christ Himself is meant. Jesus used the term of Himself to the woman of Samaria, "If you knew the gift [*dōrean*] of God, even who he is who speaks to you..." (John 4:10). Such identification avoids duplication in the series, and it is reasonable to suppose that the author would not have been redundant. The matter is not a crucial one, however, because there is an inherent connection between all of these possible identifications. Christ is God's gift to men; and when He is received by faith, He supplies the gift of salvation, involving forgiveness and eternal life, all of which are resultant from the ministry of the Holy Spirit.

Have become sharers of the Holy Spirit describes these people as partakers in some sense of the Holy Spirit. Although absence of the Greek article with **Holy Spirit** has led some to refer this to the Spirit's activity or gifts, rather than His person, this feature is not conclusive. Many times the article is omitted and the expression is regarded as a proper name which does not necessitate an article. What are the implications of **sharers** (*metochous*)? The author has used the same word in 3:1 of his readers as sharers of a heavenly calling, and in 3:14 as sharers of Christ. Hence to dilute this expression so as to make it mean anything less than genuine participation is inconsistent with the author's employment of the term elsewhere. The statement thus asserts a sharing of the Holy Spirit, and in the Christian context of this epistle, it refers to a sharing of the Spirit's indwelling presence. Normal understanding of the phrase would lead to the conclusion that such persons are viewed as regenerated, not merely exposed to the Spirit's convicting power but unresponsive to it.

Have tasted the good word of God refers to the experiencing (same metaphorical use of the participle as above) the word of God in the gospel and finding it good. Emphasis is upon the **word of God** as uttered (*rhēma*), and one should compare I Peter 1:25 and 2:3 (Ps. 34:8) for a similar thought. Because the gospel has been received and experienced, certain **powers of the coming age** have also been witnessed. In 2:4 mention was made of "various miracles" (i.e., *dunamesi,* "powers") performed by Christians as a confirmation of the supernatural character of the salvation message. They were a foretaste of what is to come when Christ returns.

Have fallen away (*parapesontas*) represents the last of the participles used in the series. The verb is employed only here in the New Testament, although it occurs in the Septuagint in passages dealing with apostasy (e.g., Ezek. 18:24; 20:27). It can hardly refer to sins committed through weakness, for which Scripture gives many examples of restoration in both Old Testament and New Testament. Because of the stated impossibility of renewal, it seems most certain that the reference is to apostasy, that is, a complete and final repudiation of Christ (as in 10:26, 27). Hence the normal understanding of these descriptive terms, in the light of the author's own usage elsewhere in the epistle, is of those who are regenerated and then repudiate Christ and forsake Him.

(2) The consequence. (6:4a, 6b)

[For it is impossible] ... *to renew* [them] *again to repentance.* ... (6:6b)

The words are stated without restriction. To qualify the meaning with suggestions that all things are possible with God, and therefore the impossibility must be only on man's side, is gratuitous. The same could be stated for all cases of repentance, since man is spiritually dead, and is always dependent entirely upon God's initiative. The statement then becomes a meaningless truism. The tenor of the passage argues for something extraordinary here. It is better to see the impossibility as just that—it is impossible for either man himself or God to bring about a life-changing repentance to salvation apart from Christ. With this understanding, the people described above have forfeited all hope of salvation. It is not a question of needing to be saved again.

(3) The reason. (6:6c)

... *since they are crucifying for themselves the Son of God and making a public exposure* [of him]. (6:6c)

The dire consequence asserted above would occur because God's only means of salvation would be rejected. Crucifying (*anastaurountas*) is always used in extra-Biblical Greek in the simple sense of "crucify" (with the prefix *ana* apparently referring to the affixing "up" on a cross), rather than "crucify again." No strong reason exists for not employing the common meaning here. The author's point is that those who experience all that Christ provides and then turn away from Him in a settled and final way are really joining the ranks of those who crucified Jesus. Such action would be saying in effect, "Christ's crucifixion was proper, and our renunciation of Him adds our consent to that momentous act." The additional description as making a public exposure (*paradeigmatizontas*) emphasizes the shameful character of apostasy. By renouncing Christ, they bring more public shame upon Him than if they had never believed at all. The verb is used in the Septuagint at Numbers 25:4 to describe a public hanging.

Now we see the reason for the impossibility of repentance in the people of this illustration. They have already tried everything God has to offer, and have then turned away from it. Hence there is nothing further that can be done for them. Such will never repent, for God has nothing further to present to them. There will be no additional gospel, no new Messiah. To turn away from God's plan of salvation is to reject the only valid plan there is.

Summary of Views on 6:4-6

A listing and brief evaluation of current interpretations may be helpful at this point. No attempt will be made to be exhaustive nor to include rare explanations not presently in vogue.

1. Saved persons who are subsequently lost.

This view interprets the description as of people who are truly regenerated, but then lose their salvation through deliberate apostasy. Lenski is one who espouses this view, as do Arminians generally.[46] This explanation properly sees the descriptives as implying a full regeneration experience, but fails to deal adequately with the Biblical teaching of election and security. To conclude that one who is truly saved actually can lose everything runs directly counter to such passages as Romans 8:28-39; John 10:28-30; Hebrews 8:12; and many others. It should also be observed that the text before us offers no help to the popular Arminian teaching that salvation can be lost and regained numerous times, for the case envisioned here has no hope of restoration.

2. Professed believers who have never really been saved.

Some explain the passage as referring to those who have been exposed to Christian truth, and may even have shown some apparent evidences of conversion, but these were abortive (like the seed sown on

---

46. Lenski, *Interpretation of Hebrews,* pp. 185-187.

the rocky ground). The apostasy is explained as the settled and final rejection of Christ (cf. the blasphemy against the Holy Spirit, Matt. 12:31, 32). Archer states, "To this limited extent an unsaved man may partake of the Holy Spirit, e.g., Judas Iscariot, who like the other disciples cast out demons and cleansed the lepers and healed the sick."[47] This view conserves the truth of the believer's security, but does so at the expense of diluting the first four participles in the description into something less than genuine salvation. To this writer, it seems a case of special pleading, and he doubts whether the same description if found elsewhere would ever be explained by these interpreters in any way other than full regeneration.

3. Saved persons who backslide.

Some recognize that the description in Hebrews 6:4, 5 most obviously refers to regenerated persons, and acknowledge also that the Scriptural teaching on the believer's security prevents the possibility of a true believer ever being lost. Thus they explain the "falling away" as a falling into sin to the extent that they are in danger of divine chastening. It must be recognized, of course, that ordinary backsliding cannot be meant; for the Bible is filled with exhortations to believers to forsake sin in their lives, but these people cannot be reclaimed. Sometimes the Septuagint usages of *parapiptō* in Ezekiel are noted as describing the covenant people Israel who fell into idolatry and were inflicted with physical death. The inference is drawn that this was simply temporal chastening, but does not imply that they were cast off from God. However, this is precarious, because all Israel was in covenant relation to God; but this by no means implied that each Israelite was a part of the spiritual remnant who were saved. It seems, rather, that the majority of Israel was apostate throughout her history (cf. 3:16-19).

By this view the impossibility stated in Hebrews 6:4 is the impossibility of starting over. The past cannot be replayed with fewer sins the next time. C. C. Ryrie has stated regarding verse 4: "There is no such thing as being saved a second time (though it might be convenient sometimes!); therefore, you cannot retreat but must make progress." [48] The interpreter must decide, however, whether the severity of the warning here is properly served if all that is meant is that you can't as

---

47. Archer, *Epistle to the Hebrews*, p. 40.
48. Charles C. Ryrie, *Biblical Theology of the New Testament*, p. 257.

Christians make a fresh start (and if you are a true Christian, you don't really need one), so you must keep moving forward from where you are.

4. A hypothetical case to illustrate the folly of apostasy.

Proponents of this view hold that the author has described a supposed case, assuming for the moment the presuppositions of some of his confused and wavering readers. To those who would suggest that they are truly regenerated but could still go back to Judaism (thus turning from an exclusive allegiance to Jesus), he warns by this description what the frightening end would be. If a person were truly enlightened and would experience everything provided in regeneration, and then would turn away in repudiation, it would be no light thing, for he would be without hope of recovery. He would have abandoned the only means of life-changing repentance. True believers would be warned by this statement to remain firm (and from the human standpoint the warnings of Scripture are a means to ensure the perseverance of the saints); for to turn from Christ would show either that they had never become true "sharers" of Christ (3:14), or else leave them with no further hope of salvation (6:6). The warning was directed to those who claimed to be saved, and took them at their own estimate of themselves to show the folly of their viewpoint. (Any readers whose faith was mere profession would also be sobered by the warning of the fearful consequences of apostasy.)

This explanation follows the normal exegesis of verses 4 and 5, regarding the description as of regenerated persons. It also treats the warning severely as verse 6 infers, and harmonizes with the severe warnings of 10:26-27 and 12:25. The hypothetical case is frequently objected to as not providing any real warning if it could not happen. Yet hypothetical and even impossible cases are not unknown in Scripture. Paul wrote in Galatians 3:12, "And the law is not of faith: but, The man that doeth them shall live in them" (but no one ever did, nor could). James 2:10 states, "For whosoever shall keep the whole law [a hypothetical condition] and yet offend in one point, he is guilty of all." Jesus said in John 9:39, "I am come . . . that they which see might be made blind" (there were none who could see, but Jesus took His hearers at their estimate of themselves, v. 41). The author of Hebrews implies that he is speaking this way in 6:9.

All things considered, the last view commends itself to the present writer as dealing most adequately with the text. This explanation is presented by Westcott, who says, "The case is hypothetical. There is nothing to show that the conditions of fatal apostasy had been fulfilled, still less that they had been fulfilled in the case of any of these addressed. Indeed the contrary is assumed: vv. 9 ff."[49] W. H. Griffith Thomas states, "The passage is apparently a supposed case to correct their wrong ideas, and the argument seems to be that if it were possible for those who have had the experiences of verses 4-6 to fall away, it would be impossible to renew them unless Christ died a second time. . . ."[50] Hewitt writes, "He is putting forward a hypothetical case. . . . There is no suggestion in the context that the sin against the Holy Spirit . . . is ever committed by true Christians."[51]

(4) The illustration. (6:7, 8)

For earth which drank the rain coming frequently upon it, and bears vegetation fitting for those on whose account it is also being cultivated, receives blessing from God. But [if it is] *bearing thorns and thistles,* [it is] *rejected and close to a cursing, whose end is for burning.* (6:7, 8)

From the natural world an illustration is drawn to show that the response to one's circumstances reflects an underlying condition, and brings its appropriate and inevitable retribution. A field is depicted on which frequent rain has fallen, and the produce is everything that was expected by the owners. Such ground is a source of joy to the farmer, and it receives his continuing care in order that it may remain as a fruitful field for years to come. It illustrates the true believer whose fruitfulness is a sign of the condition of his heart (cf. parable of the sower, Matt. 13:3-23). The mention of **blessing from God** indicates that the author has moved in thought from the agricultural illustration to its application among his readers.

The second part of the illustration describes land which received the same rainfall as the former, but whose only response was a worthless one of **thorns and thistles.** It suggests a similar parable in Isaiah 5,

---

49. Westcott, *Epistle to the Hebrews,* p. 165.
50. W. H. Griffith Thomas, *Hebrews: A Devotional Commentary,* p. 74.
51. Hewitt, *Epistle to the Hebrews,* p. 108.

where Israel was pictured as God's vineyard; but instead of producing grapes, it produced only wild grapes (v. 4). The farmer concludes that this land is not worth more expenditure of his labor, so he rejects it from further consideration. Its condition shows it as exemplifying the curse God pronounced upon the earth (Gen. 3:17, 18). It cannot be harvested, so its only prospect is to be burned over in order that windblown seed from the weeds will not infest the good ground. This illustrates those whose response to the work of God is completely worthless (cf. 6:6). The inevitable consequence will be judgment. There is no comfort in these words. **Close to a cursing** does not imply a narrow escape, but merely that it has not yet occurred. **Burning** hardly suggests here a purifying so that the ground can bear a better crop the next year. The whole tenor of the passage demands retribution and destruction as the emphatic point.

d. Reminder of the certainty of God's promises. (6:9-20)

But we are persuaded the better things regarding you, beloved, and things belonging to salvation, even though we are speaking in this way. For God is not unjust to forget your work and the love which you displayed for his name, having ministered to the saints and continuing to minister. (6:9, 10)

A fruitful olive orchard amid barren hills near Bethlehem (Heb. 6:7, 8).

The author does not think his readers have apostatized to the extent of 6:6, 8. He thinks they are truly saved, and thus would not be facing the prospect of irreversible judgment. To call the readers beloved was to assure them of the author's genuine feeling of love for them. We includes the author and probably his associates, known full well to the readers but unfortunately not to us. Even though we are speaking in this way indicates that the previous severe description has been hypothetical. It did not really describe any of the readers, but was employed for the sake of argument.

Since they were truly saved, God would not bring upon them the dire judgments of verse 8. The readers had already displayed the characteristics of the parable in verse 7, and God who is unchanging in His justice will never forget their displays of genuine conversion. Their work (*ergou*) was not the cause of the regeneration but its clear evidence. The love (*agapēs*) was that spiritual fruit produced within them which had as its object the name (i.e., the person) of God as they had come to know Him in Christ. It revealed itself in helping others (as one demonstration, at least), but it was the outgrowth of love for Christ. Previously they had ministered (aorist participle) to the saints, and this activity was still being performed (present participle). Saints does not identify these people geographically, but only as Christian believers. However, the passage does seem to rule out Jerusalem or Judea as the destination of the epistle, inasmuch as their early ministration (Acts 6) was soon curtailed by persecution and their subsequent poverty made them recipients of aid (Acts 13; I Cor. 16:1-3) rather than benefactors.

> *But we desire each one of you to display the same diligence toward the full assurance of the hope until the end, in order that you do not become sluggish, but imitators of those who through faith and longsuffering are inheriting the promises.* (6:11, 12)

The diligence displayed by the readers in their energetic concern for one another should be matched by an equal diligence in confirming their faith. They needed to be as active in strengthening their belief in Christ so as not to vacillate in the direction of Judaism as they were in manifesting Christian virtues.

Full assurance is probably the best translation of *plērophoria* in each of its four New Testament occurrences (Col. 2:2; I Thess. 1:5; Heb. 6:11; 10:22). It is a great aid to spiritual growth when the heart is fully persuaded that the Christian hope is a certainty. Many aspects of salvation are yet to be realized, and thus hope must be kept alive and firm. Without full assurance, the believer lacks the stability to make progress. He is likely to become attracted to the doctrinal aberrations that arise from time to time, because he has no settled convictions about the certainty of what lies ahead for the Christian, and can be persuaded to listen to those who speak convincingly. The full assurance can be obtained through the exercise of spiritual diligence. By devoting himself to the revelation of God's truth in Scripture (and the teaching of the apostles before the New Testament canon was complete), the believer can become grounded in the faith to the extent that his Christian beliefs develop into assured convictions, and he is ready to recognize the errors posed by unworthy teachers. This confidence needs to be nurtured until Christ returns and hope is realized.

The danger was that the readers' sluggishness in hearing the Word of God (5:11) would advance until it affected their faith and hope. Indifference to God's Word is the first step to spiritual decay, and this indifference had already begun. They must recognize their problem, and take immediate steps to interrupt the otherwise inevitable course.

One way to develop spiritual stability is to draw strength from the example of others who are not wavering. **Imitators** (*mimētai*) involves the following of an example (the English word "mimic" is a derivative). Inasmuch as humans inevitably adopt models to emulate (whether consciously or unconsciously), and too often the choices lead their followers astray, it is vitally important to have the proper human leaders. The point is not that any man is to be the object of faith or absolute emulation, but that we do properly look to others as examples. Hebrews 11 will list many Old Testament heroes to challenge us to faith. Paul in I Corinthians 11:1 urges readers, "Be followers [*mimētai*] of me, even as I also am of Christ."

Who are these models? It may be that the reference is to Old Testament saints who died in faith without seeing the realization of God's promises, but now are enjoying the fulfilment. The challenge is to follow their example of steadfastness in spite of pressures to compromise or defect. The mention of Abraham in the next verse could imply that Old Testament persons were in mind. However, the expression is sufficiently general to make possible a broader and more contemporary reference. The present participle inheriting (*klēronomountōn*) could refer to living Christians. They are presently inheriting salvation in that they are now heirs of God (Rom. 8:17). They are not wavering between Christianity and Judaism but have accepted by faith the work of Christ and exhibit longsuffering as they steadfastly endure suffering. Such believers are spiritually mature and their example can do much to guide the babes (5:12-14).

> *For when God made the promise to Abraham, since he had no greater one to swear by, he swore by himself, saying, "I will surely bless you and I will surely multiply you." And thus having patiently endured he obtained the promise.* (6:13-15)

The strongest encouragement to steadfast faith is the conviction that God's Word is trustworthy. **Abraham** is chosen as the illustration because God's promise to him was given in a very detailed way, and God's oath was added as confirmation. Furthermore, it was this promise to Abraham which had a vital relation to these readers, and to all Christians, for Christ the Savior is the promised Seed of Abraham (Gal. 3:16).

The promise to Abraham involved God's blessing upon him by the providing of a multiplied progeny, through which all nations of the earth would be blessed. (The New Testament reveals that it was through one particular Seed that the fulfilment of spiritual blessing came.) It is recorded in its various aspects in Genesis 12:1-7; 15:5; 17:5-8; and 22:15-18. A study of these passages reveals that the promise was not made just once, but was reiterated on numerous occasions. The significant feature to our author is that one of those reiterations took the form of an oath. The reference is undoubtedly to Genesis 22:15-18. When Abraham displayed his unfaltering trust in God by offering Isaac, Jehovah responded to him with the words, "By myself have I sworn" (Gen. 22:16), and stated again the basic content of the promise made earlier.

In oaths it is customary to swear by a higher power, and the greater the being sworn by, the surer the promise. The Jews of Jesus' day swore by heaven, earth, Jerusalem, and their own heads (Matt. 5:34-36). We might compare our own confirming expressions, from the courtroom "so help me, God" to the more colloquial "as sure as the world stands." The bare Word of God is itself utterly certain. However, to give men (in this instance, Abraham) more confidence, God condescended to human custom and employed an oath. There was no higher power that God could invoke to guarantee His veracity and to inflict a penalty if He spoke falsely. Therefore, he swore by himself, placing behind His promise the very integrity of God. Nothing could be surer than this. Hence Abraham was again informed that God would bless him with a greatly multiplied seed. The King James Version rendering, "blessing I will bless thee," reflects a literal translation of the Greek participle which in turn was the Septuagint method of treating the Hebrew infinitive absolute construction of Genesis 22:17. The sense to be conveyed is that of emphasis; thus, I will surely bless you.

Abraham after patient endurance finally obtained the promise. Thus he becomes a fitting example of the importance of remaining strong in faith, not wavering in the face of the promises of God. Interpretation of he obtained the promise must take into account 11:13, which speaks of Abraham and Sarah as dying in faith, "not having received the promises." To resolve the problem by explaining that 6:15 means he merely had the promise made to him, but never saw any fulfilment hardly satisfies the sense, since the "obtaining" follows upon his endurance, and that was Abraham's response to God's promise. It is better to regard the patient enduring in reference to the long testing of his faith, in which twenty-five years elapsed before Abraham finally had his son Isaac in fulfilment of the promise. Of course, this was only the beginning step of the fulfilment, for he did not see the final stage in his lifetime (11:13). To object that the birth of Isaac could not be regarded as the promise which Abraham obtained because the oath came long after Isaac was born (coming actually when Isaac was offered at Moriah) is to understand the promise in too narrow a sense. The promise was first made when Abraham had no child at all. Later statements of the promise and even the oath were a reiteration of the same promise. The birth of Isaac and the later receiving of him back (as though from the dead, 11:19) after offering him at Moriah were initial steps in the fulfilment which Abraham did receive. This in no way weakens the truth expressed in 11:13, for the ultimate fulfilment in Christ was never seen in Abraham's lifetime.

For men swear by the one greater [than themselves], *and the oath for confirmation* [is] *for them an end of all disputing.* (6:16)

The significance of an oath is impressed upon the readers, so as to emphasize the importance of God's oath as certifying the validity of His promise. Men, says the author, take an oath by invoking the power of someone (or something) greater than themselves. This greater power is usually God, and was so understood and practiced in Old Testament and New Testament times. Abraham himself called upon God in this way on many occasions (Gen. 14:22; 21:23-24; 24:3). Men have generally agreed that in matters of dispute, the oath is the statement which is legally valid, and all lesser statements are disregarded in human courts. It is what is stated under oath that is entered on the record. Confirmation (*bebaiōsin*) is a technical term involving a legal guarantee.[52] The sworn statement then is a man's last word on a given subject, that on which he stakes his integrity, and on which he is willing to be judged by God if it proves false.

Wherein God, intending more abundantly to show to the heirs of the promise the unchangeableness of his purpose, guaranteed by an oath, in order that through two unchangeable things in which [it is] *impossible for God to lie, we might have strong encouragement,* [we] *who have fled for refuge to grasp the hope set before us.* (6:17, 18)

God descended to man's level that man might have more assurance. (Of course, the oath did not make God's statement any truer; but from man's standpoint it became more emphatic.) This was grace displayed more abundantly, for the bare Word of God should have been certainty enough. Nevertheless, God, whose promise was all of grace to begin with, has made every provision for the heirs of the promise to find it reasonable to trust Him. These heirs were Abraham and his seed. Christian believers are included, at least in some sense; for the statement was intended to strengthen the faith of the readers of Hebrews who were not only Jewish but Jewish Christians. Every believer is a part

---

52. Heinrich Schlier, "Bebaiosis," in *Theological Dictionary of the NT,* I, 602, 603.

of the seed of Abraham and thus one of the heirs of the promise (Gal. 3:29).

To demonstrate beyond doubt to Abraham that His promise was unconditional and would be fully honored, God guaranteed its fulfilment by means of an oath. Guaranteed (*emesiteusen*) is a verb used only here in the New Testament. Its basic sense has to do with mediation, and with its cognates it conveys the thought of acting as umpire or negotiator. For this reason the translation "interposed" is sometimes given (so ASV), and the thought is that God interposed the oath between Himself and Abraham, or perhaps between the promise already given and Abraham. However, the sense of "guarantee" is fully attested. Oepke states, "The only possible translation [in Heb. 6:17] is 'to guarantee,' 'to vouch for.' In giving the promise, God is as it were one of the parties. But with His oath, and as its Guarantor . . . He puts Himself on neutral ground and pledges the fulfilment of the promise."[53]

The two unchangeable things are the promise and the oath. The Scriptural principle of two witnesses for establishing legality underlies this argument. Since God Himself made the promise, and there was no other person to whom appeal might be made for confirmation, He added His own oath. Now either of these two things was fully trustworthy, for they both came from God, and thus both (the Greek "which" is the plural form *hois*) are completely without falsehood for God is incapable of lying. By granting both the promise and the oath, neither of which can be altered to our hurt, we have the strongest assurance imaginable for trusting God's promises.

Believers are described under the figure of the Old Testament cities of refuge. Six of these were established in Israel, three on each side of Jordan, to provide protection against revenge for those who had slain someone accidentally (Num. 35:6, 9-32). As long as the refugee stayed within the appointed city, he was safe. He could return to his home with legal protection only after the death of the high priest. The verb used here as a substantive participle who have fled for refuge (*hoi kataphugontes*) is used in the Septuagint in Deuteronomy 4:42 and Joshua 20:9 to describe this very situation. So Christian believers,

---

53. A. Oepke, "Mesites, Mesiteuo," in *Theological Dictionary of the NT,* IV, 620.

having trusted in the promise made first to Abraham regarding his seed—a promise which culminated in Christ, the unique Seed—have fled from the prospect of coming judgment to grasp as their own the refuge provided in the Christian hope. This hope is centered in Christ Himself, and the next verses explain the sense in which believers look to Him as the very embodiment of their hope.

> *Which* [hope] *we have as an anchor of the soul, both sure and firm, and entering into the inner part of the veil, where as a forerunner for us Jesus has entered, having become high priest forever according to the order of Melchizedek.* (6:19, 20)

The figure now shifts from the city of refuge to an anchor. Christ, the believer's hope, is the anchor which insures safety from the storm. The first two descriptives of the anchor, sure (*asphalē*) and firm (*bebaian*), are joined by *te kai*, which marks an inner connection between them. They may be regarded as positive and negative aspects of the anchor itself. This anchor is secure because it is unbending. It is sure to hold because its flukes are strong and cannot be twisted out of shape nor broken. In like manner Christ in His own person is absolutely reliable and fully worthy of our trust.

A second important factor in anchors is their placement. Only if they are properly fixed in the right spot can one expect to find the safety against shipwreck for which the anchor was employed. Christ our anchor is in the safest place possible. He has entered heaven, there to appear as our high priest in the very presence of God. He is now on the inner side of the veil, a metaphor describing the veil which separated the Old Testament holy place from the holy of holies in the tabernacle and temple. Though in the figure believers may be seen as in the storm tossed ship, Christ is the one who has taken the anchor, risked the waves, and carried it to the safety of the harbor. (The illustration must not be pressed, however, to suggest that Christ was also in danger on the sinking ship.)

A third figure is now employed, in which Christ is depicted as the believer's forerunner in heaven. This need not be viewed as a mixture of metaphors (with an anchor placed in the holy of holies). The former figure was completed with the thought that the anchor was safely placed. That introduced the idea of heaven, and provided the transition to this third metaphor. As a **forerunner** Christ differs from all Old Testament priests, who were representatives of men but nothing more. To call Him a forerunner (*prodromos*) denotes the believer's prospect of eventually being where Christ now is. He is already in the actual presence of God, not just in some earthly counterpart. Thus He differs from all Levitical priests, and this explains why His priesthood is after a different order, that of **Melchizedek**. It also explains why He can be a priest **forever**, for He is in the ultimate reality, not in the passing earthly setting.

With the mention of the priestly order of Melchizedek, the author has come back to the point where he interrupted his discussion to begin the warning (5:10). Hoping to have counteracted their problem of sluggish hearing (5:11) by the previous encouragements, he resumes the main discussion.

3. The priesthood of Melchizedek. (7:1-28)

The description of Melchizedek is given in verses 1-3. Discussion centers on him because the readers were contemplating a turning from Christ to Judaism and the Levitical system in order to be true sons of Abraham. The author demonstrates that Abraham accepted the priesthood of Melchizedek, and that God Himself asserted Messiah's ministry as being after that order, not Levitical.

> *For this Melchizedek, king of Salem, priest of the most High God, who met Abraham as he was returning from the slaughter of the kings and blessed him, to whom also Abraham apportioned a tenth from all things, first being translated "king of righteousness," and then also king of Salem, which is "king of peace."* . . . (7:1, 2)

Melchizedek is mentioned in only two Old Testament passages—the historical account in Genesis 14:18-20 and the prophetic statement of Christ in Psalm 110:4. The former is in view here. **Abraham** had gone to the rescue of his nephew Lot after his capture by the coalition of five kings who had conquered Sodom and Gomorrah. God granted Abraham a most remarkable victory, and upon his return he met **Melchizedek, king of Salem**. This king of an ancient city-state (probably Jerusalem) was also a priest of the true God. He pronounced upon Abraham a priestly blessing, and in return received from Abraham a tenth of the spoils. In view of Abraham's knowledge of God at this time, it is inconceivable that he would have acknowledged the priesthood of anyone other than a representative of the true God. Melchizedek must therefore have been one of those rare persons (Abraham himself was another) who still held the true faith handed down from Noah.

The geographic identity of Salem is not important to the argument, but there are no strong reasons why it could not be understood as an ancient name of Jerusalem. In Psalm 76:2, Jerusalem is clearly so named. Furthermore, a later king in Jerusalem was named Adoni-zedek (Josh. 10:1), a fact lending support to the idea that compounds with -*zedek* were a Jebusite dynastic title.[54]

The literal meanings of the king's name (or dynastic title) and of his place of rule are picked out for special treatment. The meaning of Melchizedek is king of righteousness. This is mentioned first, not because of coincidence but because the author deliberately wants to emphasize the typology involved. Righteousness is basic to the priesthood, and peace comes from it. Melchizedek was a king whose name and realm connoted these concepts, at least etymologically. He provided a type of Christ, whose person and work accomplishes true righteousness and peace. It was Christ who was "the Holy and Righteous One" (Acts 3:14); and by satisfying the righteousness of God as our substitute, He provides peace with God for all believers (Rom. 5:1; Col. 2:20; Eph. 2:14).

> *. . . without father, without mother, without genealogy, having neither beginning of days nor end of life, but made like the Son of God, remains a priest continually.* (7:3)

The Levitical system made the priests' pedigree of utmost importance. Not only the high priest but all the priests had to be able to prove their genealogy or they would be excluded from the priesthood

---

54. John J. Davis, *Conquest and Crisis*, pp. 63, 64.

The hill of Ophel in the right foreground below the wall, site of ancient Jebusite occupation of Jerusalem. Melchizedek, "king of Salem," may have been ruler of a citystate here.

(Ezra 2:62). To be a priest, one's father needed to be a descendant not only of Levi, but of the priestly family of Aaron within that tribe. His mother needed to be an Israelite, but not every Israelite woman was eligible. No woman who was divorced or had an immoral past could be taken as a priest's wife (Lev. 21:7), not only because it would be inappropriate for her husband, but it would provide an unworthy mother for the sons who might otherwise qualify as priests.

Melchizedek, however, appears in the record without any reference to his father or mother. This does not mean that he had no human parents, but rather that so far as the record goes these were absent. This feature supplies the author of Hebrews with an interesting point for his typology. Not only do we know nothing about the immediate parents of Melchizedek, but in the record there is nothing listed of his genealogy. This does not imply that he had no ancestors or descendants, for verse 6 clearly implies that he did; but none are listed in the record and this is the basis for the typology.

Having neither beginning of days nor end of life does not mean that Melchizedek was never born and that he never died, but merely that the facts are not given in the record. These features are what made him like **the Son of God.** We note that the likeness is to Christ in His divine person, not as the incarnate Jesus; for as Son of man our Lord was born of Mary in Bethlehem and died at Calvary. In His divine nature, however, the preexistent Son of God was and remains eternal.

The main verb of the sentence is **remains** (*menei*), which has as its subject "this Melchizedek" in verse 1. All of the intervening material consists of descriptives of the subject. The assertion of the sentence is that Melchizedek remains a priest continually. To summarize the typology, our author's point is that so far as the record is concerned, Melchizedek typifies Christ because Genesis presents him as a functioning priest with no indication of beginning or ending or any dependence upon human pedigree. Thus he is a remarkable picture of Christ and His priesthood, and for this reason God Himself made this connection in Psalm 110:4.

Among some of the older commentators,[55] and occasionally among

---

55. Henry Alford apparently adopts the theophany interpretation. He states: "I would regard the epithets then as designedly used in this mysterious way, and meant to represent to us, that Melchizedek was a person differing from common men." *NT for English Readers,* pp. 1502-1506.

popular Bible teachers of the present, one finds Melchizedek identified as a theophany. This is largely due to certain statements made in Hebrews 7. However, there are compelling reasons for objecting to such an identification. (1) Melchizedek is said to be "made like the Son of God." This is strange language if the sense is that he was *actually* the Son of God. To argue on the basis of a pagan king's statement regarding the fourth figure in the fiery furnace, "one like a son of the gods" (Dan. 3:25 ASV), is hardly convincing. (2) The statement of Psalm 110:4 calls Messiah a priest "after the order of Melchizedek." This clearly differentiates Christ and Melchizedek, and it would hardly be a clarification if the text said he was a priest after the order of himself. (3) The historical record indicates that Melchizedek was king of a city-state in Canaan, a situation involving a fairly permanent residence on the part of the king. This would be totally without precedent so far as Old Testament revelation regarding theophanies is concerned. These were always temporary manifestations. (4) To argue from etymology that Melchizedek ("king of righteousness") was a theophany has its hazards. Historical and archaeological data indicate good reason to understand compounds with -zedek as reflecting a dynastic title for Jebusite kings of the area. We have the Biblical example of Adoni-zedek, king of Jerusalem, in Joshua 10:1 (whose name is even more impressive); yet it can hardly be suggested that this wicked king was a theophany.[56] The best explanation seems to be that Melchizedek was a historical human personage who typified Christ.

The superiority of Melchizedek to the Levitical order is explained in verses 4-10. Argument is given to show that the one is inherently above the other, on the basis of the Old Testament record.

Now observe how great this [priest] *was, to whom Abraham the patriarch gave a tenth of the best spoils.* (7:4)

In demonstrating the greatness of Melchizedek, the author first points out that Abraham paid a tithe to him out of the best spoils (*akrothiniōn,* literally: "top of the heap"). The term reflects the ancient custom of heaping up the spoils of battle, and then giving the top portion to the gods. No less a person than Abraham, revered by these

---

56. Davis, *Conquest and Crisis,* pp. 63, 64.

readers as the patriarch of their nation, had voluntarily given to Melchizedek a **tenth** of the spoils taken from the five kings.

> *And those of the sons of Levi receiving the priestly office*
> *have a commandment to tithe the people according to the*
> *law, that is, their brothers, although they have come out of*
> *the loins of Abraham.* (7:5)

Not all of Levi's descendants were priests. Only those descending from Aaron were eligible, and even many of those who were eligible were disqualified through improper marriages, inability to prove descent, or other reasons (Lev. 21:16-24). Those who did qualify and actually became priests had as one of their duties the task of collecting tithes from the rest of Israel. This responsibility was vested in them by the Mosaic law. Numbers 18:21 instructed the Levites to tithe Israel, and a tenth part of the tithe was given to the priests (Num. 18:26). The collection of the tithe was nevertheless under the supervision of the priests, at least in the time of Christ. Included was a tenth of all crops. Daniel-Rops states:

> These first-fruits were now taken by the priests, and not returned to
> the producer as they had been in early times, and they had become
> a due which the priests insisted upon most strictly, sending out
> Levites to collect it and insisting that everything, however small,
> should be tithed.[57]

The right to tithe someone involves a certain authority and thus a superiority. In the case of the Levitical priests, their authority stemmed from the Mosaic law. It could be considered only as an official supremacy for this specific purpose, and not some inherent superiority, for actually they were **brothers.** The Levitical priests and the remaining Israelites from whom they extracted tithes were equally descendants of Abraham, Isaac, and Jacob. Israelites paid tithes to Levitical priests only because the Mosaic law commanded it, not because their officials had any inherent right to tithe them.

> *But he who does not trace his genealogy from them has*
> *tithed Abraham, and has blessed him who was having the*

---

57. Henri Daniel-Rops, *Daily Life in Palestine at the Time of Christ,* trans. Patrick O'Brian, p. 164.

> *promises. Now without any dispute, the lesser is blessed by*
> *the better.* (7:6, 7)

Melchizedek was obviously not a Levite, inasmuch as he was a contemporary of Abraham. This passage implies that Melchizedek did have a **genealogy** or descent (see comments on 7:3), but that it was not dependent upon the Levitical line. Nevertheless, he **has tithed Abraham.** A look at the historical record in Genesis 14 indicates that this tithing was not a demand on Melchizedek's part. However, Abraham's voluntary action was accepted by the priest, so that its rightness was acknowledged. The Greek perfect tense (*dedekatōken,* has tithed) indicates the resultant condition that exists from that past act. Nothing subsequent to Melchizedek's encounter with Abraham invalidated what he did. It still stands for all to see and thus provides a valid argument for the author of Hebrews.

Not only did Abraham take the initiative in paying a tithe to Melchizedek, but Melchizedek also responded by accepting the tithe and by giving a blessing to Abraham (Gen. 14:19, 20). Again the perfect tense is used (*eulogēken,* has blessed), pointing to the lasting significance of that historic incident. Modern readers often have difficulty appreciating the argument employed here that the act of blessing someone implies superiority. Yet that is clearly the sense being conveyed. It must be understood that this "blessing" is something different from simply "praising" (as, for example, James 3:9, where men bless God, but are certainly not superior to Him). This blessing is an official pronouncement, coming from one properly authorized, which actually bestows something upon its recipient. Dods explains, "The blessing carries with it not only the verbal expression of goodwill, but goodwill achieving actual results."[58] When "blessing" is understood in this official or technical sense, the principle is readily admitted **without any dispute.** Melchizedek must have been superior to Abraham so as to be able to bestow a blessing upon him. When he blessed Abraham, his words were not just congratulatory, but were an expression of God's approval. Thus at that moment Melchizedek stood between God and Abraham and was **the better,** while Abraham was **the lesser.** All of this in spite of the fact that this was the same Abraham who was the patriarch of the Hebrew people (v. 4) and the recipient of remarkable

---

58. Dods, *Expositor's Greek Testament,* IV, 310.

promises from God (v. 6). The greatness of Melchizedek was thus recognized and experienced by Abraham, whose acceptance of his priestly blessing testifies to his superiority.

> *And here, on the one hand, dying men take tithes, but there* [it is] *testified that he lives.* (7:8)

A third superiority of Melchizedek is that his priesthood is not characterized by a whole succession of mortal men. In the Levitical system so familiar to the readers, the priests were continually dying and had to be replaced by others. **Here** (*hōde*) and the present tense of **take** (*lambanousin*) give strong support to the view that the Levitical system was still operational, and thus the epistle must be dated prior to the fall of Jerusalem in A.D. 70. Following that date, the temple was destroyed, the people scattered or deported, and there was no longer any priestly system needing to be supported by Jewish tithes. In the instance of Melchizedek the Scriptural record tells of no successors. In the "literary sense"[59] that our author employs for his references to Melchizedek, the only statements we have concern Melchizedek as alive. He does not mean that Melchizedek never died, but that the silence of Scripture on this point furnishes the basis for the typology. The writer, as one has said, gives to "the silence of Scripture the force of an assertion."[60] The fact that centuries later God speaks of the order of Melchizedek (Ps. 110:4) implies that it is not just some curiosity from the past but a living priesthood. The author concludes from the passages in Genesis and Psalms that the positive Biblical testimony is that Melchizedek lives. On these positive statements, the typology is built.

> *And one might almost say, through Abraham even Levi who takes tithes has been tithed, for he was still in the loins of his father when Melchizedek met him.* (7:9, 10)

The fourth superiority of Melchizedek is seen by the fact that Levi has been tithed by him. **One might almost say** is the rendering of the idiom *hōs epos eipein.* It may be used in the sense given above, or with the meaning "to use just the right word."[61] The former appears more

---

59. F. F. Bruce's apt term, *The Epistle to the Hebrews,* p. 141.
60. Dods, *Expositor's Greek Testament,* IV, 310.
61. W. F. Arndt and F. W. Gingrich, *A Greek-English Lexicon of the New Testament,* p. 305.

probable here. Because the argument is somewhat nonliteral, the cautionary phrase would tend to delay any hasty objections. The author may be considering the possible answer some might give that since the Levitical system came after Melchizedek, it was intended as its replacement and thus was superior to it. To this objection a most remarkable explanation is given.

Levi is viewed as being present and implicated in the action of his great-grandfather Abraham, even though he was not yet born. (In fact, even Abraham's son Isaac had not been born.) The principle involved is that there is a genuine unity in the human family, and that one is affected by the acts of his ancestors. It was not at all unusual for Hebrews to reason this way, viewing heredity in this realistic manner. One instance was the computation of the size of Jacob's family as recorded in Genesis 46. In the total of sixty-six persons who came to Egypt with Jacob (Gen. 46:26) were counted ten sons of Benjamin (Gen. 46:21), although it is quite likely that not all of these had been born to Joseph's younger brother by this time. Another instance is found in Paul's explanation that "in Adam all die" (I Cor. 15:22; Rom. 5:12). This principle is seen in many life situations. A man's citizenship bestows certain privileges as well as obligations upon his descendants, even though they may not have personally chosen that citizenship themselves. What a man does with his property affects his heirs, whether for good or for bad. Jews and Christians generally have little difficulty in seeing that the blessings God spoke to Abraham are shared by his family. Likewise, the author expects his readers to understand that other implications of Abraham's action devolve also upon his descendants. Thus while all Israelites were subjected under the Mosaic law to the Levitical priesthood and could go to no other priest, yet Levi himself was tithed by Melchizedek in the person of his great-grandfather Abraham. The hereditary implications are seen not only by looking backward from Levi to Abraham, but also by looking forward from Levi to Aaron. Levi did not personally "take tithes," for that did not occur until much later when the priestly system was set up under his descendants Moses and Aaron.

In verses 11-28, the superiority of Christ's priesthood, which is according to the order of Melchizedek, is set forth. Having already shown that Melchizedek was superior to Levi, the author now explains in detail how this demonstrates the superiority of Christ to the Levitical system.

If therefore perfection was through the Levitical priesthood (for the people on the basis of it have received the Law), what further need [was there] for another priest to arise according to the order of Melchizedek and not be called according to the order of Aaron? (7:11)

Perfection (*teleiōsis*) is used in the sense of completeness. In this context it refers to the making of men acceptable to God, which was the function of the priesthood. Something may be termed perfect or complete when it fulfils the purpose for which it was designed. Priesthood is designed to establish relations between God and sinful men. Yet the **Levitical priesthood** could accomplish this only within limits. It made possible an atonement which needed to be repeated. It could not provide complete expiation (for, as our author explains in 10:1-3, the sacrifices then would not have needed repetition). The condition (if) is assumed to be true for the sake of argument, but then the impossibility is shown.

It was on the basis of the Levitical priesthood that Israel received the Mosaic Law. It is common to think of this in the opposite way: that the priesthood existed on the basis of the Mosaic legislation. Nevertheless a Jewish writer well versed in the knowledge of his people's history could easily have thought along these lines. In the basic relationship of Israel and Jehovah, the priesthood stood at the heart. Both Moses and Aaron were chosen by God before the law was given. It was on the basis of the priestly function which God wanted performed that He issued the law at Sinai, giving the regulations for its operation.

Now if everything God required by way of making men acceptable to Him could be provided by the Levitical system, then why was Messiah not a Levitical priest? One might be disposed to argue that since the Levitical priesthood came later than Melchizedek, God must have intended it as the permanent replacement. Yet it is clear from the Old Testament that God Himself said that Messiah would be a priest after the order of Melchizedek (Ps. 110:4).

Incidentally, there is support here for the view that the original readers must have been Jewish and not Gentile. F. F. Bruce points out that Gentile converts would have been largely unaffected by this argument, for in their pagan state they had never supposed that perfection was through the Levitical priesthood; and after they had become

Christians, they would never have been encouraged to think this way. [62]
Jewish Christians, however, would find the argument here very much
relevant to their background, and possibly a problem in their present
thinking.

> For the priesthood being changed, of necessity also a
> change of law occurs. (7:12)

It has been shown in verse 11 that the fact of the Levitical priesthood necessitated the Mosaic law to support it. The two are inex-
tricably connected. It therefore follows that any basic change in the
priesthood requires a corresponding **change** in the **Law** which supports
it. If the Levitical system was superseded, the Mosaic law must also
have been replaced, an idea that will be categorically asserted in verse
18. Those who are Christians have acknowledged Jesus as the Messiah,
and on the basis of God's own statement in Psalm 110:4 Messiah is a
priest after the non-Levitical order of Melchizedek. Thus it is only
reasonable to understand that there must have been some changes in
the law as far as priesthood is concerned. To object to Jesus as the
believer's priest because He does not possess an Aaronic pedigree fails
to take into account what God has revealed.

> For the one about whom these things are said belongs to a
> different tribe, from which no one has officiated at the
> altar; for [it is] evident that out of Judah our Lord has
> descended, of which tribe Moses spoke nothing concerning
> priests. (7:13, 14)

These things are the facts about Christ's priesthood being declared as
Melchizedekian in Psalm 110:4. That passage clearly was Messianic, and
thus the one about whom (*eph' hon*) is Jesus Christ. The fact that Jesus
was not a Levite but of Judah was well known. The genealogies in
Matthew 1 and Luke 3 make this clear, as well as the birth narratives
themselves. As far as priesthood was considered, Judah was not merely
another or similar tribe (*allos*) but a **different** one (*heteras*). Nowhere in
any of the Mosaic legislation is there provision made for any of **Judah**
to minister as priests. II Chronicles 26 describes the divine wrath that

---

62. Bruce, *The Epistle to the Hebrews,* p. 144.

occurred when Uzziah, of Judaic descent, intruded into priestly functions. The Old Testament was clear that only Aaron's descendants, who were of Levi, could function as priests.

The fact that Jesus descended from Judah and yet was called a priest by God is clear demonstration that a change has occurred in the law. The tribal connection of Christ is proof that the Mosaic legislation cannot be applicable if Christ is regarded as priest. When one acknowledges Jesus as the Messiah of Old Testament prophecy, he has admitted (whether consciously or not) that certain fundamental features of the Mosaic code have been radically altered. Levitical priests had been the only allowable sort; now Jesus of Judah is termed the believer's priest. This is plainly contradictory unless the law has been changed.

Not only was Christ's priesthood planned as a successor to Aaron's (vv. 11-14), but it is superior because it is not dependent upon physical regulations but upon the power inherent in His life (vv. 15-19).

> *And it is still far more evident, if according to the likeness of Melchizedek a different priest is raised up, who has become* [priest] *not according to a law of physical commandment, but according to the power of an indestructible life, for it is testified,*
> *"You are a priest forever,*
> *According to the order of Melchizedek."* (7:15-17)

What is far more evident (*perissoteron eti katadēlon*)? An immediate connection is seen with verse 14 where Christ's descent from Judah is said to be evident (*prodēlon*). However, this hardly exhausts the author's thought. It is likely that the expression is intended to gather up all of the previous propositions in the context, such as the impossibility of perfection through the Levitical priesthood (v. 11), the fact that the law must have been changed inasmuch as the priesthood was (v. 12), and that Christ was obviously of Judah and not from Levi (vv. 13, 14). The truth of these propositions is clearly evidenced by the fact of a different priest (*hiereus heteros*) after the likeness of Melchizedek. That Christ is such a priest is not debatable, for God Himself declared it (Ps. 110:4). Hence the self-evident nature of this circumstance establishes the validity of the argument in this passage.

Of course, Christ is a different (*heteros*) priest, not just "another" (*allos*) like Aaron. The difference lay deeper than simply another in a succession. The basic difference was the principle which established the priesthood. In the case of Aaron and his Levitical successors, the priesthood was based upon a law of physical commandment. The reference is to the Mosaic law (*nomon*) with its many requirements regarding physical matters. The term *sarkinēs* ("physical," "fleshy," "carnal") refers to that which is made of flesh. It has nothing to do with sinful characteristics (for which the word *sarkikos* is used) but with constituent elements. This distinction is carefully observed in the New Testament, and is essential to the understanding of passages such as I Corinthians 3:1-3, as well as here. In the Levitical system, matters of physical ancestry, marriages, health, diet, and ceremonial performance were prominent. A man's spiritual fitness was not a vital consideration as a priestly qualification. Examples of wicked priests in the Old Testament (sons of Eli) and in the New Testament (Annas, Caiaphas, Ananias) amply confirm this fact.

Christ, however, possesses His priesthood on a different principle. It was not dependent upon external laws, but upon the power inherent in His life. God's statement in Psalm 110:4 termed Christ a priest forever. He was thus an entirely different sort from Aaron. All of the Levitical priests were subject to physical death. This necessitated regulations concerning succession so that the priestly system would not completely break down. With Christ no such need exists. The very nature of His life is different. It is indestructible (*akatalutou*). Not only will it never end in death, but it is not capable of any sort of dissolution from within or without. Aaron was made a priest only on the basis of the regulations of the Mosaic law. Inherently he was no different from his fellow Israelites. Christ, however, has His priesthood by virtue of who He is; and the life He possesses is not subject to decay or change.

The testimony of God Himself underlies the argument given above, for it was He who said of His Son, **You are a priest forever** (Ps. 110:4). Only a priest of an entirely different sort than Judaism was accustomed to could fit the description of this prophetic psalm. It is just this kind of priest—one with a superior kind of life—that believers find in Jesus Christ.

For on the one hand [there is] *an annulment of the former commandment on account of the weakness and uselessness of it (for the law made nothing perfect), and on the other hand* [there is] *a bringing in of a better hope, through which we draw near to God.* (7:18, 19)

These two verses are an expansion of the conclusion drawn in verses 12 and 16. Inasmuch as Messiah has already come (a fact freely acknowledged by these Hebrew Christian readers), and God has declared Him to be a priest after a different order, there must have been an annulment of the Mosaic law. Only if such was the case is it possible to understand God's statement about Christ's priesthood. The Mosaic law called for a priesthood that was exclusively Levitical. The Jews had no alternative to Aaron. A "setting aside" (literal meaning of *athetēsis*, "annulment") of the law was an absolute necessity before Christ could be considered a genuine priest.

This conclusion is not only demanded by the implications of God's statement in Psalm 110:4, but is also consistent with the problems inherent in the Levitical system itself. Even though the Mosaic law was given by God, it was characterized by a certain **weakness and uselessness**. The primary **weakness** in the author's mind was its inability to make its adherents **perfect** (*eteleiōsen*). The Levitical system could not in itself complete the task of saving men. The blood of animals was not valid per se (10:4, 11). Nor could the law produce the inward change which would enable men to live lives of righteousness. The law did curb many excesses, and surely served to caution men against yielding to their sinful tendencies; yet it could not create a pure heart (I Tim. 1:8-10). The concept here is similar to Romans 8:3, "For what the law could not do, in that it was weak through the flesh. . .," and Galatians 4:9, "How turn ye again to the weak and beggarly elements, whereunto ye desire again to be in bondage?"

Parallel to the annulment is the contrasting **bringing in of a better hope**. The employment of *men . . . de* shows that the one offsets the other. The ministry of Christ has abrogated or set aside the Old Testament economy. It is by Christ, whose blood gave validity to the Old Testament sacrifices (9:15), that believers **draw near** in blessed relationship **to God**, on the basis of a finished sacrifice and an eternal priesthood.

The discussion now moves to the superiority of Christ's priesthood over Aaron's because it was based upon God's oath (vv. 20-22).

> *And to the degree that not without an oath* [did he become
> a priest] *(for they without an oath have become priests,
> but he with an oath by the One who said to him, "The
> Lord swore and will not change his mind, You are a priest
> forever")*[63] *to the same degree also Jesus has become the
> guarantor of a better covenant.* (7:20-22)

This paragraph contains a somewhat lengthy parenthesis, consisting
of verses 20b and 21. The main assertion is: To the degree that not
without an oath . . . to the same degree also Jesus has become the
guarantor of a better covenant. The difference between the two priest-
hoods is considered from the standpoint of the temporary versus the
permanent. In the case of the Levitical priests, no oath of God guaranteed their perpetual validity. God was the one who had given the
Mosaic legislation, but in no Scripture is it recorded that God guaranteed by His oath the uninterrupted operation of the Aaronic order.
Aaron and his sons were formally anointed for the exercise of their
office, but God did not bind Himself with an oath that their priesthood
was established forever.

Christ's priesthood was different. God not only established it, but
did so with an oath to insure its perpetual validity. The fact of the oath
is recorded in the same passage which revealed Christ's priesthood (Ps.
110:4). God's simple word is sufficient to insure truthfulness, but the
addition of the oath provides additional confirmation to men. The
statement goes on to emphasize the permanent character of God's
announcement, for it means that He will not change his mind (*ou
metamelethesetai*). Thus the oath stressed the permanence of the new
priesthood in contrast to the provisional or transitory nature of the old.

To this same degree (*kata tosouto*) is Christ superior to Aaron. His
priesthood has been established by an oath which guaranteed its operation forever. Those who look to Christ find in Him their guarantor
(*enguos*) that the new and better covenant will be met in all its
provisions. A mediator of a covenant is the one who gets all parties
together and devises the terms of the agreement. A guarantor is one
who assumes responsibility that the obligations imposed will be carried

---

63. The words "according to the order of Melchizedek" appear in some
ancient manuscripts, but not those usually considered the most reliable. It is easy
to see how interpolation could have occurred from verses 11 and 17.

out. This is the only New Testament occurrence of *enguos,* although it is common in the papyri, and is also found in the Septuagint.[64] For whom does Jesus serve as guarantor? Does He guarantee to men that God will stand by His promises (since the covenant is basically that which God promises to man)? Or does He act as guarantor to God for man by assuring that men will truly accept its provisions and ultimately enjoy its full blessings? Perhaps a choice need not be made inasmuch as both are true, and the unique character of this covenant and its guarantor transcend strict human analogy. F. F. Bruce suggests:

> But Jesus guarantees the perpetual fulfilment of the covenant which He mediates, on the manward side as well as on the Godward side. As the Son of God, He confirms God's eternal covenant with His people; as His people's representative, He satisfies its terms with perfect acceptance in God's sight.[65]

In verse 22 appears the first of seventeen occurrences of *diathēkē* ("covenant," "testament") in Hebrews. The word was a technical term for a "last will and testament" in Greek legal circles in every period, and carried this meaning popularly as well.[66] Only rarely was it employed among the Greeks in the sense of treaty or agreement (another word, *sunthēkē,* was the regular term employed for covenant or agreement negotiated by two parties on equal terms). The illustration cited by Behm of *diathēkē* in the sense of treaty is "a treaty between two parties, but binding only on the one according to the terms fixed by the other."[67] In the sense of disposition or ordinance the term was also employed. It denoted "an 'arrangement' made by one party with plenary power, which the other party may accept or reject, but cannot alter. A 'will' is simply the most conspicuous example of such an instrument, which ultimately monopolised the word...."[68] In the Septuagint *diathēkē* (rather than *sunthēkē*) was used to translate the Hebrew *berît* (covenant). This did not imply that the Hebrew concept of a covenant equaled exactly the Greek idea of a will or testament, but

---

64. Herbert Preisker, "Enguos," in *Theological Dictionary of the NT,* II, 329.

65. Bruce, *The Epistle to the Hebrews,* p. 151, fn.

66. See the excellent discussion by Johannes Behm in *Theological Dictionary of the NT,* II, 104-134, on which much of the following discussion is based.

67. Behm, p. 125.

68. James H. Moulton and George Milligan, *The Vocabulary of the Greek Testament,* p. 148.

that the one-sided character of God's covenant was the point to be conveyed. Arndt and Gingrich explain:

> Another essential characteristic of a testament is retained, namely that it is the declaration of one person's will, not the result of an agreement betw. two parties, like a compact or contract. This is without doubt one of the main reasons why the LXX rendered *b^erît* by *d.* In the "covenants" of God, it was God alone who set the conditions....[69]

The problem facing the English translator is that no one English word contains the breadth of *diathēkē* and could be properly used in all cases. "Covenant" conveys the idea of agreement but also suggests negotiation. "Testament" denotes a one-sided legal arrangement, but also necessitates the death of the one making it, a fact not applicable to all uses of *diathēkē* in Scripture. Probably the best approach is to translate most occurrences as "covenant" with the understanding that the sense is a "testamentary or one-sided covenant." Only in 9:16, 17 is the narrower English sense of "testament" clearly indicated.

> *And they have become priests more* [in number] *because they were prevented by death from continuing; but he, because he remains forever, has the priesthood unchangeable.* (7:23, 24)

The superiority of Christ's priesthood is next indicated by the fact that it is not interrupted by death (vv. 23-25). The Levitical system required a succession of priests because death continually made replacements necessary. Thus there were more (*pleiones*) than one, or perhaps "more" as compared to Melchizedek.[70] Now, of course, the Levitical system contained specific instructions as to the procedure for selecting a replacement for the high priest. Nevertheless, the very fact that the operation of the priesthood was periodically confronted with such interruption is here viewed as a weakness. The constant and inevitable change left the way open for a breakdown in proper representation. A

---

69. Arndt and Gingrich, *Greek-English Lexicon,* p. 182.

70. The first century Jewish historian Josephus counts eighty-three high priests from Aaron to the destruction of the temple in A.D. 70. *Antiquities of the Jews* 20. 10. 1.

faithful priest who had the confidence of the people might be succeeded in office by a worthless son. Even if this did not occur, the possibility always remained for the next replacement.

With Christ our great high priest, the situation is far different. The unending life of Christ, which insures a perpetual priesthood, has already been alluded to in verses 8 and 16. The death of Christ on the cross does not weaken the author's point because it was Calvary which provided the once-for-all sacrifice. The primary function of our great high priest is His representation of believers in heaven, and this involves His postresurrection and ascension ministry. In this capacity He is no longer subject to death, and thus His priesthood will never be interrupted. It is therefore unchangeable (*aparabaton*). Although contextually and etymologically one could find reason for interpreting the term as "without a successor" (etym. "not passing along [to another]"), this meaning is not found elsewhere.[71] The well-attested sense of "permanent, unchangeable" yields good sense, and therefore should be retained.[72] Because Christ will never need personal replacement, all of His superiorities and their advantages for believers are without termination. Whenever men need the services of their priest (and is there ever a time when this is not so?), they are assured that Christ is available. He will never die, retire, nor be replaced.

Is there a difference to be understood between the statements of Christ's life as "indestructible" (*akatalutou,* v. 16) and of His priesthood as "unchangeable" (*aparabaton,* v. 24)? Careful consideration of the context suggests that the answer is to be found in noting to what the assertions about Christ are contrasted. In verse 16 the contrast is between Christ and the Levitical regulations which were largely physical and external in nature. Christ, however, functions by virtue of His inherent life which is not subject to physical restrictions, dissolution, or decay. In verse 24 the contrast is between Christ and the Levitical succession of dying priests. Christ, by virtue of His deathlessness, guarantees a priesthood not subject to the weakening effect of a constant need of replacements.

---

71. Arndt and Gingrich, *Greek-English Lexicon,* p. 80.
72. Arndt and Gingrich, p. 80.

> *Wherefore he is able also to save to the uttermost the ones*
> *coming to God through him, since he is always living to*
> *make intercession for them.* (7:25)

Wherefore (*hothen*) introduces a summary from the previous discussion. Christ is able to save **to the uttermost** (*eis to panteles*). The sense of this phrase has been understood by some as "completely," and by others with the temporal idea of "forever." The only other New Testament usage occurs at Luke 13:11 of the woman with a spirit of infirmity whose body was bent and could not be straightened "completely." It must be noted, however, that extra-Biblical uses in the temporal sense of "forever" do occur (see listing by Arndt and Gingrich). Contextually, either sense fits well. The meaning "completely" has the support of the only other New Testament use, accords well with the sense of the cognate adverb *pantelōs,* and actually would include the idea of time also. Christ, in contrast to the priests of the former system, is able to save **men completely**. His priesthood does not depend upon validation by anyone else (as animal sacrifices did), nor did it require repeated offerings. By saving men **completely**, there is no need for subsequent redemptive acts. Hence Christ's saving work was also "forever." This priesthood, of course, is not universal in its operation. It serves only those who come **to God through him**. The statement is reminiscent of the upper room discourse, in which Jesus explained, "I am the way, the truth, and the life: no man cometh unto the Father, but by me" (John 14:6).

The way in which Christ's saving ministry as a priest is carried on is indicated as His **always living to make intercession for them**. This is not a repeated offering of His blood (as Jewish high priests on the annual Day of Atonement), for this was done once and its efficacy abides continually. It rather refers to Christ's present ministry exercised in heaven on behalf of believers, in which He serves as their Advocate. F. F. Bruce calls attention to Christ's words to Peter on earth, "I have prayed for you that your faith fail not" (Luke 22:32), and to His prayer in John 17, as illustrative of Christ's intercessory work for believers, a work which is doubtless still being performed for them in heaven.[73]

---

73. Bruce, *The Epistle to the Hebrews,* pp. 154, 155.

The final superiority of Christ's priesthood to be mentioned is that it is performed by one with superior personal fitness (vv. 26-28).

> *For such a high priest was also fitting for us, holy, guileless, undefiled, separated from sinners, and having become higher than the heavens; (7:26)*

After the incompleteness of the Levitical system, it was appropriate that the messianic **high priest** be complete in His person and work, so as to bring salvation to its proper culmination. This our great high priest was (and is) fully able to do because in His own person He possesses in the absolute sense what the former priests reflected only to a limited degree and in some cases merely in a ceremonial way.

Christ is **holy** (*hosios*), possessing the quality of personal piety, with no hint of pollution. The meaning may be clarified by examining the negative term *anosios,* which describes "impious" acts which transgress laws or reject sacred obligations.[74] The positive term describes the nature of one who is pious, acting always out of regard for God's requirements.

He is **guileless** (*akakos*), one who does no evil but is morally pure and upright. In Him is no malice or badness of any sort. The active sense of not performing evil seems prominent here since the following term stresses the passive idea of being defiled. Christ is **undefiled** (*amiantos*). Not only does He do no evil, but no evil attaches itself to Him. His purity goes far beyond ceremonial requirements of clean garments and observance of physical taboos. He is morally unstained with anything that could possibly mar His effectiveness as high priest in the very presence of God.

Separated from sinners employs a perfect participle, denoting the present condition resultant from a past act. This has been interpreted of Christ's present location in heaven (see next phrase), where He is removed from this sinful world and thus can carry out His ministry without any possibility of defilement. Sometimes reference is made to the later Jewish custom of having the high priest move from his home to the sanctuary precincts a week before the Day of Atonement so as to

---

74. Friedrich Hauck, "Hosios, Anosios," in *Theological Dictionary of the NT,* V, 489-493.

avoid all possibility of contamination.[75] However, it is not the teaching of Scripture elsewhere that this was the purpose of the ascension and exaltation. Christ did not return to heaven to escape worldly defilement. It is better, therefore, to regard the statement as describing Christ's permanent state throughout His incarnation (and continuing, of course, today). Though He entered true human life, He was always separated from sinners as far as contracting defilement was concerned. He mingled freely with publicans and sinners (and drew the disapproval of the ceremonially scrupulous Pharisees), but never partook of their sin nor was ever honestly suspected of doing so. "Which of you convicteth me of sin?" asked Jesus of His enemies (John 8:46).

Having become higher than the heavens denotes Christ's present abode and the place of His priestly ministry. The epistle has already indicated that Christ has passed through the heavens (4:14), that He is seated at God's right hand (1:13), and is crowned with glory and honor (2:9). The statement may imply not only that He is in heaven, but also that He is higher than all other beings in heaven (the Father excepted).

> . . . *who does not need daily, as the high priests, to offer sacrifices first for his own sins,* [and] *then for those of the people; for he did this once for all when he offered himself.* (7:27)

Christ's personal sinlessness sets Him in a superior position to Levitical priests, for He had no necessity of making sacrifices for any sins of His own. The mention of **daily** (*kath' hēmeran*) poses a problem. Surely the author does not erroneously suppose that the high priest offered the atonement sacrifice daily rather than yearly, for he clearly shows his precise knowledge of the ritual in 9:7 and 10:1. Numerous suggestions have been made to resolve the difficulty. It has been argued that the author has merely telescoped the annual sacrifice with the daily sacrifices (for which the high priest was responsible for having them carried out).[76] Others try to show that the daily sacrifices had a similar

75. Gustav F. Oehler, *Theology of the Old Testament,* trans. George E. Day, sec. 140, p. 311. Also Wilhelm Moller, "Atonement, Day of," in *International Standard Bible Encyclopedia,* ed. James Orr, I, 327, 328, based on Mishnah tract "Yoma."

76. Hewitt, *Epistle to the Hebrews,* p. 127.

twofold significance as the annual celebration.[77] However, the careful distinction drawn in verse 27 between his own sins and those of the people strongly suggests that the Day of Atonement ritual was uppermost in the writer's mind. Even though the Old Testament did make provision for the sin offerings of the priest himself on days other than the annual one (Lev. 4:3), there is no hint that such were to be daily. One must go to Philo and other extra-Biblical traditions for the idea that this twofold operation was involved in the daily offerings.

Daily can hardly be understood as the series of annual days, one after another year by year, for the proper way to express that concept is used by the author in 9:7 (*hapax tou eniautou*, "once a year") and in 10:1 (*kat' eniauton*, "yearly"). The best explanation notes that the position of **daily** in the sentence is connected solely to Christ. It is He who does not have this daily need. The point is that every time the high priest interceded for his people (which in the Levitical system was yearly), he first had to make a sin offering for himself (see Lev. 16 for the Old Testament illustration). In the case of Christ, however, every time He intercedes for believers (which is not one day a year but every day, i.e., continually, always, 7:25), He has no such need.[78]

The reason is that the sin offering by Christ has already been made once for all (*ephapax*). The unique character of Christ's offering is here asserted. It was not repeatable as the Levitical ones were. Of course, the one-for-all offering of Christ was not for sins of His own, since His sinlessness has already been asserted (4:15; 7:26) and was presumably acknowledged by the readers. His sin offering did not require to be offered twice, once for Himself (Lev. 16:6, 11) and afterward for the people (Lev. 16:15). When our Lord died upon the cross as a sin offering it was totally vicarious. When He offered himself, He did what no other priest could ever do successfully, for no other person could offer himself as an absolutely perfect sacrifice. This is the first mention in Hebrews of Christ's priestly offering as being Himself, but the subject will be elaborated in the next section.

> *For the law appoints men as high priests having weakness,*
> *but the word of the oath, which* [came] *after the law,*
> [appoints] *a Son perfected forever.* (7:28)

---

77. F. F. Bruce, *The Epistle to the Hebrews,* pp. 157, 158.

78. This is the view of Westcott, *Epistle to the Hebrews,* pp. 195, 196, and Alford, *NT for English Readers,* p. 1513.

The superior personal fitness of Christ as high priest is summarized by this concluding statement of the section. The priests of the Levitical system were duly appointed according to the regulations spelled out in the Mosaic law. Yet their personal **weakness** was recognized from the start, so that special notice was taken of the fact ceremonially (5:2-3; 7:27; cf. Lev. 16). God's **oath** regarding the messianic priest came long after the Mosaic legislation, being announced by David in Psalm 110:4 more than four hundred years after Moses. This priest, rather than being one characterized by weakness, is God's own Son. Absence of the article with *huion* stresses the quality of "son-ness" possessed by Christ. Thus in His very essence relative to God He is far superior to any other priest. As such He has been **perfected** (*teteleiōmenon*) or brought to completion and fully equipped to exercise His priesthood in heaven on behalf of believers. The once-for-all nature of His sacrifice coupled with the personal qualifications of the priest Himself as God's own Son make the eternal character of His priesthood a certainty, immeasurably superior to the Aaronic order.

E. CHRIST'S MINISTRY IS SUPERIOR TO THE OLD TESTAMENT MINISTRY. (8:1–10:18)

Having set forth the superiority of Christ to prophets, angels, Moses, and Aaron, the epistle now considers how this leads to the inescapable conclusion that Christ as the believer's high priest performs an incomparably better priestly ministry. This ministry operates from a better covenant, in a superior sanctuary, and with an offering whose efficacy is beyond question.

1. Introduction. (8:1-6)

> *Now the main point in the things being said* [is this] : *we have such a high priest who sat at the right hand of the throne of the Majesty in the heavens, a minister of the sanctuary and of the true tabernacle which the Lord erected, not man.* (8:1, 2)

Main point is preferable to "sum" as the translation of *kephalaion*, inasmuch as a present participle *tois legomenois* (the things being said) is used rather than an aorist or perfect ("things which were said"). The author is not just providing a summation of previous material, but is picking out the main point of the discussion presently being conducted. In fact, some of the material given as part of the *kephalaion* has not been mentioned before, and thus could not properly be a summary (e.g., the true tabernacle).

We have such a high priest emphasizes the present operation of Christ's priesthood on believers' behalf and in terms of the description in chapters 5–7. He is far superior to Aaron for He serves not on earth, but in heaven. He is not still making sacrifice, but has taken His seat at **the right hand of the divine Majesty** (a periphrasis for "God"). He is thus established as an exalted and regal priest.

Christ as our high priest officiates in the **sanctuary.** The Greek term here is *tōn hagiōn,* a plural form of the word meaning "holy." The interpreter must proceed most carefully in identifying the precise meaning of this and similar expressions throughout Hebrews. Attractive as the notion might be that the variations which occur between the uses have reference to specific distinctions, it appears impossible to adopt this as a rigid hermeneutic in Hebrews. For example, the singular *to hagiōn* in 9:1 apparently refers to the whole earthly tabernacle, including all its parts. In 9:2 the first chamber of the tabernacle is designated as *hagia* ("holy place"), and in 9:3 the second chamber is called *hagia hagiōn* ("holy of holies"). However, it is impossible to insist that all uses of the term be interpreted according to this pattern, for such instances as 9:12 and 25 use the simple *hagia* (although with the article) in the sense of the holy of holies. The interpreter must then determine the meaning in each instance by the demands of the specific context. In 8:2 it is most probable that the reference to Christ as "high" priest demands the understanding of the holy of holies here, although not the earthly one.

What is the **true tabernacle** (*tēs skēnēs tēs alēthinēs*)? Efforts to explain it as Christ's glorified body (based on our Lord's statement of the "sanctuary of his body," John 2:21), or the Church as God's dwelling place seem strangely disconnected from the context. A much simpler view sees in this phrase a further explanation of the preceding one, with *kai* being treated as even. The **sanctuary** looks at the priest's ministry as in the holy presence of God, and the further description as the **true tabernacle** regards this priest as ministering in the actual dwelling place of God, not the representational one of Old Testament days. (*Alēthinos* means "true" as the opposite of counterfeit, unreal, or merely apparent. It does not mean "true" as the opposite of false.) Which the Lord erected, not man points to the difference in nature between the Old Testament tabernacle and the sanctuary in which Christ performs as high priest. The reference is to heaven itself, where Christ is presently enthroned (8:1), and where His representation of believers is exercised (4:14; 9:24). There does not seem to be any compelling reason to insist upon some sort of edifice in heaven, corresponding to each item in the Mosaic tabernacle. (If so, certain changes need to be introduced, especially removal of the veil between the holy place and the holy of holies.) The author equates the holy of holies with "heaven itself" in 9:24.

> *For every high priest is appointed for the offering of both gifts and sacrifices, hence* [it is] *necessary for this* [high priest] *also to have something which he may offer.* (8:3)

The thought now moves to the fact that Christ must of necessity minister in heaven, because He would be disqualified on earth under the Old Testament Levitical system (vv. 3, 4). The concept is developed by stating the basic function of the **high priest** to be that of offering **gifts and sacrifices** (*dōra te kai thusias*). A similar description was given in 5:1. The two terms apparently denote the categories of voluntary thank offerings and required sacrifices for sin. The present tense of the infinitive *prospherein* ("to offer") is used in view of the iterative character of these offerings. Inasmuch as the offering of sacrifices is the very essence of being a priest, it follows that Christ must also have something to offer. (The author has already stated in 7:27 what this offering was, but he does not intend to enlarge upon this truth until 9:12.) It is of considerable interest to note that the verb **offer** at the end of the verse is an aorist (*prosenengkēi*), suiting admirably the one sacrifice of Christ in contrast to the repeated offerings of the Levitical priests.

The necessity of an offering requires also an acceptable sanctuary in which to offer it. The point has already been asserted in 8:1, 2 that Christ ministers in heaven. Could this have been regarded as a disadvantage by some of these readers who felt the lack of an earthly priest?

The following explanation shows the importance and superiority of the heavenly sanctuary in the functioning of Christ's priesthood.

Now indeed, if he were on earth, he would not even be a priest, inasmuch as there are those who are offering the gifts according to law; (8:4)

Christ as our high priest must of necessity function in heaven. If He were still on earth, He would not even be an ordinary priest, much less a high priest. The reason is that the Levitical system was already established, and it left no room for a non-Levite (see discussion on 7:13, 14). Jesus had come from the tribe of Judah, and as long as the Mosaic legislation was operative within God's covenant nation of Israel, any other priest was a violation of the law. Furthermore, the Levitical regulations contained no provision for the kind of offering Jesus made (7:27; 9:12). Hence Christ is not just another priest of the same general sort, but a different kind of priest, for whom even the place of ministering must be radically different.

The interpreter must proceed with care at this point lest he erroneously conclude that Christ's priesthood did not begin until the ascension. If so, then the offering of Himself in once-for-all sacrifice cannot be regarded as a priestly act, even though it is at the very heart of priestly ministry. It is much better to regard the statement of verse 4 as relative to the author's standpoint as he writes. Theologically, the death of Christ rent the veil and brought to a close the Old Testament economy. Thus Christ's sacrifice was no violation of the divinely established Mosaic system. On the other hand, from the human standpoint the sacrifices were not ended until the destruction of the temple forty years later in A.D. 70. Thus at the time of writing there were still priests carrying on the established ritual. If Christ had been on earth at that time, He would have been disqualified from officiating in the temple in any priestly way. Nevertheless, His death and His subsequent representation of believers in heaven are all aspects of His high priestly work.

Incidentally, there is indication in the present tense of the participle those who are offering that the epistle was written before A.D. 70, while the Levitical system was still operating.

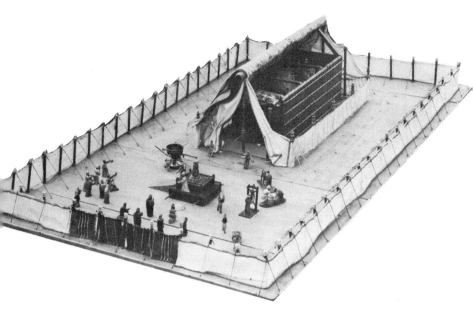

Model of the tabernacle by Conrad Shick.

> . . . who serve a copy and shadow of the heavenly things,
> even as Moses has been instructed as he was about to erect
> the tabernacle, for "See [to it], he says, "you shall make all
> things according to the pattern which was shown to you on
> the mountain." (8:5)

If (incredible as it seems) service in the heavenly sanctuary be
regarded by the readers as something less significant or of less practical
relevance than earthly priests, then let them know that the Levitical
system was only a reflection of the heavenly reality. It had no real
validity of its own. It was merely a copy (*hupodeigmati*) and a shadow
(*skiāi*). The use of *hupodeigma* here is similar to the Septuagint practice
of treating *hupodeigma* and *paradeigma* as interchangeable [79] with the
sense of model or copy. Other New Testament uses of *hupodeigma*
meaning "copy" or "example" are found in John 13:15 (Christ's
example in washing the disciples' feet), Hebrews 4:11 (rebellious Israel's example in the wilderness), Hebrews 9:23 (the tabernacle furniture as copies of the heavenly realities), James 5:10 (Old Testament
prophets as examples of patience in suffering), and II Peter 2:6 (Sodom
and Gomorrah as examples of the consequences of ungodly living).

---

79. Schlier, "Deiknumi," in *Theological Dictionary of the NT,* II, 32, 33.

This point is clearly demonstrated in the reference to Moses, for in Exodus 25:40 Moses was divinely instructed (common meaning of *chrēmatizō* is to denote a supernatural revelation from God, an angel, a prophet, or some oracle) to follow precisely the pattern shown to him on Sinai. What was subsequently erected was thus not an original but a copy. Now what did Moses see in the mountain? He was shown a *tupon*. The meaning is surely that of archetype, exemplar, or pattern. Inasmuch as the passage stresses that Moses was shown something, it can hardly be explained as merely instruction regarding spiritual truths which Moses was then to illustrate by constructing a physical tabernacle. Much better is it to understand that Moses was actually shown not only something approximating blueprints but even an architect's scale model. The tabernacle which was then constructed was a copy of the pattern or model shown to him on Sinai. Of course, this does not demand that a spatial building existed in heaven. All that is implied is that the heavenly truths were represented in the visual pattern for construction shown to Moses, and that the resultant tabernacle was a copy of this pattern.

But now he has obtained a more excellent ministry, by as much as he is also mediator of a better covenant, which has been enacted on the basis of better promises. (8:6)

Christ's priestly ministry is more excellent than any Levitical high priest. Some reasons for substantiating this assertion have already been given, such as the fact that Christ's ministry is carried on in the heavenly sanctuary. However, the particular idea in the author's mind here is that Christ's ministry is superior because He mediates a better covenant. As mediator (*mesitēs*) He is the "middleman" who gets the parties together and makes possible the agreement. Moses is called the mediator of the covenant made at Sinai (Gal. 3:19). Christ, however, is the mediator of the better covenant (called in 9:15 "mediator of a new covenant") in a far higher sense than Moses was of the old. Moses was merely the representative of the people to whom God chose to convey His law. But Christ is mediator in that by His very person and death He accomplished the reconciliation that was needed.

The covenant by which Christ officiates in His priesthood is better than the former one. The point is not that the Mosaic law was evil, for it was God who gave it. The better character of the covenant lay in the better promises which it conveyed. They were better because of what was promised and because of their unconditional nature. The Mosaic law contained a large emphasis upon physical and earthly matters. At the same time, fulfilment of them depended upon Israel's meeting of certain conditions (see Exod. 19:5-8; 24:3-8). The new covenant, however, is far more unqualified in its promises than the old, and its provisions deal primarily with spiritual rather than physical blessings. The general nature of this covenant will be noted shortly in the quotation from Jeremiah.

The reader can hardly miss the emphasis in verse 6 upon Christ's ministry as "more excellent . . . better . . . better." This relentless insistence upon the superiority of Christian truth to the superficial attractions of the Levitical system reveals again the nature of the hostile ideas the author is refuting.

2. The two covenants. (8:7-13)

> *For if that first* [covenant] *were faultless, a place would not be sought for a second one.* (8:7)

This is the same sort of argument as pursued in 7:11. There the author argued that the Levitical system must have been envisioned by God as inadequate, inasmuch as He announced a replacement with a different kind of priest. Here the reasoning is that the Mosaic covenant must not have been able to accomplish all that was needed, since God saw fit to plan another covenant. Even during Old Testament times, such a replacement was declared by Jeremiah; and ever since that prophetic announcement spiritually sensitive Israelites were looking for that place in history when the promise would be fulfilled.

> *For finding fault with them, he says:*
> *"Behold days are coming, says the Lord,*
> *And I will accomplish with the house of Israel*
> *and with the house of Judah a new covenant."* (8:8)

Although the first covenant was inferred to be faulty in verse 7, the actual fault lay not in the covenant itself but in the people who did not keep their part of the agreement. The inadequacy of the covenant was its inability to insure that the people could live up to it.

In the days of Jeremiah God announced a new covenant. Those were dark days for the nation of Israel. The northern kingdom had already been led captive by the Assyrians. The southern kingdom (Judah) was nearing its destruction by the Babylonians. Jeremiah began his ministry during the reign of Josiah, and lived into the period of the seventy-year captivity. He had witnessed the revival that occurred when the law was rediscovered in Josiah's eighteenth year (II Kings 22—23); but he must also have been aware that the spiritual awakening was not permanent. It was just a matter of time until judgment would fall upon the nation. Jeremiah himself lived to see the captivity begin. It was during those days that he received the prophecy of the new covenant, recorded in Jeremiah 31:31-34. The speaker was God Himself, who promised to the suffering nation a new covenant in which there would be the accomplishment of those things which the first covenant was not designed to achieve.

Verse 8 indicates that the new covenant would be made with the houses of **Israel** and **Judah.** The clear implication is that there would be a reunited nation. Jeremiah's contemporaries would also have understood the reference literally as God's promise to the Jewish people of a new kind of relationship to them. It would be accomplished when the people were regathered to their land (Jer. 30:1-3), after the time of their greatest suffering known as "Jacob's trouble" (30:7). All their enemies would be destroyed (30:16), and their ancient homeland would be rebuilt (30:17, 18). The new covenant would bring about a spiritual transformation individually as well as nationally. The prophecy was thus a ray of hope for a downtrodden people.

> *"Not according to the covenant which I made with their fathers in the day when I took hold of their hand to lead them out of the land of Egypt, because they did not continue in my covenant, and I did not care about them, says the Lord."* (8:9)

The new covenant God promised would be a different sort from the first one. This verse (quoted from Jer. 31:32) makes it clear that the first covenant in view is the Mosaic one, given at Sinai after God had miraculously delivered Israel in the Exodus. In spite of the solemn promise of their forefathers (Exod. 19:7, 8; 24:3-8), Israel had failed to keep the provisions of the covenant. Because the covenant was a conditional one, Israel's abandonment of it caused God likewise to withdraw from it.

> *"For this is the covenant which I will make with the house of Israel after those days, says the Lord, giving my laws into their mind, and I will write them upon their hearts, and I shall be to them a God, and they shall be to me for a people."* (8:10)

The basic promises of the new covenant, which have been termed "better" in verse 6, are given in verses 10, 11, and 12. The first (quoting Jer. 31:33) concerns the inward knowledge of God. God's laws would not be an external code inscribed on stone, but implanted in the very minds and hearts (Hebrew synonymous parallelism) of the people. Compliance would thus be by inner desire, not by outward compulsion. The transformation described here is the essence of regeneration. This promise of an inner change was made also by Ezekiel: "A new heart also will I give you, and a new spirit will I put within you: and I will take away the stony heart out of your flesh, and I will give you an heart of flesh. And I will put my spirit within you, and cause you to walk in my statutes, and ye shall keep my judgments, and do them" (Ezek. 36:26, 27).

Even before the days of Jeremiah and Ezekiel, Hosea had prophesied: "For ye are not my people, and I will not be your God. . . . And I will sow her unto me in the earth; and I will have mercy upon her that had not obtained mercy; and I will say to them which were not my people, Thou art my people; and they shall say, Thou art my God" (Hos. 1:9; 2:23).

It is not implied that no one under the Mosaic covenant had the proper sort of heart, any more than one would say that no Israelite knew the experience of having Jehovah as his God. The point is that the covenant itself did not provide this experience, and many lived under its provisions and yet died in unbelief. The new covenant, however, guarantees regeneration to its participants.

> *"And they shall not teach each one his fellow-citizen and each one his brother, saying, 'Know the Lord,' because all shall know me from small to great of them."* (8:11)

The second promise embodied in the new covenant (quoting Jer. 31:34a) assures that the covenant provisions will be uniformly efficacious, for each participant will have a personal knowledge of God. Because many under the old covenant had no personal experience of God as far as spiritual knowledge was concerned and the revelation itself was not complete, there was constant need for the priests and prophets to make known the latest word from God. They did this by teaching and writing, and the knowledge of God was spread by this means as one man told another. In the new covenant the knowledge of God will be planted in the heart of believers by God Himself (only true believers participate in the new covenant), and the indwelling Holy Spirit will provide an intuitive knowledge of God to every believer without exception.

Jesus taught that this was the experience of all who truly followed Him: "It is written in the prophets, And they shall be all taught of God. Every man therefore that hath heard, and hath learned of the Father, cometh unto me" (John 6:45). The same truth was explained by the apostle John: "But ye have an anointing from the Holy One, and ye all know" (I John 2:20, literal rendering), and "the anointing which ye have received of him abideth in you, and ye need not that any man teach you" (I John 2:27). The Holy Spirit residing in each believer provides the basic enlightenment. John did not mean that no teachers are ever needed by believers (John himself was teaching in his epistle), but that the function of human teachers is to clarify and unfold, rather than to convey new revelation from God. That revelation has already come, and the indwelling Spirit provides the intuitive knowledge which in germ at least is possessed equally by all believers.

> *"Because I shall be merciful to their iniquities, and their*
> *sins I will no longer remember."* (8:12)

The third of the "better promises" in the new covenant (quoting Jer. 31:34b) bestows complete forgiveness upon those covered by its provisions. Forgiveness, of course, was no new concept to Israel. Personal forgiveness of sins was always available to the contrite and obedient Israelite. Even for him, however, the very fact of repeated sacrifices served as a reminder that no final sacrifice for sin had yet been offered (10:3, 4). Nationally, however, the sins of Israel caused her to be set aside as God's special people (Hos. 1:9); but the new covenant will insure her restoration, at which time her sins will be finally forgiven (Hos. 2:23). This will occur on a nationwide basis because it will also occur on an individual basis. Sins will be remembered no longer with repeated sacrifices because the mediator of the new covenant has provided the once-for-all sacrifice which expiated sin completely (10:17, 18).

> *In saying "new," he has declared the first* [covenant] *old; now the thing declared old and becoming obsolete* [is] *near vanishing.* (8:13)

A conclusion is now drawn from the terminology of the Jeremiah passage. When God called the covenant which He proposed to make with Israel a new covenant (8:8; cf. Jer. 31:31), He implied that the first covenant (the one given at Sinai) was old. Our author then elaborates this concept by reasoning that what is old and obsolescent is doomed to eventual destruction. Hence the thought of replacing the first covenant with a second should not seem strange. This is all the more understandable when it is recognized that the first covenant was implied as "old" around 600 B.C. (i.e., the time of Jeremiah). Surely the readers of Hebrews should not feel uneasy at the thought of the former economy being superseded.

The Church and the New Covenant

A crucial question is the identity of the beneficiaries of the new covenant. Who fulfils it? Has it been fulfilled? Suggestions are many, and whatever explanation one adopts reflects something of his hermeneutics as well as his general theological position regarding eschatology.

The expression "new covenant" occurs six times in the New Testament:

> Likewise also the cup after supper, saying, This cup is the new testament [*hē kainē diathēkē*] in my blood, which is shed for you (Luke 22:20).

> After the same manner also he took the cup, when he had supped, saying, This cup is the new testament [*hē kainē diathēkē*] in my blood: this do ye, as oft as ye drink it, in remembrance of me (I Cor. 11:25).

Who also hath made us able ministers of the new testament [*kainēs diathēkēs*]; not of the letter, but of the spirit: for the letter killeth, but the spirit giveth life (II Cor. 3:6).

For finding fault with them, he saith, Behold, the days come, saith the Lord, when I will make a new covenant [*diathēkēn kainēn*] with the house of Israel and with the house of Judah (Heb. 8:8).

And for this cause he is the mediator of the new testament [*diathēkēs kainēs*], that by means of death, for the redemption of the transgressions that were under the first testament, they which are called might receive the promise of eternal inheritance (Heb. 9:15).

And to Jesus the mediator of the new covenant [*diathēkēs neas*], and to the blood of sprinkling, that speaketh better things than that of Abel (Heb. 12:24).

Several other New Testament passages, some of them in the same context with the above, use the word "covenant" alone and presumably are references also to the new covenant (Matt. 26:28; Mark 14:24; Rom. 11:27; Heb. 8:10, 13; 9:15b; and 10:16). It should be noted in passing that the word "new" in the Hebrews 12:24 reference is different from the one used in all the others.

Four views are current today regarding the relation of the church to the new covenant:

View 1. The church has replaced Israel as the participant in the new covenant. This is the viewpoint of amillennialists, who see the nation of Israel as permanently displaced and all the blessings promised to her now fulfilled by the church. Lenski is representative of this position as he writes concerning the mention of "the house of Israel" in Hebrews 8:8:

> Right here we have the universality of the new testament. Lost among the Gentiles and turned Gentile, the gospel goes out to all nations to bring the new testament in Christ's blood to all.[80]

Oswald T. Allis comments in the same vein regarding the new covenant:

---

80. Lenski, *Interpretation of Hebrews,* p. 263.

> The passage speaks of the new covenant. It declares that this new covenant has been already introduced and that by virtue of the fact that it is called "new" it has made the one which it is replacing "old," and that the old is about to vanish away. It would be hard to find a clearer reference to the gospel age in the Old Testament than in these verses in Jeremiah.[81]

One accepts this view only to the extent that he is willing to interpret "the house of Israel and the house of Judah" as the Christian church in the present age.

View 2. The new covenant is with the nation of Israel only. This is one of several views suggested by various dispensational premillennialists. It interprets the words of Jeremiah literally and sees no warrant for inclusion of the New Testament church. J. N. Darby has written:

> The first covenant was made with Israel; the second must be so likewise, according to the prophecy of Jeremiah. . . .

> We enjoy indeed all the essential privileges of the new covenant, its foundation being laid on God's part in the blood of Christ, but we do so in spirit, not according to the letter.

> The new covenant will be established formally with Israel in the millennium.[82]

The two views above represent the extremes—one seeing the church exclusively in the new covenant, and the other seeing Israel only.

View 3. There are two new covenants, one with Israel and one with the New Testament Church. This explanation recognizes the demands of a strict grammatico-historico hermeneutic for the Jeremiah passage, and at the same time acknowledges that some of the New Testament passages cannot ignore the church's relation to the new covenant. This view was expressed by Chafer as follows:

> Reference at this point is to the new covenant yet to be made with Israel and not to the new covenant now in force in the Church.

> There remains to be recognized a heavenly covenant for the heavenly people, which is also styled like the preceding one for Israel a "new covenant." It is made in the blood of Christ (cf. Mark 14:24) and continues in effect throughout this age, whereas the new covenant made with Israel happens to be future in its application. To suppose that these two covenants—one for Israel and one for the Church—are the same is to assume that there is a latitude of

---

81. Oswald T. Allis, *Prophecy and the Church,* p. 154.
82. J. N. Darby, *Synopsis of the Books of the Bible,* V, 329, 330.

common interest between God's purpose for Israel and His purpose for the Church.[83]

Among others holding this view are C. C. Ryrie[84] and J. F. Walvoord.[85] J. D. Pentecost presents the position at some length, but does not indicate categorically his personal commitment.[86] These three were all students of L. S. Chafer.

By this view one is required to differentiate among the New Testament references those referring to the new covenant promised to Israel from those describing the new covenant with the church.

View 4. There is one new covenant to be fulfilled eschatologically with Israel, but participated in soteriologically by the church today. This view recognizes that Christ's death provided the basis for instituting the new covenant, and also accepts the unconditional character of Jeremiah's prophecy which leaves no room for Israel's forfeiture. At the same time it also notes that the New Testament passages definitely relate New Testament Christians to this covenant. Perhaps the best-known representative of this position is the Scofield Reference Bible. At Hebrews 8:8 the following notes appear:

> The New Covenant secures the personal revelation of the Lord to every believer (v. 11); . . . and secures the perpetuity, future conversion, and blessing of Israel.[87]

> The New Covenant rests upon the sacrifice of Christ, and secures the eternal blessedness, under the Abrahamic Covenant (Gal. 3:13-29), of all who believe.[88]

Among the reasons supporting this interpretation are the following:

(a) The normal way of interpreting the several uses of the expression "the new covenant" is to refer them to one covenant, rather than to posit two distinct covenants with the same name (and apparently with the same or at least very similar contents).[89]

---

83. L. S. Chafer, *Systematic Theology,* IV, 325; VII, 98, 99.

84. C. C. Ryrie, *The Basis of the Premillennial Faith,* pp. 105-125.

85. J. F. Walvoord, *The Millennial Kingdom,* pp. 208-220, particularly pp. 218, 219.

86. J. D. Pentecost, *Things to Come,* pp. 116-128.

87. C. I. Scofield, ed., Scofield Reference Bible, p. 1297. The New Scofield Reference Bible (p. 1317) is virtually the same, although the mention of "Israel" is expanded to read "a repentant Israel, with whom the New Covenant will yet be ratified. . . ."

88. Scofield, p. 1298.

89. It is surprising that some dispensationalists who strongly argue that

(b) The author is writing to Christians when he mentions the new covenant. It is granted that they are Jewish Christians, but the fact remains that they are Christians.

(c) To assign arbitrarily the references to the new covenant to Israel exclusively in some cases and to the New Testament church exclusively in other cases so as to imply the existence of two new covenants encounters difficulty at Hebrews 12:23, 24, where both the church ("church of the firstborn") and Old Testament saints ("spirits of just men made perfect") are related to the new covenant (not two covenants).

(d) Christ spoke of the new covenant in the upper room discourse (Luke 22:20), and the apostles who heard Him must certainly have thought in terms of Jeremiah 31. Yet they were being made ready for the church. Christ's mention of the new covenant was a part of His institution of the bread and the cup, and this was understood by the apostles as intended for the church to perpetuate.

(e) The apostle Paul shows a clear connection between the new covenant and the church in his two uses of the term. In I Corinthians 11:25, he uses it in quoting our Lord's upper room instruction, where the sense conveyed to the apostles must surely have been the concept in Jeremiah 31. At the same time Paul is urging the observance of this ordinance by the Gentile Christian church at Corinth. In II Corinthians 3:6 he calls himself and his associates "ministers of the new covenant."

(f) Hebrews 8 argues that the title "new covenant" implies a corresponding "old covenant." The Mosaic covenant is obviously the old covenant insofar as Israel's relation to the new covenant is concerned. If the church has a totally separate new covenant, what is its "old covenant"?

All things considered, view 4 offers the least hermeneutical problems. It allows the new covenant as announced for Israel by Jeremiah to find its fulfilment with the nation when Christ returns. At the same time it recognizes that after the analogy of the Abrahamic covenant, in

---

"Israel" must be interpreted consistently wherever it is found, abandon that principle when it comes to interpreting the term "new covenant." For example, Ryrie says, "If language means anything at all, this means the natural descendants of Abraham through Jacob"; Yet he concludes that the "new covenant" is the name given to two distinct covenants (Basis of the Premillennial Faith, pp. 124, 125).

which present believers through their union with Christ (the "Seed" of Abraham, Gal. 3:16) enjoy God's blessing as "Abraham's seed" (Gal. 3:29) even though the Abrahamic covenant will not find its complete fulfilment until the millennium, so Christian believers depend for their blessing upon the blood of Christ which instituted the new covenant. Romans 11:17 ff. depicts the same truth as Gentile believers are described as grafted into the good olive tree (and at present the natural branches—Israel—are broken off). Yet the Jewish branches will someday be grafted back in (Rom. 11:24), and God's new covenant will find its fulfilment as Jeremiah predicted.

3. Operation of the first covenant. (9:1-10)

Then even the first [covenant] *was having regulations of divine service and the sanctuary belonging to the world.* (9:1)

Although the word "covenant" is not in the text, it is clearly implied by 8:13 and the rest of the preceding context. In this discussion of the sanctuary inaugurated with the first covenant, there is no attempt by the author to disparage the former system. He speaks of it with dignity and in some detail before proceeding to show the superiority of the heavenly sanctuary. It is true, he says, that the first covenant (i.e., Mosaic) was God given. It had **regulations** pertaining to the official **service** to God which was to be conducted. It had also **the sanctuary**, the one place on earth which God had designated for His manifested presence. In this passage the singular form (*to . . . hagion*) is used for the entire structure, and the plurals which follow (*hagia, hagia hagiōn*) differentiate the two parts. It should be noted that the tabernacle is in view here, not any of the succeeding temples. Proof is seen in 9:4, which describes the contents of the holy of holies. In Herod's temple, the one destroyed in A.D. 70, this chamber was empty. Hence nothing can be deduced as to the tense **was having** (imperfect *eiche*), as though implying the temple no longer stood, for the reference is not to the temple but to the tabernacle.

Belonging to the world (*kosmikon*) identifies the tabernacle as mundane, being part of this world's scene and built by man (8:2; 9:11, 24). There is no implication of evil in the expression here.

Interior panel on the Arch of Titus in Rome depicting the candelabrum and the table of showbread from the Second Temple in Jerusalem being carried away by the Romans in A.D. 70. These items were patterned generally after the tabernacle furniture (Heb. 9:2).

For a tabernacle was prepared, the first one, in which were
the lampstand and the table and the presentation of the
bread, which [first chamber] *is called the holy place.* (9:2)

In this description of the wilderness tabernacle, each of the two
chambers is called a *skēnē* ("tent," "tabernacle"), with the first tabernacle referring to the outer room, and the tabernacle after the second
veil referring to the inner chamber. Instructions for building this structure and its furniture are given in Exodus 25—40. The entire sanctuary
was approximately 45 feet long (30 cubits), 15 feet wide (10 cubits),
and 15 feet high. The enclosed space was divided into two rooms
(Exod. 26:33), with the first or outer room commonly thought to have
been about twice the size of the second or inner chamber.[90]

The furniture mentioned as belonging in the first room (holy place)
consisted of the lampstand and the table for the showbread. The
lampstand was a candelabrum constructed to hold seven lamps (Exod.
25:31-39; 37:17-24). There were no windows in the tabernacle, and the
lamps were thus required to provide illumination for the daily service of
the priests in the forechamber. When Solomon built a permanent
temple in Jerusalem, his structure contained ten lampstands (I Kings
7:49; II Chron. 4:7); but in the later temple destroyed by the Romans
in A.D. 70 there had apparently been a return to one lampstand (I
Macc. 1:21; 4:49). The Arch of Titus, erected in Rome to commemo-
rate the conquest of Jerusalem, depicts the conquerors carrying off the
single candelabrum.

Although the table and the bread are named separately, the reference is to the one item of furniture, together with the naming of its use.
The table was made of acacia wood covered with gold (Exod. 25:23-30;
37:10-16). On it were placed weekly the twelve cakes of bread (Lev.
24:5-9).

And after the second veil [was] *a tabernacle which is called*
the holy of holies, having a golden altar and the ark of the
covenant overlaid on all sides with gold, in which was a
golden pot holding the manna, and the rod of Aaron which
budded, and the tables of the covenant, and over it cher-

---

90. There is difficulty in reconstructing the tabernacle exactly from the data
given in Exodus. For detailed discussion see T. Whitelaw, "Tabernacle," in
International Standard Bible Encyclopedia, V, 2887-2898.

ubim of glory overshadowing the propitiatory cover; concerning which things it is not now [fitting] *to speak in detail.* (9:3-5)

The second veil (*katapetasma*) separated the two rooms of the tabernacle (Exod. 26:31-33). It is called the second veil to distinguish it from the curtain screen at the entrance to the holy place (Exod. 26:36, 37; 36:37). The room to which the veil led was the holy of holies, whose measurements apparently formed a cube 15 feet (10 cubits) in each dimension. This was the chamber which only the high priest could enter, and he only once a year.

The phrase *chrusoun echousa thumiatērion* ("having a golden altar/censer") poses at least two problems: the identity of *thumiatērion* (altar? or censer?) and its relation to the holy of holies. As to the first of these difficulties, the King James Version has translated the term as "censer," referring it to the instrument used to carry coals from the brazen altar into the holy of holies on the Day of Atonement (Lev. 16:12). Support for this translation is found in the Septuagint, which uses *thumiatērion* for "censer" but never for "incense altar" (II Chron. 26:19; Ezek. 8:11; IV Macc. 7:11). To some, this explanation may seem to avoid the problem caused by locating the incense altar in the holy of holies (although a similar problem yet remains by the improbability that the *censer* was kept in the holy of holies). This view, however, is not without its difficulties. In addition to the fact that Scripture nowhere calls this censer golden (although admittedly there is no reason why it could not have been, and some noncanonical Jewish literature so terms it), a more serious objection is seen in the omission of any mention of the incense altar if *thumiatērion* is treated as "censer."

Favoring the identification as "incense altar" is the likelihood that this key item of tabernacle furniture would not have been overlooked. Furthermore, *thumiatērion* is used of this altar by the Jewish writers Philo and Josephus, by the Christian writers Clement of Alexandria and Origen, and in the versions of Theodotion and Symmachus at Exodus 30:1. Finally, Scripture explicitly calls the incense altar "gold" in the description of its construction (Exod. 30:1-10). For these reasons most recent interpreters treat the term as altar.

The second problem concerns the relation of this altar to the holy of holies. Actually, this problem exists regardless of the view one adopts regarding *thumiatērion,* for it is impossible that either the altar or the censer were kept in the holy of holies. (The high priest had to enter the inner chamber *with* the censer; thus it could not have been stored there during the year.) Did the author err in locating the incense altar in the holy of holies? This is unthinkable since he knew that the daily service of the priests (v. 6) involved the golden altar, and knew also that the holy of holies was entered only once a year (v. 7). The intimate knowledge of details which the author obviously had argues strongly that any confusion rests with later readers, not with him. The use of the general expression having (*echousa*) rather than the more explicit "in which" (cf. *en hēi,* regarding the ark as *containing* the golden pot) provides some leeway in interpretation (although this is weakened somewhat by the use of "having" to describe the relation of the manna to the pot).

The best answer to this puzzle is to note the author's statement as being influenced by liturgical function at this point rather than by strict physical location. In so doing he is following precisely the thinking as well as the terminology of the Old Testament which also describes the incense altar in relation to the veil and the ark, rather than in terms of the chamber in which it actually was placed. "And thou shalt put it before the vail that is by the ark of the testimony, before the mercy seat that is over the testimony, where I will meet with thee" (Exod. 30:6); "And thou shalt set the altar of gold for the incense before the ark of the testimony. . ." (Exod. 40:5). The same sort of description was used of the altar in Solomon's temple: "And the whole house he overlaid with gold, until he had finished all the house: also the whole altar that was by the oracle he overlaid with gold" (I Kings 6:22).

The altar of incense was thus described in this fashion because of its close association with the Day of Atonement ritual, for the high priest took burning incense from that altar with him into the holy of holies so that the smoke of it would cover the mercy seat and protect him from death (Lev. 16:12, 13).

Within the holy of holies proper was the ark or chest covered with gold (Exod. 25:10-15). The ark originally contained a golden pot holding the manna from the wilderness (Exod. 16:33, 34) and Aaron's rod that budded (Num. 17). Neither the pot nor the rod was existent in Solomon's time (I Kings 8:9; II Chron. 5:10), and it may be safely concluded that they disappeared at the time of the Philistine capture of the ark (I Sam. 4:10, 11). In the ark were placed also the two stone tables from Sinai (Exod. 25:16, 21; 40:20). These were still in the ark at the time of Solomon's temple dedication (I Kings 8:9; II Chron. 5:10), but were not in the Second Temple. The Roman general Pompey who entered the temple in 63 B.C. found only the furniture belonging to the first chamber.[91] Apparently the ark and the tables of stone disappeared at the destruction of Solomon's temple by the Babylonians under Nebuchadnezzar in 586 B.C. (II Kings 25:8, 9). The postexilic temple of Zerubbabel contained only a stone slab on which the high priest placed his censer on the Day of Atonement.[92]

The cherubim of glory are described in Exodus 25:18-22 as being two-winged creatures of beaten gold facing one another. These were placed upon the lid of the chest containing the tables of stone. The term *hilastērion* is the Septuagint translation of the Hebrew *kapporet* ("covering"), and is somewhat interpretive as it recognizes the propitiatory purpose for which the cover of the ark was employed. The translation **propitiatory cover** is a fair rendering of the term, conveying as it does the fact that "covering" involved the covering of sin, not just the covering of the ark. This cover was made of pure gold and upon it the blood of atonement was sprinkled by the high priest (Exod. 25:17; 37:6; Lev. 16:14).

---

91. Josephus *Antiq.* 14. 4. 4.
92. W. Shaw Caldecott and James Orr, "Temple," in *International Standard Bible Encyclopedia,* V, 2936, citing the Mishna tract "Yoma," 5.2.

Plan of the tabernacle sanctuary, showing the main pieces of furniture.

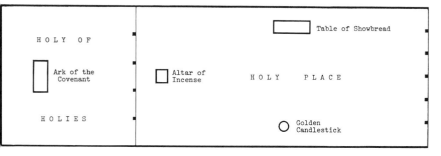

The author did not wish to discuss the above individual terms in greater detail because he desired to emphasize Christ's superior ministry, not the types that foreshadowed Christ. Thus he proceeds after the briefest mention to the service which was carried on in the tabernacle.

> *Now these things having been so prepared, into the first tabernacle the priests go continually accomplishing the divine services. . . . (9:6)*

After the tabernacle was constructed and properly furnished, the priestly functions could be performed within it. The first tabernacle (*tēn prōtēn skēnēn*) refers to the outer compartment, the holy place (as in v. 2). The common priests entered it daily to observe the ritual prescribed in the law. Incense was offered morning and evening upon the golden altar at the same time that the candelabrum was tended (Exod. 30:7, 8). The showbread was changed weekly (Lev. 24:5-8). In later years when the order of priests became so numerous that they had to be divided into twenty-four groups (I Chron. 24:1-19), the selection of the priest who would burn the incense was settled daily by casting the lot (Luke 1:9), and was regarded as a high privilege. Zacharias was engaged in this honorable task when the angel announced to him the coming birth of John the Baptist.

> *. . . but into the second* [tabernacle] *the high priest* [went] *alone once a year, not without blood, which he offers on behalf of himself and the ignorances of the people. . . .* (9:7)

The ministry in the second chamber was exceedingly more restricted. First, it was off limits to everyone except the high priest. All ordinary priests were excluded. By this means God pictured vividly the barrier that sin has posed between His holy presence and sinful men. Access to God must be on God's terms, and depends upon expiation of sin. Second, even the high priest could enter the holy of holies only once a year. The reference, of course, is to the annual Day of Atonement on the tenth day of the seventh month. This does not deny the fact that on that occasion the high priest actually entered the holy of holies several times—at least twice, and perhaps three or four. He entered with the blood of a bullock as the sin offering for himself and his household, and again with the blood of a goat as the sin offering for the people. Furthermore, the taking of the censer of burning coals and the incense into the holy of holies may have required an additional entrance (Lev. 16:12, 13) and perhaps its removal necessitated yet a fourth entry. By "once a year" the author means the one annual celebration, without pausing to separate the various steps in the ritual.

The third restriction was the mandatory offering of blood, without which even the high priest could not enter the holy of holies. This was required for his personal sins as well as those of the people he represented. Ignorances takes into account the Mosaic distinction between sins of ignorance and sins of presumption (Num. 15:27-31). In the case of the former, atonement was available. For the latter, the sin was that of deliberate rebellion against God, and no sacrifice was provided.

> ... the Holy Spirit indicating this, that the way into the holy of holies[93] was not yet manifested while the first tabernacle was still having a position. ... (9:8)

The Old Testament tabernacle was the visible demonstration by the Holy Spirit (viewed here as the Father's agent in revealing these truths to men) that perfect access to God by all people did not yet exist. The reference to the first tabernacle in verse 8 has been understood in two ways. Some interpret it as the entire earthly structure in contrast to the heavenly reality.[94] The term *tōn hagiōn* is understood as the sanctuary in heaven. It appears more natural, however, to treat the first tabernacle the same way it has been used throughout this paragraph (vv. 2, 6) to denote the outer chamber (holy place), and the holy of holies would then most likely refer to the earthly inner compartment.[95] As long as the tabernacle existed with two chambers, the position of chamber one barred the way to chamber two.

> ... which [first tabernacle] is a parable for the season [then] present according to which both gifts and sacrifices

---

93. Greek, *ton hagion.*
94. So F. F. Bruce, *The Epistle to the Hebrews,* pp. 194, 195.
95. So Dods, *Expositor's Greek Testament,* IV, 330, 331; Carl Bernhard Moll, "The Epistle to the Hebrews," in *Commentary on the Holy Scriptures,* ed. John Peter Lange, trans. A. C. Kendrick, pp. 152, 153.

>*are being offered* [which are] *unable to bring to comple-*
>*tion in conscience the one who worships,* [these sacrifices
>being] *only, as regards foods and drinks and various wash-*
>*ings, regulations of flesh, being imposed until a time of a*
>*new order.* (9:9, 10)

These two verses set forth the typical significance of the earthly tabernacle. Not only was the tabernacle in general an object lesson for God's people, but in particular the presence of the "first tabernacle" or forechamber served as a **parable** or teaching figure of the principal lesson God wanted to convey. As long as God was pleased to demonstrate His presence in a tabernacle with two chambers, He was showing men that real freedom of access to His presence was not available. The holy place had a curtain at the front to prevent the common people from entering, and the second veil kept the ordinary priests from the holy of holies.

The season [then] **present** (*ton kairon ton enestēkota*) should be understood of the Old Testament period. As long as the tabernacle stood with its first chamber intact (and one may enlarge the concept to include the temples which succeeded it if he does not suppose the author to regard the current sacrifices as still valid), it offered testimony to its adherents of the continued presence of a barrier to God.

The gifts and sacrifices were the voluntary gifts brought to God by the worshiping Israelite, as well as the bloody offerings required for sin. The present tense **are being offered** (*prospherontai*) may be a historical present, or may be an indication that the same sort of offerings were continuing in the temple at Jerusalem.

Now these Jewish sacrifices had distinct limitations. They were unable **to bring to completion in conscience** the adherents of this system. The Levitical offerings never enabled the worshiper to have the inner consciousness that he was completely and permanently cleansed (otherwise they would not have needed repetition, 10:2). This does not imply that no Old Testament believer ever achieved a cleansed conscience, but that animal sacrifices per se could not grant this inner consciousness of God's favor. Such was the result of the Spirit of God acting in response to the faith of the believing Israelite (e.g., Ps. 51). In fact, it was only when sacrifices were offered in obedience out of a heartfelt contrition and faith that they were acceptable to God (Ps. 51:16-19).

Old Testament ritual for purification involved physical things, such as foods and drinks and ceremonial ablutions. Only certain specified kinds of animals were allowable as sacrifices. Some foods could not be eaten. Strong drink was not allowed to those taking a Nazarite vow (Num. 6:3). Priests had to bathe themselves ritualistically before the Day of Atonement celebration (Lev. 16:4). Yet these matters were all regulations regarding the flesh, and actually had no connection with the heart (except as expressions of heartfelt obedience to God's instructions). Thus it is always possible for persons to satisfy themselves that they have fulfilled their obligations to God merely by observing traditional ceremonies. Many in Israel did just that, and although their faithful conformity to Mosaic law maintained them in their civil and religious privileges, their hearts were far from God and they knew little or nothing of God's forgiveness. Was this part of the problem of the original readers? As Hebrew Christians whose spiritual growth was abnormally slow (5:12), they could well have placed undue confidence in the ritual of Judaism, and found its attractions almost irresistible. This would explain the author's repeated emphasis upon the inadequacy of Levitical sacrifices (7:11, 18, 19; 9:9, 10, 13, 14, 23; 10:1-4, 11).

The Old Testament tabernacle and its ministry was intended only as a type. It was temporary, an external figure dealing with material matters to represent basic spiritual truths. The value lasted only until the time of a new order. That new order had its inauguration when Christ offered Himself as the perfect and final sacrifice for sin. He fulfilled the previous types and shadows, and in this new order the Spirit brings about an inward change, far more basic than ceremonial cleansing. This new order has as its basis the new covenant discussed in chapter 8. Now that Christ has died, there is no cause for anyone to be occupied with the ceremonial cleansing embodied in Judaism.

4. Operation of the new covenant. (9:11–10:18)

a. General description. (9:11, 12)

But Christ having arrived [as] *a high priest of the good things which have come, through the greater and more perfect tabernacle not made with hands, that is, not of this creation . . . (9:11)*

In contrast to the symbolic operations under the first covenant, Christ has now arrived as the great high priest (4:14), and has instituted the good things of the new covenant discussed in 8:10-12. Many manuscripts read *mellontōn* ("about to come"), perhaps influenced by 10:1.[96] This yields the sense either that these good things are still future, or else that they were future in relation to the Old Testament prophecy regarding Messiah's priesthood (Ps. 110:4). However, there seems to be no compelling reason to abandon the consensus of textual critics in choosing *genomenōn* ("having come").[97] The passage then states that the good things of the new covenant have already come in the sense that Christ has secured them and believers have begun to enjoy many of them.

Christ's priestly work is performed through the greater and more perfect tabernacle. Some expositors, particularly the older ones, have regarded through (*dia*) as local in sense, and have identified the "tabernacle" as corresponding in some sense to the outer chamber of the earthly sanctuary through which the high priest passed to reach the divine presence. It is explained then as the local heavens, traversed by Christ at the ascension. Other identifications of this tabernacle as Christ's flesh, His glorified body, and even the saints themselves have all been proposed. Several factors argue strongly against such identification. First, this tabernacle is said to be "not of this creation" (*ou tautēs tēs ktiseōs*); yet Christ's flesh was certainly part of this physical creation. Pink's argument that Christ's humanity was of "a totally different order"[98] than ours is unfortunate, for Hebrews 2:11 argues in exactly the opposite direction in showing that He is one in His humanity with His brethren. The heavens also are part of this creation, and thus do not qualify. Second, it is inappropriate to insist upon an anteroom any longer, since 9:8 has argued that the presence of the anteroom indicated that the way into the holy of holies was not yet open. Christ's death, however, opened the way, so that any action of Christ subsequent to Calvary would not involve something comparable to the outer chamber. Third, the point has already been made by the author that the spiritual

---

96. So Aleph, A, and the vast majority of later manuscripts of the Byzantine type. The King James Version follows this reading.

97. So B, D (and P[46] similarly). This reading is adopted by Westcott and Hort, Nestle-Aland, and the United Bible Societies.

98. Pink, *Exposition of Hebrews,* p. 488.

reality corresponding to the material tabernacle is located in heaven (8:1-2, 5), and 9:24 will confirm this. Fourth, it is more consistent to treat "through" (*dia*) the same as in the rest of the sentence (v. 12), where "through [*dia*] blood of goats and calves" and "through [*dia*] his own blood" cannot be local but rather denote instrumentality or means.

Much simpler is the identification of this more perfect tabernacle as the heavenly reality (explained in 9:24 as heaven itself), of which the earthly structure was only a type. It is not made with hands as was the building erected by Bezaleel and Aholiab and their crew (Exod. 35:30-35; 36:1-4; 38:22, 23). It is not a part of this created order of heavens and earth. Christ acts as high priest in a far better sanctuary— the actual presence of God.

> . . . *neither through blood of goats and calves but through*
> *his own blood he entered once for all into the sanctuary,*
> *having obtained eternal redemption.* (9:12)

Not only is the place of Christ's activity a great improvement over the Old Testament priest's, but so is the offering. Goats (*tragōn*) and calves (*moschōn*, a variation of *taurōn*, "bulls," v. 13) were the animals whose blood was utilized in the Day of Atonement ritual. The high priest first entered the holy of holies with the blood of a bullock for his own sin, and then reentered with the blood of a goat for the sins of the people (Lev. 16). Christ, however, entered once for all (*ephapax*) into the heavenly sanctuary. The plural form *ta hagia* is used of the earthly holy of holies in 9:25 and 13:11, and of the heavenly counterpart (used with the genitive case) in 8:2 and 10:19. With such an offering repeated expiatory sacrifices were unnecessary. It achieved eternal redemption for its beneficiaries, in contrast to the annual atonement required in the former system. The annual duty emphasized that the atonement obtained was only temporary.

Verses 11 and 12 have stated in brief the essentials in the operation of the new covenant. Christ serves in the more perfect tabernacle on the basis of a far superior offering. The author then follows this general statement with a more detailed discussion of three important items that are vital to the operation of the new covenant: Christ's death (9:13-22), His presence in heaven (9:23-28), and His once-for-all offering (10:1-18).

b. Christ's death. (9:13-22)

For if the blood of goats and bulls and ashes of a heifer sprinkling the ones defiled sanctify toward the purity of the flesh, how much more shall the blood of Christ, who through the eternal Spirit offered himself without blemish to God, purify our conscience from dead works to serve the living God. (9:13, 14)

The sacrificial blood of animals had primary relevance to ceremonial purity. Goats and bulls were the sacrifices on the Day of Atonement (Lev. 16). Ashes of a heifer refer to the ceremony of the red heifer (Num. 19), in which this animal was slain, burned completely, and then the ashes were stored for future use. Whenever a person contracted ceremonial defilement by touching a dead body, or entering the tent of one who had died within it, or touching a human bone or a grave, he could be cleansed by being sprinkled with water in which the ashes of the heifer had been mixed. Perhaps this particular practice was selected because it illustrates so clearly the largely ceremonial nature of the purity provided by Old Testament sacrifices. In the cases needing this sprinkling, the defilement was purely ceremonial, and the cleansing provided restoration to the congregation of Israel (Num. 19:13, 20). It really had nothing to do with spiritual defilement. We must not think that the conscience was not involved at all, since a defiled person who failed to obtain this purification would have a bad conscience. But the point is that the ceremonial cleansing satisfied the Jew's conscience regarding that physical matter only.

Christ's blood is far more efficacious. He offered himself to God as the sacrifice without blemish. Animals may have had a physical perfection, but only Christ was the morally and spiritually spotless victim, and no animal could ever offer himself. This Christ did through the eternal Spirit (*pneumatos aiōniou*). Absence of the article with Spirit leads some to deny any reference to the Holy Spirit here, and to explain it as denoting Christ's own divine nature.[99] There is no disharmony, however, in seeing the Holy Spirit at this point; for no article is required for such identification. The Holy Spirit is consistently

---

99. So Lenski, *Interpretation of Hebrews*, p. 298; Alford, *NT for English Readers*, p. 1529.

represented in Scripture as anointing Christ, empowering Him for His work, and guiding in all His activities. [100] If behind the author's concept lies the revelation of the Suffering Servant in Isaiah 53 who "bore the sin of many" (Isa. 53:12; cf. Heb. 9:28), then the statement of God about His servant in Isaiah 42:1 seems pertinent: "Behold my servant . . . I have put my spirit upon him."

Christ's sacrifice of Himself makes it possible to **purify our conscience**. Animal sacrifices could not do this (v. 9; cf. 10:1, 2). Christ's blood dealt with the realities and the ultimate issue, not just the externals. Appropriation of His merits brings to the regenerated soul true peace of conscience through the knowledge that eternal redemption has been secured. **Dead works** are here viewed not just as useless or inactive but as defiling and causing the need for cleansing. Involved are legalistic ceremonies which cannot impart life (cf. 6:1), seen not only as mere externals which are not defiling per se, but as the expressions of sinful hearts bent on spurning the grace of God in favor of a system of works righteousness.

> *And on account of this he is mediator of a new covenant, in order that a death having occurred for redemption of the transgressions at the time of the first covenant, those who have been called might receive the promise of the eternal inheritance.* (9:15)

In discussing the death of Christ (a problem for Jewish people generally, and to some extent apparently even for Jewish Christians) the author emphasizes two factors which made this radical act nevertheless a reasonable one for God to allow. First, Christ's death was a sacrifice, and as such it was more efficacious than that of animals (vv. 13, 14). Second, it validated a new covenant (vv. 15-22).

On account of this, that is, on account of the fact that Christ by His blood accomplished what the former covenant issued at Sinai could not, a **new covenant** was in order. This has been discussed already in 8:6-13 (see comments in loco). Again the term *diathēkē* is used, the one regularly employed for "will" or "testament" among the Greeks, but used in the Septuagint for the Hebrew *bᵉrit* ("covenant"), because the

---

100. So F. F. Bruce, *The Epistle to the Hebrews,* p. 205, Archer, *Epistle to the Hebrews,* p. 54.

translators recognized that the Old Testament covenants were divine dispositions, not agreements arrived at by mutual formulation (see comments on 7:22).

Now this **new covenant** not only made possible the provisions prophesied by Jeremiah (31:31-34), but also had an effect upon the guilt of those who lived under the former Mosaic covenant. Transgressions committed at the time of the **first covenant** were "covered" (i.e., "atoned") by animal sacrifices, but this provided no true expiation. Old Testament atonement by animal blood depended for its value upon the death of Christ to come. The **death having occurred** is clearly Christ's death, and **redemption of the transgressions** means redemption of the sinner from the accumulated debts which were against him. **Those who have been called** identifies these redeemed ones as Old Testament saints. This is similar language to some of Jesus' parables which spoke of the elect as those who have been invited ("called") to the kingdom (see Luke 14:16-24; Matt. 22:1-14). By the death of Christ all of those who have been effectively called by God, whether from the Old Testament economy or from New Testament times onward, have the promise of an **eternal inheritance** validated for them. The mention of the provisions of the new covenant as an **inheritance** stresses the testamentary aspect of the covenant and paves the way for the statement which follows.

> *For where a testament is* [there is the] *necessity for the death of the testator to be brought on, for a testament* [is] *in force* [only] *in the case of dead ones, since it is never in effect when the testator is living.* (9:16, 17)

At this point the author employs for illustration the more restricted but very common usage of *diathēkē* as a will or **testament**. Because English does not use the word "covenant" in this exact sense, we must adopt another translation—testament—for the uses of *diathēkē* in verses 16 and 17. Efforts to treat the word as "covenant" in all places, although strongly asserted, [101] are forced, because it just is not true that the slaying of the animal in all Old Testament covenants represented the death of the one making the covenant. Did the death of the

---

101. Westcott, *Epistle to the Hebrews*, p. 265.

animals at Sinai (Exod. 24:8) represent the death of God who made the covenant? Much better is the explanation of Bruce:

> Christ, says our author, is the Mediator of the new *diathēkē*, and there is one kind of *diathēkē* that serves particularly well to illustrate this aspect of His ministry—namely, the testamentary *diathēkē* which does not come into effect before the death of the person who makes it.[102]

This is a general proposition that is true to this day. No provisions of a will are effective prior to the death of the one whose testament it is. A person may periodically change his will as his circumstances alter, and this is entirely legitimate because the will is not in force as long as the testator is still alive.

> *Hence not even the first* [testamentary covenant] *has been inaugurated without blood. For when every commandment had been spoken according to the law by Moses to all the people, having taken the blood of the calves,*[103] *with water and scarlet wool and hyssop, he sprinkled both the book itself and all the people saying, This is the blood of the covenant which God commanded you.* (9:18-20)

To any who may have been finding fault with the idea of Christ's death as a necessary feature of the new covenant, the reminder is given that not even the Mosaic covenant was inaugurated without blood. If some of these were actually contemplating a return to Judaism, let them remember that the use of sacrificial blood was involved in that covenant as well.

The events at Sinai recorded in Exodus 24:1-8 are the basis for the author's remarks, although a few of the details must have come from traditional sources. As given in Exodus, the events were as follows: Moses reported to the Israelites all that the Lord had declared, and the people promised, "All the words which the Lord hath said will we do"

---

102. F. F. Bruce, *The Epistle to the Hebrews,* p. 213.
103. The reading adopted here is supported by P46, a corrector of Aleph, K, Ψ, numerous minuscules, the Peshitta, Harkleian, and Palestinian forms of the Syriac, Origen, Chrysostom, and is used in the text of the United Bible Societies Greek Testament with a "C" rating. The alternatives all combine *tragōn* (goats) with *moschōn* (calves) in some way.

(24:3). Moses then wrote all the words, and the next morning he erected an altar and the twelve pillars (24:4). Burnt offerings and peace offerings were sacrificed, half of the blood was collected in basins, and the other half was sprinkled on the altar (24:5, 6). Moses next read the book in which had been written the terms of the covenant, and again the people stated their acceptance of its provisions and obligations (24:7). Whereupon Moses took the remaining blood (the half collected in basins) and sprinkled it upon the people to signify the official institution of the covenant (24:8).

The narrative in Hebrews mentions **calves** in conformity to Exodus 24:5 (KJV "oxen"). Those manuscripts which add "and goats" [104] may appeal for support to the fact that goats could be used for burnt offerings (Lev. 1:10; 4:23; 9:2), even though goats are not specifically mentioned in Exodus 24. **Water and scarlet wool and hyssop** find no mention in the Exodus account, although some means had to be employed for the sprinkling. In the ceremony of the red heifer (Num. 19:6) already alluded to in 9:13, water and hyssop and scarlet were used. Hyssop had been used previously in Egypt to apply the blood of the passover lamb to the doorposts of every Israelite home. Exactly how our author obtained information that such was the procedure at Sinai is not known, but there is nothing improbable about it. The sprinkling of **the book** itself which contained the covenant provisions is another feature not noted in the Old Testament account. Westcott's observation that the book was outwardly the work of man and thus needed the purifying blood to be applied indicates the reasonableness of the act. [105]

At the conclusion of the impressive inauguration at Sinai, Moses declared the significance of the blood which he had just sprinkled as **the blood of the covenant** (Exod. 24:8). These words were strikingly similar to those of Jesus, "For this is my blood of the new covenant, which is shed for many for the remission of sins" (Matt. 26:28), a similarity of which our author was doubtless well aware. The blood inaugurated the Mosaic covenant and put its various provisions in force, both in precept and in ceremony.

---

104. Aleph, A, C, D, Coptic, Old Latin, and the Byzantine family.
105. Westcott, *Epistle to the Hebrews*, p. 268.

> *And both the tabernacle and all the vessels of the ministry he likewise sprinkled with the blood. And with blood almost all things are purified according to the law, and without shedding of blood there occurs no forgiveness.* (9:21, 22)

The sprinkling of the tabernacle and all the vessels must have occurred some time later than the event described in verses 19 and 20, since the tabernacle had not as yet been built. At the dedication of the tabernacle, the Old Testament records an anointing of the structure and everything in it with oil (Exod. 40:9), but no mention is made of blood. In Numbers 7:1, however, reference is made to the fact that Moses "anointed it and sanctified it," and perhaps the latter term involved a sprinkling with the blood. The Old Testament does speak of Aaron and his sons being installed in office through an anointing with the blood of a ram, and this blood was also applied to the altar (Lev. 8:22-24). Josephus mentions the same fact as the author of Hebrews:

> And when Moses had sprinkled Aaron's vestments, himself, and his sons, with the blood of the beasts that were slain, and had purified them with spring waters and ointment, they became God's priests. After this manner did he consecrate them and their garments for seven days together. The same he did to the tabernacle, and the vessels thereto belonging, both with oil first incensed, as I said, and with the blood of bulls and of rams, slain day by day one, according to its kind.[106]

Thus both apparently record a correct Jewish tradition.

The word almost (*schedon*) stands at the beginning of the sentence just after and, and probably is intended to govern both clauses which follow. Thus the sense is: "It is almost the case that the law requires all things to be purified with blood, and that without bloodshedding no remission occurs." Almost does allow for exceptions, but they are clearly exceptions and the norm is blood. Purification, particularly of things in contrast to persons, was sometimes accomplished by water (Exod. 19:10; Lev. 15:5; 16:26, 28; 22:6) and by fire (Num. 31:22, 23). Blood, however, was the characteristic means of purifying in the Mosaic law, especially of persons. The clause without shedding of blood there occurs no forgiveness refers to the requirement of a bloody

---

106. Josephus *Antiq.* 3. 8. 6.

sacrifice for all sin offerings. There could be an exception made in the case of the man too poor to afford the price of an animal, but even in that instance it was clearly noted that the flour and oil mixture was a substitute for blood, with blood remaining as the norm (Lev. 5:11-13). Furthermore, this substitute offering was burned "on the altar upon the offerings of Jehovah made by fire" (Lev. 5:12 ASV), and was thus apparently placed on top of previous bloody offerings and burned in conjunction with them. The author is therefore making the point that the principle of sacrificial death was clearly established even in Old Testament practice, and it would be folly to turn from Christ on account of His dying.

c. Christ's presence in heaven. (9:23-28).

Therefore there was a necessity on the one hand for the copies of the things in the heavens to be cleansed with these [animal sacrifices], but on the other hand the heavenly things themselves with better sacrifices than these. (9:23)

The next feature of the new covenant's operation to be given special discussion is the fact of Christ's presence in heaven (vv. 23-28). Is there a hint that the Christian teaching of a high priest in heaven was somehow less impressive to some of the readers than the earthly priests who seemed more accessible? Whether or not such was the case, the importance of Christ's presence in heaven is set forth in three respects.

First, it cleansed the heavenly things (vv. 23, 24). The necessity that the earthly sanctuary be cleansed with the sacrifices mentioned above was found in the Mosaic law which demanded certain ritual. The tabernacle and its furniture, however, were only copies of the things in the heavens (see 8:5). Whatever cleansing was achieved by the sacrifices offered in the tabernacle was thus performed in a place that was in a certain sense secondary. Now if the earthly sanctuary and practice were a copy, there must be a corresponding need for cleansing in the heavenly counterpart, for the earthly was a copy of some definite thing. The heavenly things themselves surely must be interpreted as the spiritual realities in heaven to which the tabernacle and its ritual gave visible representation. The discussion in 8:1-5 corroborates this view. Since the earthly copies required cleansing by animal sacrifices, surely it is obvious that the heavenly originals needed even better sacrifices than these. Christ's blood provided this better sacrifice. (The plural *sacrifices* is used because the statement gives a general principle and is made parallel to the previous clause referring to animal "sacrifices.")

In what sense did the **heavenly things** need cleansing? Perhaps the answer lies in the fact that heaven was the scene of Satan's rebellion, and thus needed cleansing from the defiling effects of that sin. One may compare Colossians 1:20, which speaks of Christ's death as reconciling all things to God, including things in heaven. Another explanation may be that just as the furniture in the tabernacle needed cleansing, not because of itself but because it was the place where sinners were restored to God's presence, so the heavenly realities, consisting of God's righteous presence, needed cleansing, not because of sin in heaven but because sinful men need to be reconciled to God's offended righteousness. What animal sacrifices accomplished ceremonially and typically, Christ's sacrifice achieved actually. Christ's blood fully satisfied God's wrath against sin, and thus His presence in heaven provided an incalculable advance over the ministrations of any earthly priest.

> *For not into a sanctuary made with hands did Christ enter,*
> *a copy of the true one,* [107] *but into heaven itself, now to*
> *appear before the face of God in our behalf.* (9:24)

It is true that Christ never ministered in the temple in Jerusalem nor in any other **sanctuary made with hands**. His tribal connections would have prevented it (7:13, 14). This is no disadvantage, however; for the earthly tabernacle (and the temples which succeeded it) were but a **copy of the true one**. As a copy (*antitupa*), the tabernacle corresponded to the model or pattern (*tupon*) shown to Moses in the mount (8:5). It was only a copy or representation, not the original.

Christ has entered **heaven itself**. This is the author's definition of the heavenly sanctuary. If he had meant for his readers to understand a heavenly structure corresponding to the earthly one board for board and curtain for curtain, this would have been the obvious place to indicate it. However, heaven itself is the Biblical place of the divine presence, and answers to all the truth conveyed by the symbolism of

---

107. *Antitupa tōn alēthinōn* is plural in form (literally, "copies of the true ones"), agreeing with the plural *hagia* ("sanctuary"); but the sense in English is best represented by the singular "a copy of the true one."

the earthly holy of holies. It is in the actual and not just the representational presence of God that Christ our high priest has entered now to appear before the face of God. He is not in a smoke clouded chamber where God's glory needed to be obscured lest the high priest die. He appears in our behalf in the very presence of God, the only place where final priestly representation can be made.

> *Neither* [is it necessary] *that he should be offering himself often, even as the high priest enters into the sanctuary yearly with blood of another, since it would have been necessary for him to suffer often from the foundation of the world; but now once at the consummation of the ages he has appeared for* [the] *putting away of the sin through his sacrifice.* (9:25, 26)

Second, Christ's presence in heaven indicates that sin has been put away forever (vv. 25, 26). It does not need annual atonement as in the Old Testament system. Readers must not conclude that Christ has entered heaven in order to secure access for repeated offerings. His one offering cared for the problem of sin forever. It has been questioned whether this reference to offering himself refers to Christ's death on earth (cf. vv. 14, 26), or to the presentation of Himself before the Father in heaven, corresponding to the high priest's entry into the holy of holies (v. 25b). Perhaps it is unnecessary to be so precise. What is paramount in the author's mind is Christ's fulfilment of the entire Day of Atonement ritual, and that included both shedding of blood and presentation in the holy of holies. Thus he refers to both the entry into the sanctuary and blood of the sacrificial victim in the same clause.

To suppose that Christ's priestly ministry required repeated offerings is to press the Aaronic analogy erroneously, and actually to deny the basic difference in character between the two offerings. In the earthly ritual the blood offered was that of another (*allotrioi*), being actually the blood of an animal. It was an example and a shadow (8:5) but was not expiatory in itself (9:9; 10:4). To conclude that repeated offerings were still necessary denies the abiding efficacy of Christ's sacrifice. If Christ's one offering was not sufficient in itself for the putting away of the sin, then it really accomplished little more than the Old Testament series of sacrifices and needs periodic repetition. If that were the case, Christ should have sacrificed Himself frequently ever since the foundation of the world because sin has been a problem since Adam and Eve. Yet this has obviously not happened. God sent His only begotten Son once (*hapax*), in clear indication that his sacrifice (i.e., Christ's) was of a character that did not need periodic reoffering to care for all sins since creation. Christ's sacrifice was made at the consummation of the ages. This designation of Christ's death uses *sunteleiāi* (consummation) to emphasize the focal nature of Calvary. It was the event which was the focus of redemptive history, that in which the various facets of God's plan of salvation came together. One has expressed it: "All previous ages led up to this; all succeeding ages are governed by this!"[108]

The putting away of the sin was the overriding purpose of the incarnation. The term *athetēsis* (putting away) occurs only one other time in the New Testament. It is used in Hebrews 7:18 of the "annulment" of the law which was necessitated before Christ could be considered as a priest. Thus the debt of sin which holds every man in its grip was fully paid and its penalty is now set aside or annulled for all those who avail themselves of Christ's sacrifice.

> *And just as it is appointed for men to die once, and after this* [is] *judgment, so also Christ having been offered once to bear* [the] *sins of many shall appear a second time apart from sin to those who await him for salvation.* (9:27, 28)

The third significance of Christ's presence in heaven is that it insures God's favorable verdict, and Christ's reappearance will confirm it.

Just as (*kath' hoson*) introduces an analogy, one drawn from human life. It is appointed for men to die once names the principle in view. This principle has its exceptions; for Enoch and Elijah escaped death, Lazarus probably died twice (his raising by Jesus was apparently a return to mortal existence), and the generation of believers who are living when Christ returns will not die at all. Nevertheless, the rule is still normative for human beings. And after this [is] judgment. Death ends man's opportunity to alter his circumstances. He does not get a second chance, nor die over and over. Death closes the earthly scene for him, and then he must face the eternal issue of his life. This was an important point to remember as these early readers compared Christ's

---

108. William R. Newell, *Hebrews Verse by Verse*, p. 323.

sacrifice to the Levitical ones. The reason why Christ's sacrifice does not need frequent repetition as was true of animals in Old Testament times is because Christ's sacrifice consisted of Himself (v. 25). It was a human sacrifice, and men die but once and then must face the results of their lives. Inasmuch as this particular human was the God-Man, the analogy is all the more forceful.

Christ was offered once. The repetition of once (*hapax*) throughout this context shows the author's emphasis (9:26-28). Were the first readers enamored with the annual sacrifice of the Jewish high priest rather than with the one sacrifice of Christ? **Once**, of course, means "once for all." Christ's death brought its irrevocable result. He cannot come to die again. Whatever He achieved by the offering of Himself is finished and settled for all time. His purpose in coming was to **bear [the] sins of many**. The expression seems indebted to Isaiah 53:12. Although His was the death of just one individual, yet it availed—because of who He was—for many others. In actuality it provided full expiation for all who trust Him for their salvation.

Christ's first coming was as the sinbearer. That task has been finished forever. His priestly work of making sacrifice is done, and His representation of believers in the sanctuary of God's presence is now being accomplished (v. 24). There remains one final action of this high priest. Even as the Jewish priest emerged from the holy of holies, signifying by the very fact of his emergence that his sacrifice had been accepted (otherwise he would have been divinely stricken in the inner chamber), so Christ will also appear a second time. **Those who await him** are all true believers, for whom Christ's second coming will mean the consummation of their **salvation**. All of the blessed results of Christ's sacrifice will be brought to fulfilment. At Christ's second coming, His purpose will be **apart from sin**, for that was dealt with by His once-for-all sacrifice when He came the first time. For believers, salvation in its fullest realization will occur as they share God's blessed presence for eternity.

Three "appearings" of Christ have been mentioned in these verses. He now appears on our behalf in heaven (v. 24). This is based upon the perfect sacrifice of Himself which He made when He appeared on earth as the sinbearer (v. 26). Believers now look with expectancy to His next appearing to bring salvation to its fullest realization (v. 28).

Model of Herod's temple prior to the destruction of A.D. 70. It was in this temple that sacrifices were offered when Hebrews was written (Heb. 10:1).

d. Christ's once-for-all offering. (10:1-18).

For the law having a shadow of the good things that were coming, [but] not the very image of the things, is never able yearly with the same sacrifices which they offer continually to bring to completion those who draw near; (10:1)

The third feature of the new covenant to be singled out for special treatment is Christ's once-for-all offering (vv. 1-18). The subject is developed by showing first the inadequacy of animal sacrifices (vv. 1-10), and then the efficacy of Christ's offering (vv. 11-18).

Animal sacrifices were proved to be inadequate by their very repetition (vv. 1-4). The Mosaic law contained instruction for these sacrifices but they were only a shadow of the good things that were coming. They depicted the barrier that sin had caused, the necessity for expiation, and the provision of forgiveness on the basis of an appropriate sacrifice, but they did so only as shadow. They were not the very image. The contrast between these two terms is important. Some understand image (*eikona*) in the sense of true form in contrast to the shadow (*skian*). [109] Others treat image in the sense of three-dimensional likeness, and explain the phrase as meaning the law was only a shadow and not even a three-dimensional image of the reality. [110] Elsewhere in the New Testament *eikōn* conveys the idea of exact representation. In Colossians 1:15 it denotes Christ as the *eikōn* of the invisible God. Thus the contrast is between the law as containing in its sacrificial system only the barest shadow outline of the spiritual truths involved. It was not (nor could it be) the exact replica of what God would do about sin, for no animal nor any other finite creature could convey adequately all that God would do in His program of redemption.

Yearly points to the sin offerings of the Day of Atonement. These **same** animal sacrifices had been offered annually for centuries (continually), although interrupted at various times because of exile or foreign oppression. When the author says **they offer continually**, his usage of the present tense argues that the temple with its priestly system was still operating. He therefore must have written before Jerusalem's destruction in A.D. 70. In spite of such extended observance, those animal sacrifices were unable to bring their offerers **to completion** (*teleiōsai*). The basic purpose of sacrifices was not accomplished by the endless series of animal offerings. Proof of this is indicated by the author's rhetorical question.

> . . . for otherwise would they not have ceased being offered,
> because the worshippers having once been cleansed would
> have had no more consciousness of sins? (10:2)

The point is obvious. Since the sacrifices of the Day of Atonement were invariably the same, no one of them was any better than the ones

---

109. So Arndt and Gingrich, *Greek-English Lexicon,* p. 221.

110. Westcott says: "The words contain one of the very few illustrations which are taken from art in the N. T. The 'shadow' is the dark outlined figure cast by the object . . . contrasted with the complete representation (*eikōn*) produced by the help of colour and solid mass." *Epistle to the Hebrews,* p. 304.

of previous years. Not one was complete or final so that the series could be terminated. The use of not (*ouk*) indicates that an affirmative answer is expected to this question.

The passage does not imply that no forgiveness of any sort was possible under the Old Testament system; that was plainly not the case (Lev. 4:20, 26, 31, 35). What is asserted is the absence of any complete or final cleansing. **Having once been cleansed** (*hapąx kekatharismenous*) stresses the once-for-all character of the forgiveness in view. The participle is in the perfect tense, signifying the resultant or completed state, and the adverb *hapax* reinforces the concept. The kind of forgiveness contemplated is that which is fully efficacious, not needing repeated validation. Annual sacrifices (or even more frequent daily ones) by very definition have not secured such cleansing. The fact that they continued to be offered showed that the worshipers had no assurance of permanent forgiveness. Day of Atonement offerings brought forgiveness "up to date," but subsequent sins required further sacrifices, and the passing of another year necessitated the cycle to begin again.

To have **no more consciousness of sins** does not mean that true believers are henceforth blissfully unaware of sinfulness in their lives. The statement refers to the consciousness of sin's guilt as being still objectively unremoved. The Old Testament saint indicated by his repeated sacrifices that new sins brought guilt which needed objective removal. Since Christ's offering of Himself, the situation is different. That perfect sacrifice has removed the guilt of all sin once for all. When Christians sin (and they do) they are subjectively conscious of their failure and their need of confession and cleansing, but they must also recognize that the sacrifice which removed their guilt has already been made by the once-for-all sacrifice of Christ. Dods expresses it clearly: "The sinner once cleansed may, no doubt, be again defiled and experience a renewed consciousness of guilt. But in the writer's view this consciousness is at once absorbed in the consciousness of his original cleansing."[111]

> But in them [there is] *a remembrance of sins yearly, for* [it is] *impossible for blood of bulls and goats to take away sins.* (10:3, 4)

---

111. Dods, *Expositor's Greek Testament,* IV, 342.

In them refers to those sacrifices of animals mentioned in verse 1. As the author argues that the repetition of animal sacrifices proves their inadequacy, he shows that the atonement ritual actually provided a remembrance of sins yearly. This striking approach must have given his readers pause for some sober reflection. Did not the ritual provide an annual removal of sins? Was it not the means God had ordained whereby their forefathers could obtain forgiveness? None of this is denied by the author, but his point is that the existence of the Day of Atonement focused attention upon the sins committed since the previous Day of Atonement. The very fact of an annual Day showed that Israel never had the conception of sins put away permanently through animal sacrifices. It reminded them of sin, the guilt it brings, and the need for its removal. All of this should have demonstrated that it is impossible for blood of bulls and goats to accomplish the final expiation which is promised in Christ. No reflection is cast upon the value of Old Testament sacrifices, as long as they are viewed in proper perspective. What must be remembered is that their atoning value was temporary and typical, depending for their efficacy upon the coming sacrifice of Christ to whom they pointed. Although the inherent nature of animal sacrifices (being nonrational, nonmoral, nonspiritual) may be implicit in the reference, no point is made of this fact here. The argument turns on the feature of their constant repetition as pointing up their incompleteness.

> *Wherefore, coming into the world, he says,*
> > *"Sacrifice and offering you did not desire, but a body*
> > *you prepared for me;*
> > *Whole burnt offerings and* [sacrifices] *for sin you did*
> > *not approve.*
> > *Then I said,*
> > > *'Lo, I have come (in the roll of the book it has been*
> > > *written concerning me) to do your will, O God.' "* (10:5-7)

Animal sacrifices were also shown to be inadequate by direct Scriptural statement (vv. 5-9a). A portion of Psalm 40 is cited and interpreted typologically of Christ. It is shown that the Christian attitude toward animal sacrifices is not a radical concept but had Old Testament roots.

Coming into the world is the author's statement (i.e., not part of the psalm) which relates the quotation to Christ's incarnation. The present participle coming (*eiserchomenos*) does not restrict the reference to the nativity, the beginning of public ministry, or to any other specific moment. Nor can one find in the Gospels any instance where Jesus uttered these words. The reference is rather to the incarnation considered as a whole, and the psalmist's words are viewed as characteristic of Christ's continual attitude toward the Father. The specific portion of the psalm to be applied typologically to Christ consists of verses 6-8 (Ps. 40:12 speaks of the psalmist's iniquities, and is thus not applicable to Christ).

Sacrifice and offering looks at the tabernacle ritual from the standpoint of the material nature of the sacrifices. Sacrifice (*thusian*) refers to the animal victim; offering (*prosphoran*) denotes the meal or drink offering. The next clause contains a Hebrew parallelism, but the terms are not completely synonymous. Whole burnt offerings (*holokautōmata*) describes the voluntary sacrifices brought to the tabernacle by grateful worshipers. Sacrifices for sin (*peri hamartias*) were the required sin and trespass offerings. This last pair has represented the two classes of offerings as to their function.

As Messiah (typified by the psalmist) is depicted as addressing God and stating God's attitude to be one which did not desire and did not approve animal sacrifices, we must recognize that this was not an otherwise unknown concept in Old Testament times. Frequently, and especially in the prophets, are found similar assertions.

> To what purpose is the multitude of your sacrifices unto me? saith the Lord: I am full of the burnt offerings of rams, and the fat of fed beasts; and I delight not in the blood of bullocks, or of lambs, or of he goats (Isa. 1:11).

> To what purpose cometh there to me incense from Sheba, and the sweet cane from a far country? Your burnt offerings are not acceptable, nor your sacrifices sweet unto me (Jer. 6:20).

> For I desired mercy, and not sacrifice; and the knowledge of God more than burnt offerings (Hos. 6:6).

> I hate, I despise your feast days, and I will not smell in your
> solemn assemblies. Though ye offer me burnt offerings and your
> meat offerings, I will not accept them: neither will I regard the
> peace offerings of your fat beasts (Amos 5:21, 22).

The point, of course, is not that God disapproved of animal sacrifices,
for it was He who had instituted them. But God does not want mere
sacrifices, for animal sacrifices per se were valueless, nor does He want
them forever. What God desires, and always has, is the heartfelt devo-
tion of the person. Such may be present when sacrifices are made, and
in the Old Testament such sacrifices pleased God. The animal alone,
however, did not satisfy Him.

In the quoted line, **a body you prepared for me**, a problem exists.
The Old Testament at Psalm 40:6 has the words, "mine ears hast thou
opened." The Septuagint says, "a body you prepared for me" (Ps.
39:6).[112] The Epistle to the Hebrews has followed the Septuagint
rendering. One must first ascertain what the psalmist meant. Although
it is frequently suggested that the basis lay in the custom of boring a
servant's ear to indicate that he had voluntarily renounced his freedom
(Exod. 21:6; Deut. 15:17), the use of the plural "ears" makes this
reference unlikely. More probable is the explanation that the Septuagint has interpreted the Hebrew idiom, and thus conveys properly its
thought. The fact that Hebrews cites this rendering would support the
idea that the Septuagint translation was a legitimate paraphrase. The
psalmist meant that God had shaped his ears and had made them
responsive to His will. This thought was expressed in paraphrase in the
Septuagint, which stated that God had prepared the psalmist's body so
that he might perform the will of God.

The psalmist acknowledged his willingness to do the will of God.
David claimed that he was willing to do more than merely offer
sacrifices. He desired to perform the will of God with his whole life.
For David the specific purposes of God had been revealed by Samuel
and other prophets and were recorded in the roll of the book, that is, in
Scripture. The term translated roll (*kephalidi*) means "little head" and
apparently denoted the knob on the end of a scroll, used here by

---

112. This is the reading found in the leading manuscripts of the Septuagint:
Vaticanus, Sinaiticus, and Alexandrinus. Instead of *sōma* (body), however, the
Psalterium Gallicanum version reads *ōtia* (ears).

metonymy for the scroll itself. In the next clause of the psalm which immediately follows the portion being quoted, the words are: "Yea, thy law is within my heart" (Ps. 40:8). Hence David may be understood to say: "God's instruction in Scripture is concerning me." Thus he acknowledges his obligation to fulfil the precepts of Scripture, inasmuch as they are the expression of the will of God. Whether what is written in the book is regarded in this latter general sense of spiritual obligations incumbent upon all God's people, or whether it is understood as the specific information about David's kingship, in either case David's response was the positive one of dedicating himself to do thy will, O God. Our author, however, sees David as prefiguring Christ in these words. What was true to a limited degree in David found far greater expression in the Son of God whose body was prepared by the Father that He could fulfil the divine will of saving men. Likewise, Christ in His earthly career accepted for His own life the righteous obligations of Scripture, as well as fulfilling many of the specific references which spoke in advance of His messianic office.

> [When] *saying* [in the lines quoted] *above, "Sacrifices and offerings and whole burnt offerings and* [sacrifices] *for sin you did not desire nor approve," which are offered according to the law, then he has said, "Lo, I have come to do your will."* (10:8, 9a)

The author repeats his quotation from Psalm 40, and divides it into its two parts in order to emphasize his particular point. He reminds us that the first part of the quotation, which mentioned that God did not desire animal sacrifices, dealt with matters prescribed by the Mosaic law. Thus the law must not be regarded as God's final provision for man. The law demanded the ritual of animal sacrifices; yet God was not primarily interested in the ritual.

The second part of the quotation spoke of God's messianic servant who would perform that in which God was chiefly interested. In contrast to inadequate sacrifices, Messiah presents Himself to God in the psalm as ready to do the will of God.

> *He takes away the first in order that he may establish the second. In which will we have been sanctified through the offering of the body of Jesus Christ once for all.* (10:9b, 10)

The final indication given by the author that animal sacrifices were inadequate is Christ's replacement of the former system (vv. 9b, 10). After dividing his quotation from Psalm 40 into two sections, the first dealing with animal sacrifices and the second referring to Messiah's performance of God's will, he declares of Christ that he takes away the first. By Christ's fulfilment of the types and shadows in the old system, He provided the actual expiation that animal blood could only symbolize. In the purpose of God, therefore, the former system was abolished that he may establish the second. The second refers to Messiah's coming to do voluntarily the will of God, particularly in offering Himself as the sacrifice for sin. This purpose has been achieved, for Christ has come and has done the Father's will. "I have finished the work which thou gavest me to do," said Jesus to His Father on the eve of crucifixion (John 17:4). Inasmuch as this second part of the quotation has now been established, it follows that the ritual system of animal sacrifices has been annulled (even though thousands of Jews continued offering them meaninglessly until A.D. 70).

In which will refers to the will of God which Christ came to do, and it is further identified as the offering of the body of Jesus Christ once for all. Everything which Jesus said in His earthly teaching and performed throughout His life and ministry was precisely the will of God (John 12:49, 50; 5:19). In view here, however, is the death of Christ, the culmination of His ministry and that toward which His ministry was ever moving (Matt. 20:28). The performing of God's perfect will even to the death of the cross was what accomplished man's redemption. The somewhat unusual reference to the body of Jesus Christ is clearly patterned after the mention of "body" in the quotation above (v. 5). Just as previously in this section, emphasis is made upon the once-for-all (*ephapax*) character of Christ's sacrificial death (note also 9:12, 26, 28). It is this sacrifice of Christ that has completed the work of expiation and rendered unnecessary further sacrificial victims. The blessed effects of this perfect expiation were enjoyed by the author and his readers, for we have been sanctified, he says, by Christ's offering. Sanctified (*hēgiasmenoi*) occurs here as a perfect participle in a periphrastic construction used as an alternative for the perfect passive tense form. The sense is that the offering of Christ brought about the completed state of sanctification in believers. This sanctification is objective and judicial, for it was accomplished by Christ through His death. It denotes the act of God which "set apart" (literal meaning of *hagiazō*) believers from the spiritual contamination they had and the condemnation which they deserved to a perfect position before God, so that they are acceptable to Him. This is the status of every Christian, and for this reason they are frequently termed *hagioi* (saints) in the New Testament. (This does not describe present or practical sanctification, which is to be progressively developed in believers' lives.)

And every priest stands daily ministering and offering many times the same sacrifices, which are never able to take away sins. But this one having offered one sacrifice for sins forever sat down at the right hand of God, henceforth waiting until his enemies be placed under his feet. (10:11-13)

The closing lines of the previous discussion provided the transition to this second phase. Previously it had been demonstrated that animal sacrifices were inadequate. For that reason Christ has replaced the former system. Now the discussion moves to a consideration of the efficacy of Christ's offering (vv. 11-18). In the previous paragraph the emphasis was upon the inferior nature of the animal sacrifice. Here the argument is based upon the superior performance of Christ as a priest. What Christ did is shown to have been efficacious, first by virtue of His present exaltation (vv. 11-14).

The high priest's sacrifice on the Day of Atonement did not keep the people sanctified, not even till the next year. Consequently **every priest stands daily ministering.** The common priests in the order of their courses served daily at the altar. As the worshipers came, these priests continued **offering many times the same sacrifices.** Sin and trespass offerings were offered for individuals repeatedly throughout the year. The author has already demonstrated that these sacrifices were **never able to take away** sins, for if they could have taken them away in any final sense, they would not have needed endless repetition (10:2). No Old Testament Scripture gave any assurance to those bringing animal sacrifices that such would care for the sin problem forever.

Attention should also be paid to the contrast between the Old Testament priest who **stands** while engaging in his ministry, and Jesus Christ who **sat down.** Standing, of course, was the normal posture of the priest as he carried out his various liturgical duties. To our author, however, it pointed up the fact that the priest's work of offering sacrifices was never really finished. There were no chairs in the tabernacle. With Christ came a radical change. The sacrifice which He offered was His own life, and this would be offered only once (9:27, 28). It was sufficient per se to expiate sin forever. Consequently, this priest, having entered the heavenly presence of God, does not need to offer continually, but has **sat down at the right hand of God.** He not only sat as indicating His offering was concluded, but the place of this seating was the position of honor and authority in the very presence of God.

Forever (*eis to dienekes*) appears between one sacrifice for sins and sat down, and it is difficult to ascertain whether it should be construed with what precedes or with what follows. Does it mean that Christ made "one sacrifice for sins forever," or that He "forever sat down"? The Greek text allows both, and to insist that a grammatical probability exists for either alternative may reflect more bias than insight. If the former is chosen, the thought is the same as previously expressed in 7:27; 9:12, 25-28; and 10:10, 14. If the latter alternative is selected, the thought is that Christ's priestly offering is finished, and He will never again stand to offer the sacrificial blood. (To deny the latter thought on the basis of Christ's subsequent "standing" at the death of Stephen [Acts 7:55], or His leaving of heaven at the second advent [I Thess. 4:16; Rev. 19:11] is an unwarranted pressing of the statement here. "Sat" is in obvious contrast to "stands" in verse 11, and must be explained within the limits of that contrast. The point is, He will never again stand to offer sacrifice.) On the whole, to construe **forever** with **one sacrifice for sins** seems to this writer more consistent with the author's emphasis in the paragraph, and leaves verse 13 to give further description of Christ's exaltation to the place of divine authority.

The sacrifice of Christ in regard to sin was done once-for-all. Now He sits in royal dignity with the Father, **waiting until his enemies be placed under his feet.** This is the third usage of Psalm 110:1 in Hebrews (cf. 1:3, 13). Verse 4 of the same psalm has been used extensively to prove Christ's priesthood after the order of Melchizedek (Heb. 5:6, 10, 20; 7:11, 15, 17, 21). Here the royal dignity of the messianic King is in view, and the final subjugation of all things to Him is specifically asserted. This will occur at Christ's second coming, but even now Christ is at the right hand of the Father.

For by one offering he has perfected forever those who are being sanctified. (10:14)

This verse summarizes the discussion just preceding. Christ's one offering was sufficient for all time. This is why He is able to sit at the Father's right hand, for His task is finished and was fully successful. The **one offering**, of course, was the perfect life of Christ which was sacrificed at Calvary. By this offering, Christ **has perfected forever** the beneficiaries of His sacrifice. This perfection could not come by the law or the Old Testament priesthood (7:11). Only Christ's offering was sufficient to bring men near to God (7:19) and save them to the uttermost (7:25). The basic idea involved in the verb *teteleiōken,* translated "perfected," is to bring to completion, to accomplish fully, to reach the goal. This concept of perfecting is found throughout Hebrews in verb form (2:10; 5:9; 7:19, 28; 9:9; 10:1, 14; 11:40; 12:23), in nouns (6:1; 7:11; 12:2), and in an adjective (5:14; 9:11). It is this bringing to the goal that God accomplishes for believers through the redemptive work of Christ.

Those who are made complete by Christ's offering are here called **those who are being sanctified** (*tous hagiazomenous*). The expression is an alternative designation for believers, denoting them as ones who have been set apart from sin and made acceptable to God through the merits of Christ. The use of the present tense of the participle ("being sanctified") suggests several possible interpretations. Sanctification is presented in the New Testament as having three aspects involving believers. The past aspect was accomplished by the blood of Christ shed on man's behalf, and as a result every believer is entitled to be called a saint (Heb. 13:12; I Cor. 1:2). Past sanctification is positional and admits of no degrees. At the moment of regeneration every believer receives the benefits of past sanctification and has as much right to God's presence as any other Christian. There is also a present phase of sanctification which is progressive during the Christian life (John 17:17; Eph. 5:25, 26). It is practical rather than positional, and is accomplished as believers submit to the control of the Holy Spirit and walk in the light of God's Word (I Peter 1:15). The future aspect of sanctification will occur when Christ returns and the believer's present sanctification is completed (I Thess. 5:23; 3:12, 13). The present tense employed here in Hebrews could denote the fact that believers are those who are presently experiencing the process of sanctification in their lives, a process not yet completed. Another possibility is to refer the present participle to the progressive occurrence in this age as one after another responds to the gospel and experiences the sanctification which Christ's offering obtained.

> *And the Holy Spirit also testifies to us, for after he said:*
> *This* [is] *the covenant which I will make with them after those days,* [then] *says the Lord,* [I will be] *giving my laws upon their heart, and upon their mind I will write them. . . .*
> (10:15, 16)

The efficacy of Christ's offering is also indicated by the testimony of the Holy Spirit (vv. 15-18). The **Holy Spirit** is appealed to as the author of Scripture, and the mention of **also** shows that He adds His testimony to that of Christ previously referred to in Psalm 40. The passage cited is Jeremiah 31:33, 34, which has been used at greater length in Hebrews 8:8-12. In the more abbreviated quotation here, the author has cited somewhat freely, [113] and has also divided it into two parts in order to emphasize the second. The words **says the Lord** are actually part of the quotation, but they are used by the author of Hebrews to separate the two parts and introduce the second portion.

When this passage in Jeremiah was used earlier in the epistle (8:8-12), the purpose was to demonstrate that God intended to replace the Mosaic covenant with a new one, and that the prophecy of a "new" covenant implied that its predecessor was approaching obsolescence. Now, however, the same passage is utilized to show that in the new covenant the sins of the people were completely remitted. The argument is that since sins are no longer remembered, there is no need for further sacrifices.

In the quotation the Lord announced that He would make a covenant that would be subsequent to the Mosaic one. But the important thing to our author is the character of this new covenant. It would produce an inward change, not just another legal code.

> *. . . and their sins and their lawless deeds I will no longer remember.* (10:17)

---

113. There is considerable verbal variation from the Septuagint also (Jer. 38:33, 34).

At this point in the discussion the most significant feature in this quotation regarding the new covenant is its provision concerning sin. The Lord promised that sins and lawless deeds will never again be remembered against them. In view of the righteous character of God, this could only be so if the blood of Christ which instituted the new covenant accomplished the complete remission of sin.

> *Now where* [there is] *remission of these things,* [there is]
> *no longer offering for sin.* (10:18)

Here is the grand conclusion to the doctrinal section of the epistle. God promised that in the new covenant He would remember sins no more. Inasmuch as Christ's death provided the blood of the new covenant, it follows that those who are the beneficiaries of its provisions have had their sins fully and finally remitted. It should then be obvious to all that if full remission has occurred, there is no longer any necessity for sin offerings of any sort.

The logic should have been compelling to every reader. First century recipients of this letter, particularly those Jewish Christians who were toying with the notion of returning to Judaism, should recognize the foolishness of such a step. Since Christ's offering secured complete remission of sin, no further need exists for Levitical sacrifices or any other kind. The argument is no less relevant to modern readers. When a large segment of Christendom regularly reoffers the sacrifice of Christ in the Mass, it is obvious that the forthright implications of this verse need to be more clearly understood and proclaimed.

PART II
Practical Exhortations
10:19 - 13:17

A. AN EXHORTATION TO USE THE NEW ACCESS TO GOD. (10:19–31)

1. Draw near in faith. (10:19-22)

Therefore, brethren, having boldness for the entrance of the sanctuary by the blood of Jesus, which recent and living way he initiated for us through the veil, that is, his flesh. . . . (10:19, 20)

This section of Hebrews consists of a series of exhortations based upon the great doctrinal truths set forth previously. The superiorities of Jesus Christ as sacrifice and as priest should have been fully apparent to every reader. These truths, however, must not remain as abstractions, but must issue in appropriate conduct. These exhortations to Christian practice are not mere moralizing, or admonitions to follow some new external code. They are the believer's logical and appropriate response to the benefits secured for him by his Lord and priest, Jesus Christ.

The first exhortation is based squarely upon the argument just concluded. Christ's death was the once-for-all sacrifice (10:14), and He is now in the heavenly sanctuary, not only as the believer's priestly representative (9:24) but also as his forerunner (6:20). Thus every believer may have the utmost confidence to make use of his access to God. **Boldness** is the rendering of *parrēsian,* a term occurring four times in Hebrews (3:6; 4:16; 10:19; 10:35). Although the word is probably best translated "boldness" or "confidence," it denotes not primarily a subjective attitude but something objective.[1] It is the believer's freedom of access to **the sanctuary** (*tōn hagiōn*). Now that expiation has been permanently made, believers are not restricted to the outer courts as in the earthly tabernacle, but have full rights to the heavenly presence of God Himself. This is not through any merits of their own, but **by the blood of Jesus** (*en tōi haimati Iēsou*). By virtue of Christ's sacrificial blood given once-for-all at Calvary, believers may enter the presence of God without hindrance and without need for further sacrifices.

This access to God's presence was **initiated** (*enekainisen*) for us as something new. (To translate as "consecrated" [KJV] may imply that it had previously existed and was now being dedicated, and this would be incorrect.) It is a **recent and living way.** The term **recent** (*prosphaton*) means "freshly slain" etymologically, and it is attractive to find this meaning here because of the sacrificial metaphor being employed. However, the etymology seems to have been lost sight of much earlier, and the word should be understood merely as "recent" or "new." The death of Christ had occurred well within the lifetime of most of the original readers. This new way to God's presence was also far superior to any other because it was a living (*zōsan*) way. Even though this access was provided by the sacrificial death of Christ, it is no slain and hence lifeless animal on whom we depend but upon the resurrected and living Son of God.

The new way of entrance into the true sanctuary was provided **through the veil, that is, his flesh.** The imagery is drawn from the inner veil of the tabernacle, the one separating the holy place from the holy of holies (see diagram, p. 165). It was this veil which kept the holy of holies beyond the view of and off limits to everyone except the high priest, and he but once a year. Some have felt that identification of this veil with Christ's flesh poses a serious problem, for Christ was not a

---

1. See the excellent discussion by Heinrich Schlier, "Parrēsia," in *Theological Dictionary of the New Testament,* ed. Gerhard Kittel, trans. Geoffrey W. Bromiley, V, 871-886.

barrier but was the entrance to God's presence. For example, Westcott protests, "It is most unlikely that the Apostle would describe Christ's 'flesh' as a veil hiding God from men, through which they too must pass. . . ."[2] It is proposed that flesh should be regarded as in apposition with recent and living way. There is no doctrinal objection to this way of treating the text. However, it should be observed that the Greek word order would more naturally suggest the connecting of flesh with veil. Furthermore, it is certainly possible to understand the veil as marking the way by which the high priest entered the holy of holies, as well as a barrier to keep others out. Bruce has also observed that if "flesh" and "blood" may both denote Christ's life given sacrificially, then it is no more incongruous to speak of entering the sanctuary through Christ's "flesh" than it is to say the same thing regarding His "blood" (9:12; 10:19).[3] If the author had in mind the rending of the temple veil at the crucifixion, the imagery employed here is most appropriate. It was the sacrificial death of Christ which rent the veil and opened it permanently for believers' access to God.

> . . . and [having[4]] a great Priest[5] over the house of God, let us draw near with a true heart in full assurance of faith, having been sprinkled in our hearts from an evil conscience and washed as to the body with pure water. (10:21, 22)

Believers not only have the benefits of a matchless sacrifice, but they also have the services of an incomparable priest. He is a **great Priest** (cf. 4:14) because of His own person as the Son of God, as well as because of His position within the heavenly sanctuary. He is **over the house of God**, as the sovereign of God's household of faith (cf. 3:6). Even though He has opened the way for our direct approach to God, Christ does not cease His ministration on our behalf. He continues as our great priest, guiding, strengthening, encouraging, and interceding.

These two advantages (access to God, and a great priest) should give constant encouragement for a continual approach to God. Israel's unregenerate condition caused their hearts to be far from God (Isa.

---

2. B. F. Westcott, *The Epistle to the Hebrews,* p. 320.
3. F. F. Bruce, *The Epistle to the Hebrews,* in *The New International Commentary on the New Testament,* pp. 248, 249.
4. Implied from verse 19.
5. Not "high priest" (*archierea*) but *hierea megan.*

29:13; Matt. 15:8), but believers can approach God in prayer and fellowship because of God's gracious work upon their hearts. **Full assurance of faith** should characterize the believer's approach. There should be no wavering, no looking back to the old system. Proper understanding of the doctrinal truths explained earlier in the epistle should cause the objective grounds for confidence there set forth to be transformed into a firm assurance of faith. **Having been sprinkled in our hearts** states the situation of these Christian readers. Old Testament saints depended for their access to the manifested presence of God and to their covenant privileges upon an external sprinkling of blood upon a material altar. New Testament believers may look back in faith to Christ's work at Calvary, and rejoice in that inward purification obtained by the blood of the Lamb of God and applied to the guilt of an evil conscience. The author has found the fulfilment of Old Testament ritual in the reality of the Christian's spiritual experience.

Washed as to the body with pure water has been interpreted in different ways. Many see in this expression a reference to Christian water baptism, as the outward rite corresponding to the inward cleansing denoted by the previous phrase. Others regard it as depicting spiritual cleansing, just as the former phrase. The Old Testament background may have been provided by the priestly bathing before the Day of Atonement ritual (Lev. 16:4), and by the requirement for washing at the laver before every entrance into the tabernacle and every ministration at the altar (Exod. 30:18-21). The statement here is also reminiscent of Ezekiel 36:25, 26: "Then will I sprinkle clean water upon you, and ye shall be clean.... A new heart also will I put within you. . . ." Perhaps the twofold thought is that just as the Old Testament priest entered the divine presence by the sprinkling of blood and by virtue of bathing his flesh with water, so the Christian believer may confidently exercise his approach to God on the basis of a heart purified judicially by the blood of Christ and with a life that is cleansed from defilement by the Word of God (Eph. 5:25, 26).

2. Hold fast the hope. (10:23)

Let us hold fast the confession of the hope without wavering, for faithful is He who promised. (10:23)

Hope[6] is the proper word in this sentence. The author has employed the familiar triad of faith (v. 22), hope (v. 23), and love (v. 24) in this section. By the mention of hope the reader is caused to think of his future prospect. He is reminded that his confession of faith in Christ not only brought him immediate pardon for his sins and many other present blessings, but also secured for him the promise of heaven at last. Faithful is He who promised refers to God who has given to men the promise of entering into His rest (4:1). This faithfulness of God is an oft repeated theme, and it has never disappointed those who truly trust Him (see I Cor. 1:9; 10:13; I Thess. 5:24; Heb. 11:11).

3. Encourage one another in love. (10:24, 25)

And let us consider one another for stirring up to love and good works, not deserting the assembly of ourselves, as [it is] *a custom to some, but encouraging* [one another], *and so much the more as ye see the Day drawing near.* (10:24, 25)

As Christians these readers needed also to give proper consideration to the needs of one another within their group. Consider denotes careful observation and attention of the mind so as to acquire proper perception. The purpose is the fostering of love and good works. Such demonstrations of spiritual growth and activity should characterize every true Christian assembly. They are manifestations of the Spirit's presence and of His operation in individual lives (Gal. 5:22, 23; Col. 1:10). Here, however, the author says that Christians play a part in enabling fellow Christians to love and to perform good works. The Holy Spirit is the ultimate source of spiritual fruit and activity, but many times His work is resisted by the very believers in whom He is longing to work. Paul commands Christians, "Be filled with the Spirit" (Eph. 5:18), and by this he means that believers should submit to the control of the Spirit. Christians may help one another to submit to the Spirit's

---

6. Although the King James Version has "faith," it is without manuscript support. Nestle-Aland list no alternatives for the reading *elpidos*, except for the possible inclusion of *hēmōn* ("our"). Pink's assumption that "faith" has some manuscript support is apparently ill advised (Arthur W. Pink, *An Exposition of Hebrews*, I, 595).

control by the proper sort of influence which they impart through Christian fellowship.

Stirring up (*paroxusmon*) is a term used elsewhere in the New Testament with the unfavorable sense of "provoking" (Acts 15:39).[7] Here, of course, the meaning is to stir up for a good purpose. Rather than insist upon some new meaning for the word, perhaps we should regard the usage as a play on words. There may have been far too much stirring up of the congregation to anger and evil actions. What was needed was for them to "stir up" their brethren toward a greater love.

The means of carrying out this injunction is stated negatively and then positively. Not deserting the assembly of ourselves cautions against anyone's abandonment of the Christian group. The close connection of this phrase with the preceding statement suggests that a few had done some "stirring up" in the more usual sense, and had finally withdrawn from the assembly. Such factiousness was probably due to the chief problem confronted by this epistle—that of some being enamored with Judaism and threatening a return to its ceremonies. Even though the clause as [it is] a custom to some sounds a bit casual, and leads many to explain the reference merely to erratic attendance or slothfulness on the part of some Christians, the term deserting (*enkataleipontes*) seems too strong for that idea. Its commonest usage was with the sense of "forsake," "abandon," or "desert." Furthermore, the close connection of this statement with verse 26 (note the use of the inferential conjunction "for"), which has a most serious situation in view, argues against mere indolence as the point at issue.

The noun assembly (*episunagōgēn*) occurs only one other time in the New Testament, where it refers to the gathering of believers with Christ at His return (II Thess. 2:1). The addition of the prefix *epi* to the common word for the Jewish congregation has led some to conclude that a distinctively Christian meeting appended to the Jewish synagogue is referred to.[8] It was this special meeting of Christians which was being abandoned by some out of fear or other considerations emanating from their Jewish brethren. However, it cannot be established that it meant

---

7. The cognate verb *paroxunomai* is also used in the sense of irritate or provoke (Acts 17:16; I Cor. 13:5).

8. The possibility is entertained by William Manson, *The Epistle to the Hebrews*, p. 69.

anything other than "assembly." Thus it is probably best to understand it here as the distinctive Christian gathering (but with no special relation to the Jewish synagogue).

Positively, each reader was to promote spiritual growth in the church by encouraging (*parakalountes*). This encouragement might take the form of exhorting those who wavered, urging them to steadfastness, comforting those whose Christian commitment had brought trouble and distress, or by lending a strengthening hand to whoever needed it. How much better is this positive attitude of helpfulness toward others than the abandonment of the assembly that some had done. It also would serve to prevent such defection, for one who is genuinely involved in assisting others usually has little time to indulge his fears or nurse resentments which might cause him to forsake the fellowship of the saints.

Another reason to increase Christian steadfastness was the believers' knowledge of the Day drawing near. In all likelihood these words were written before the fall of Jerusalem and the destruction of the temple with its sacrificial system (see introduction). Thus the day of that destruction as predicted by Jesus (Matt. 24:1, 2) was of great interest to these Jewish Christians. However, the consistent New Testament use of expressions such as "the Day," or "the Day of the Lord," or "the Day of Christ" points rather to eschatological times. In view is the day of Christ's return. This simplest of designations is used elsewhere in I Corinthians 3:13 and I Thessalonians 5:4. The return of the Lord, with all of the glorious blessings that this entails, as well as the sobering prospect of rendering an account to Christ, should provide encouragement to believers to remain faithful to Christ and their Christian brethren.

FOURTH WARNING PASSAGE (10:26-31)

The mention of deserting the assembly provided the transition to this paragraph of warning, in which the consequences of rejecting the sacrifice of Christ are stated in sobering terms. Abandoning the Christian congregation may be symptomatic of a far more serious condition, and it is this to which the author addresses himself in this fourth warning passage.

*For if we are sinning wilfully after receiving the knowledge
of the truth, no longer for sins is there left a sacrifice but
some frightful expectation of judgment and a zeal of fire
about to consume the adversaries.* (10:26, 27)

In explaining this warning we must remember what the particular
problem was which confronted these readers. It lay in the attractions of
Judaism which continued to exert a pull upon many Jewish Christians
and caused them to consider abandonment of their Christian profession
and reversion to the old ritual. The warning here is similar to the one in
6:4-8, where the inability of a believer once enlightened to be brought
back to repentance if he defected was set forth. Here the warning is
directed to the same problem, but the approach is based upon the fact
that there is no other sacrifice than Christ's, and if that is finally
rejected, then only judgment can ensue.

The persons in view are regarded as previously **receiving the knowledge of the truth.** No hint is given that this knowledge (*epignōsin*) was
deficient. Just as in the case of the previous warnings, it should be
understood that the readers are Christians. **Sinning wilfully** (*hekousiōs
gar hamartanontōn*) thus refers to sinning subsequent to salvation. The
use of the present tense with its emphasis upon durative action prevents
us from identifying this as isolated acts of sin for which repentance may
follow and forgiveness be obtained. Not only does the tense of the
participle argue against this but the clear teaching of the New Testament elsewhere (even in Hebrews) asserts that Christians who sin may
be restored (Gal. 6:1; I John 2:1, 2). It is one of the functions of the
believer's high priest to help Christians in times of spiritual weakness
(Heb. 2:17, 18; 4:15, 16). The sinning referred to here is a condition,
and is described as being done **wilfully** or deliberately. Inasmuch as
Christ's offering has been explained as being once-for-all, this wilful
sinning must refer to rejection of that means of expiation since it is
stated that no sacrifice is available for it. The close connection with
verse 25 reinforces the idea that deserting the faith is in view.[9] For a
Christian Jew to abandon Christ meant that he had no place to go.

---

9. The conjunction *gar* ("for") in verse 26 indicates that what follows is a
logical inference from what precedes.

Jewish ritual had no efficacy per se apart from the reality which Christ's death supplied for it. To abandon the Christian faith was therefore to depart from the living God (3:12). It is apostasy from the Christian faith which our author warns against.

The only prospect in view for such sinning is a **frightful expectation of judgment**. The word *ekdochē* has not been found elsewhere with the meaning "expectation"; yet that sense is demanded here, and is so listed in the lexicons.[10] The **judgment** awaiting those who will not trust for their salvation in the sacrifice of Christ must consist of eternal loss in hell. It is pictured as a fire that is almost personified and is possessed of zeal which is about to consume[11] the opponents of Christ.

> *Anyone having set aside the Law of Moses dies without mercy before two or three witnesses. Of how much worse punishment do you think he will be counted worthy who trampled underfoot the Son of God and counted as common the blood of the covenant by which he was sanctified, and insulted the Spirit of grace?* (10:28, 29)

These two sentences present an *a fortiori* argument. Reference is made to the regulations under the Mosaic code in which the sentence for certain offenses was capital punishment. No sacrifice was provided for these offenses. The perpetrator was to be stoned to death by the people, as long as the guilt was clearly established by two or three witnesses (Deut. 17:2-7). Prominent among such offenses was the crime of rebellion against God and abandonment of true worship. This was the sin of presumption, or the sin "with a high hand" (Num. 15:30, 31). No sacrifice was provided because the perpetrator was a rebel against God's revelation and had shown his disregard for the real import of the law God had given (which embodied the system of sacrifices).

The argument is that if apostates from Israel's worship suffered physical death as retribution for their deeds, how much greater would

---

10. So W. F. Arndt and F. W. Gingrich, *A Greek-English Lexicon of the New Testament,* p. 238.

11. Greek: *esthiein,* to eat.

be the punishment for rejecters of the Son of God. These rejecters are described as guilty of three terrible deeds. First, they have **trampled underfoot the Son of God**. It was bad enough to disregard the stipulations of Moses' law. How much worse it would be to turn one's back on Christ Himself, especially since He has been revealed as the very Son of God. To trample underfoot implies not only rejection but also contempt.

Second, they **counted as common the blood of the covenant**. This, of course, was the blood of Christ which was shed in His once-for-all sacrifice to establish the new covenant (9:14, 15). To treat this blood as common is tantamount to calling it "unclean" (Acts 10:14, 15). Counting Christ's blood as common is to take the position that His death was no more efficacious than that of any other man. How unthinkable that any Christian would regard the blood of Christ **by which he was sanctified** in this blasphemous way. Some would explain this sanctification (which refers to the apostate, not to Christ) as merely an external dedication to God entered into by profession of faith; but by far the commonest usage of this terminology describes the person who has been set apart from sin to God. Inasmuch as this is said to have been accomplished by the blood of the covenant, an actual experience of covenant relationship would seem to be called for.

Third, such persons have **insulted the Spirit of grace**. It is the work of the Holy Spirit to bring men to Christ and to sanctify them. To apostatize is to reject all such activity. The divine Spirit is called the "Spirit of grace" in Zechariah 12:10. It is by the grace of God that the work of salvation was prepared and carried out. The action of the Spirit in convicting and regenerating is thus a demonstration of God's grace to sinners in bringing them to salvation in Christ.

Are true Christians ever guilty of complete apostasy? The Arminian says yes, and interprets this passage as denoting true believers who lose their salvation.[12] Calvinists, however, recognize that salvation is eternally secure for true believers, and interpret this passage in other ways. Some regard the apostates as mere professors who finally depart.[13] It might be tempting to weaken the punishment so as to make it less than loss of salvation, but this expedient has not satisfied many in the light

---

12. So Westcott, *Epistle to the Hebrews*, pp. 327-332.
13. W. R. Newell, *Hebrews Verse by Verse*, p. 357.

of the nature of the offense. A more reasonable explanation would seem to be that the passage warns true believers what the outcome would be if apostasy would occur. The author does not say that it has occurred, and comparison with 6:4-9 provides additional reasons for seeing this as a somewhat hypothetical argument. To object to the value of an argument which "cannot happen" is to misunderstand the difference between God's perfect knowledge of His program and the means He employs for achieving it. Several examples may be helpful. Jesus "would not walk in Judea because the Jews sought to kill him" (John 7:1). Yet from the divine standpoint, Christ's death was set for a certain time, and His hour had not yet come. Therefore, the Jews surely could not have killed Him prematurely. Nevertheless, Jesus avoided Judea at that time, and this was the means whereby God's plan was effected. On the voyage to Rome, Paul was divinely instructed that all on the ship would survive the storm and shipwreck. Although this was now certain to occur, Paul later told the soldiers, "Except these abide in the ship ye cannot be saved" (Acts 27:31); and this was the means of accomplishing God's purpose (even though the purpose was certain). Although it was not possible that Herod the Great could kill the infant Jesus and thus thwart God's purposes planned for Calvary, Joseph was nevertheless warned to take Jesus and Mary to Egypt to escape the slaughter of the children at Bethlehem. His heeding of the warning was the means God employed to bring about the results which in God's plan were already certain of fulfilment. Hence it is proper to see in warnings such as this one in Hebrews the means whereby God achieves the goal of keeping true believers faithful to the end (3:14). We should not forget that those who truly loved the Lord and accepted the certainty of His plan nevertheless heeded the warnings.

> *For we know Him who said,*
>   *"Vengeance* [belongs] *to me, I will repay";*
> *and again,*
>   *"The Lord will judge his people."*
> *A frightful thing* [it is] *to fall into the hands of the living*
>   *God.* (10:30, 31)

The two Scripture citations are drawn from Deuteronomy 32:35, 36, and the latter one appears also in Psalm 135:4. Of particular interest is the fact that the first quotation differs slightly from the

Hebrew text (which reads, "To me vengeance and recompense") and also from the Septuagint ("In a day of vengeance I will recompense"), and yet it occurs in exactly the same form in Romans 12:19. Either it must have commonly circulated in the church in this form, or the writer of Hebrews may have used Romans as his source, or else Paul wrote both passages.

In saying **we know Him who said**, the author infers more than mere identification. The thought is that God who spoke those words through Moses was no stranger to these readers. They not only possessed the Scripture which revealed Him, but had seen countless evidences in history which demonstrated His absolute justice. The first quotation stresses God's judgment as the appropriate recompense for men's deeds. **Vengeance** and **repay** convey the thought of requital. Men cannot reject God with impunity. In the song of Moses from which these words were taken, the apostates in Israel who had sacrificed to demons and rejected the true God (Deut. 32:17) were threatened with the divine vengeance of destruction (Deut. 32:24). To Jewish readers the citation should have been all the more impressive as it reminded them that many of their ancestors experienced the vengeance of God because they were not the true spiritual seed of Abraham. When God finally moves in retribution, His judgment will not be forgetful of the enormity of men's rejection of Christ's perfect sacrifice.

The second quotation is found in the following verse in Deuteronomy (32:36). It stresses that God's **people** will not escape. No one deserving God's vengeance may avoid it simply by claiming to belong to God's people, for when He moves in judgment, He will purge out all hypocrites and rebels. If any Jewish Christians thought they could escape the consequences of apostasy from Christ by simply reverting to Judaism, let them be reminded that in the Old Testament a mere outward connection with Israel without a spiritual relationship to God was no insurance against judgment. Many Israelites perished under the vengeance of God because they had turned away from the God of Israel (Deut. 32:15-16). To turn away from Christ, even if one held on to his Judaism, was to turn away from the living God whom Christ had revealed (Heb. 3:12).

In summary, it is a most awesome prospect to face the judgment of God. **To fall into the hands** of someone is to come under his authority and be incapable of further resistance. A somewhat contrasting use of this phrase occurs in II Samuel 24:14, where David chose to fall into the hand of the Lord rather than into the hand of man because God's mercies are great. In Hebrews, however, the reference is certainly to the apostate, for whom such a prospect can only be terrifying. As the living God, He is fully aware at all times of men's deeds, and is always capable of exercising His power and His judgment with absolute justice. Those who truly love the Lord will heed the warning and strengthen their trust in Christ as the one sacrifice which is valid for sin. May those whose understanding of God's truth has never been clear find instruction in this solemn warning and flee from the day of vengeance to the Son of God, whose blood shed at Calvary provides the only perfect sacrifice.

B. AN EXHORTATION TO REMEMBER FORMER EXPERIENCES. (10:32-39)

> *But remember the former days, in which after being enlightened ye endured a great contest of sufferings, sometimes being publicly exposed to reproaches and afflictions, and sometimes by having become companions of the ones being so treated.* (10:32, 33)

In a milder vein, the writer appeals to his readers to keep remembering[14] the time shortly after their conversion. **Enlightened** is the same word employed in 6:4, and denotes the spiritual enlightenment that came with their regeneration. At that time these Hebrew Christians had apparently been subjected to severe persecutions. **A great contest of sufferings** depicts these afflictions somewhat figuratively as a contest (*athlēsin*), in which their enemies or perhaps the trials themselves are viewed as fighting against them. The important thing to notice is that they had **endured** these sufferings without flinching. In the first bloom of their faith, the fact of suffering for the name of Christ was taken for granted, just as in the case of the early believers in Jerusalem (Acts 5:41). At times their persecution took the form of personal **reproaches and afflictions**. Accepting Jesus as the Messiah immediately laid them

---

14. Greek present imperative *anamimnēskesthe*.

open to attacks of all kinds by their unconverted countrymen, pagan neighbors, and civil as well as religious authorities. Examples of such treatment are frequent in the Book of Acts (e.g., 4:1-3; 5:17-18; 6:9-14; 17:5; 18:12). **Publicly exposed** (*theatrizomenoi*) does not demand that they were actually put on display in some amphitheater, although the incident at Ephesus was one occasion where such did happen (Acts 19:29). This is the only occurrence of the word in the New Testament, and the meaning is probably a general exposure to disgrace (much as the cognate noun is used in I Cor. 4:9).

Sometimes their sufferings were caused, not by themselves being the objects of attack but by their willingness to identify themselves as companions of their fellow Christians, even when remaining silent might have meant escape. To stand up and be counted in times of persecution was no easy thing. Yet their commitment to Christ had been so strong that they had done so without hesitation, even though it could bring more suffering. Instances in the New Testament where this occurred may be the devout men who buried Stephen (Acts 8:2),[15] and Onesiphorus, who brought assistance to Paul in spite of Paul's chain (II Tim. 1:16-18).

> *For both with the prisoners you sympathized and accepted with joy the seizure of your possessions, knowing that you have yourselves as a greater and abiding possession.* (10:34)

Verse 34 gives specific instances (in reverse order) of the sufferings mentioned in verse 33. The reading **the prisoners** (*tois desmiois*) is preferred by most textual critics, and is found in early Alexandrian and Western sources as well as Byzantine. Several variants are also found, such as "the bonds" (*tois desmois*), or "their bonds" (*desmois autōn*), or "my bonds" (*desmois mou*). The last of these has been utilized by some interpreters in the interest of proving Paul's authorship.[16] If the first reading above is adopted, the reference is to the readers' sympathy with all of their group who were mistreated because of their faithfulness to Christ.

---

15. It is possible, however, that these were not Christians, but Jewish friends of Stephen from the synagogue who deplored his stoning. Non-Christian Jews were called devout men in Acts 2:5.

16. So John Owen, *Exposition of the Epistle to the Hebrews*, VI, 10, 568.

Not only had they been sympathetic when their Christian friends had suffered, but they also had known what it was to suffer personally. They had experienced seizure of their possessions, and the inference from the previous clause is that they might have escaped some suffering and loss if they had not openly sympathized with other suffering Christians. Yet this confiscation of goods had been accepted with joy. The abiding joy of their new life in Christ could not be extinguished by material losses. This response to their trials was explainable only on spiritual grounds. They had accepted without despair or cowardice their losses because of their firm faith in the spiritual realities which they had acquired. In the phrase knowing that ye have yourselves as a greater and abiding possession, several textual variants occur regarding the word "yourselves." Many manuscripts contain it as "knowing in yourselves that ye have. . ." (*heautois* or *en heautois*). The reading preferred by most textual experts has "yourselves" as the direct object of the verb "have" (*echein heautous*). The sense is that by becoming Christians, though they may lose the whole world, they have gained their souls (cf. Luke 9:25). This idea is reinforced by verse 39, which speaks of the preservation of the soul. By acquiring eternal life, they have secured themselves from ultimate loss, and this is far better than any temporal possession.

The nature of this persecution has provided data which shed some light on the situation of these first readers and their possible location. They had suffered reproaches and afflictions (10:33), imprisonment and loss of possessions (10:34), but none of them had been killed (12:4). This would appear to rule out Jerusalem, which had witnessed the execution of Stephen (Acts 7:60), James (Acts 12:1), and perhaps others (Acts 9:1; 22:4; 26:10). Some have traced certain similarities to the situation in Rome prior to the fire in A.D. 64. During the days of Claudius in A.D. 49, Jews were expelled from Rome because of troubles caused by "Chrestus."[17] It is not inconceivable that this was a misspelling of the name Christ and refers to Jewish opposition to the preaching of the Christian message. When the Jewish community became riotous (note the similar situations in Acts, such as at Pisidian Antioch, Iconium, Lystra, Thessalonica, and Corinth), the authorities expelled the whole Jewish population. Thus Aquila and Priscilla left

---

17. Suetonius *Life of Claudius* 25.

Rome, apparently being already Christians, and became acquainted with Paul at Corinth (Acts 18:1, 2). This expulsion was not permanent, however, since Christian Jews were back in Rome at the time of the writing of the Epistle to the Romans (A.D. 56) and at Paul's arrival there (A.D. 59, 60). The above circumstances would fit well with the data supplied about the readers in Hebrews, but of course it is not conclusive. Similar circumstances could have existed elsewhere of which we have no present knowledge.

> *Do not cast away, therefore, your confidence, which has a great reward, for you have need of patience in order that when you have done the will of God you may receive the promise.* (10:35, 36)

They must not throw away their confident faith which had expressed itself so admirably in past days. To turn aside now to Judaism would be to lose their great prospect of reward in the eternal future. As Jesus said regarding those suffering persecution, "Rejoice, and be exceeding glad; for great is your reward in heaven: for so persecuted they the prophets which were before you" (Matt. 5:12). Loss of confidence[18] would mean loss of conviction about the truth of the Christian faith, and this would also mean loss of boldness in their witness and in their response to their persecutors.

All Christians have need of patience in times of stress. Otherwise the temptation to despair, to discouragement, and even to abandonment of the fellowship of the saints may become too strong to resist. Patience (*hupomonēs*) denotes endurance, a willingness to remain under adverse circumstances without compromise or defection. They needed to allow the trials they faced to develop this steadfast endurance in them (James 1:4). Now the goal in view is that they **may receive the promise**. Similar expressions occur elsewhere in Hebrews (6:12, 15; 9:15; 11:13, 17, 39). In some of these instances the assertion is that the persons did not receive the promise during their lifetime, and in other passages it is said that they did. The variation is to be explained as the difference between introductory aspects and complete fruition. In this passage the complete fulfilment is in view. The author looks ahead to the consumma-

---

18. Greek: *parrēsian.* The word meant "boldness of speech," and from that developed the sense of courage, confidence, fearlessness.

tion of salvation at the coming of Christ (note v. 37), and urges that their **patience** be increased through their trials so that nothing may hinder the full experiencing of the **promise** of salvation, a promise described earlier as entering into God's rest (4:1, 9).

Before one reaches the final enjoyment of this goal, there must have been the doing of **the will of God.** This is not restricted to the initial acceptance of Christ, but is that which will have been completed by the time the full substance of the promise is fulfilled. It is the faithful performance of God's will in the Christian life, particularly the continual walk of faith which looks to Christ as the great high priest for every need and does not turn away from Him.

> *For yet in a very little while He who cometh will come and will not delay; but my righteous one shall live by faith, and if he should turn back, my soul shall have no pleasure in him.* (10:37, 38)

This passage is a rather free citation of Habakkuk 2:3, 4, with an introductory phrase borrowed apparently from Isaiah 26:20. The words from Isaiah, **a very little while,** may have been used because they referred specifically to the second coming of Messiah, a point which the author of Hebrews also had in view.

Our author transposes some of the phrases in the Habakkuk passage, and makes other slight changes. He had as much right to quote freely as we do, and the sense is not basically altered. He chose this passage because it spoke of the fact that Messiah is on the way and men should be ready, not turning away in cowardice. Habakkuk wrote in view of the coming of the Chaldeans (Hab. 1:6), who would be God's instrument of judgment upon Judah. The prophet was understandably concerned about what God would ultimately do in judging the Chaldeans and vindicating His people. The prophecy was then given that judgment would eventually come. In the Septuagint this was translated more precisely as a reference to Messiah's coming, and it is this latter understanding which the author of Hebrews also supports. By associating Isaiah 26:20 with Habakkuk 2:3, 4, the identification of Messiah as the deliverer at the final "appointed time" which shall be at "the end" is made clearer (Hab. 2:3). **The coming one** was a common designation of Messiah even at His first coming (Matt. 11:3; Luke 7:19, 20; John 1:27; Rev. 1:4, 8; 4:8; 11:17).

There is textual variation regarding the use of "my" in the expression **my righteous one**. The Hebrew text does not employ this possessive in Habakkuk, and the Septuagint uses it with "faith" rather than with "righteous one," understanding it either as referring to God's faith (i.e., God's faithfulness) or else as the righteous one's faith in God (i.e., "faith in me," understanding God as the speaker). Among the Greek manuscripts of Hebrews, some place it with "righteous one,"[19] some place it with "faith,"[20] and some omit it altogether.[21] No doubt the variation between the Hebrew and Septuagint texts was largely responsible for the textual uncertainty among New Testament manuscripts. Fortunately the argument of the passage does not hinge upon any of these alternatives.

The **righteous one** is the believer, the one who has been justified by faith. This quotation is used also in Romans 1:17 and Galatians 3:11. The emphasis here is upon the exercise of **faith**, the very opposite of apostasy. These are God's own words, spoken through the prophet Habakkuk centuries earlier but every bit as valid to these readers and to all subsequent believers. By "faith" is meant not only the initial act of faith but the continuing attitude of trust in God which looks to Him for final salvation.

If he should turn back is the proper rendering, not "if any man" as in the King James Version. The subject of the verb is undoubtedly the same person who is called the "righteous one" in the previous clause. The statement is drawn from the Septuagint (where it precedes the assertion about the righteous one living by faith), but is considerably different from the Hebrew text, at least in the form of that text available to us. Certainly God could not be pleased if one of His children should abandon the faith. It should not be inferred from this verse, however, that some had done so. On the contrary, the next verse clearly states that such had not occurred. The passage is therefore a statement of God's displeasure with lack of faith, and must have been somewhat hypothetical as it sketched the prospects for a righteous one who would turn back. It is a cautionary passage, pertinent to all, but Scripture is clear that a true Christian will not finally apostatize.

---

19. Papyrus 46, Aleph, A.
20. This is the original reading in D.
21. Papyrus 13, corrector of D.

> *But we are not of* [the] *turning back to perdition, but of*
> *faith to preservation of* [the] *soul.* (10:39)

The author is confident that neither he nor his readers are such as will turn back to eternal loss. Perdition (*apōleian*) means destruction or ruin, and is used commonly in the New Testament of eternal destruction. Such passages as Matthew 7:13; Romans 9:22; Philippians 1:28; 3:19; and I Timothy 6:9 reveal this aspect of the word. Both Judas and the Antichrist are called "the son of perdition" (John 17:12; II Thess. 2:3), because of the eternal torment and ruin which their heinous deeds will bring. The usage of *apōleia* here makes it clear that the judgment described in this context is not just a chastening of God's people but the final destruction of apostates.

These readers, however, were those whose spiritual condition was characterized by faith. Of course, it is a particular kind of faith in view: faith that has been placed in Christ so as to obtain eternal salvation. **Preservation of** [the] **soul** employs the term *peripoiēsin*, which has the meanings of obtaining (I Thess. 5:9), possessing (I Peter 2:9), and preserving. The latter sense is predominant here, used as the opposite of *apōleian*. To possess and preserve one's soul is the essence of salvation. The gospel is proclaimed in the New Testament as the means whereby one may escape eternal destruction in hell and may have eternal life (Matt. 10:28, 39; 16:25, 26; I Peter 1:9). This harmonizes also with the view taken in verse 34, "You have yourselves as a greater and abiding possession." Even though the author has spoken severely about the importance of unwavering faith and the dire consequences of apostasy, he is confident also that true faith will emerge in victory.

C. A REVIEW OF THE ACHIEVEMENTS OF FAITH. (11:1-40)

Having just discussed the importance of maintaining faith and not turning back, the author proceeds to a demonstration that it was this principle of faith even in Old Testament times that God was most interested in. Steadfast endurance in the face of obstacles is the evidence of true faith, and it was this very feature which the Old Testament heroes here mentioned exemplified in their lives. For the readers to give up their present faith in order to escape censure or suffering would be contrary to the stalwart examples of these Old Testament greats whose memories were justly honored. One would not be showing respect for Old Testament religion, even if he reverted to Judaism, by abandoning the very essence of his ancestors' worship. Hence the burden of this section is to set forth the vital importance of Biblical faith.

1. Introduction. (11:1-3)

> *Now faith is confident assurance of things hoped for, conviction of things not being seen. For in this the elders were testified to.* (11:1, 2)

A formal or complete definition of faith is not given, but rather there is a description of what faith does. The terms *hupostasis* and *elenchos* have several uses, and our versions reflect this. In the case of *hupostasis*, the King James Version has rendered it as "substance," giving it the same sense as it has in 1:3. Of course, faith is not actually the real substance or essence of what is hoped for; therefore, it must be understood in some such subjective sense as "lending substance to." On the other hand, the American Standard Version translates it as "assurance," understanding it in the same sense as its use in 3:14. This yields good sense without the need of any manipulation. The usage of *hupostasis* meaning "title deed"[22] in the papyri has intrigued some interpreters. This usage suggests an interpretation analogous to the Pauline terminology of the Spirit as being the earnest or down payment which guarantees the ultimate possession of our inheritance in Christ (Eph. 1:14). On the whole, the translation **confident assurance** is the simplest and is supported by the parallelism of the next clause.

The King James Version translation of *elenchos* is "evidence." The term occurs only here in the New Testament. The American Standard Version renders it as "conviction." Lexicons stress the basic idea as being a proof or means of proof with a view to convincing or refuting. Although Arndt and Gingrich suggest the possibility that it could mean "inner conviction,"[23] Büchsel denies that it can ever be used as subjective persuasion. He concludes that the objective sense of persua-

---

22. J. H. Moulton and G. Milligan, *The Vocabulary of the Greek Testament*, pp. 659, 660.
23. Arndt and Gingrich, *Greek-English Lexicon*, p. 248.

sion must be retained, but that the sense in Hebrews 11:1 demands that it be regarded as "the divinely given conviction of things unseen."[24] Hence faith is the confident assurance which the believer has because God has provided conviction about unseen realities.

The faith here described is operative both for future matters (**things hoped for**) and also for things not visible to the physical eye even though they may presently exist (**things not being seen**). Included would be the future blessings of Christ's return, the believer's final glorification, his entrance into the heavenly rest, and all the other benefits of salvation's culmination (Heb. 9:28), as well as the present values of Christ's high priestly ministry, the believer's access to God's presence in prayer, the full pardon for sin, and the constant experiencing of spiritual growth. This description does not discuss how faith is arrived at, but merely states its essential nature. A fuller definition of Biblical faith would need to include the fact of divine revelation on which true faith is based. Faith in the Biblical sense is the assurance and conviction that what God has said is true, and is to be acted upon by the believer.

It was in this (i.e., faith) that the elders of the Jewish people were immortalized in Scripture. The reference is to the illustrious ancestors of the readers, whose lives exhibited the kind of patience in adversity and willingness to follow God's leading that pointed unmistakably to their trust in God's revelation. Many of them are named in the succeeding verses. They were testified to in the pages of holy Scripture as being pleasing to God because they trusted Him.

> By faith we understand that the ages have been framed by God's word, so that what is seen has come to pass not out of things that appear. (11:3)

Before beginning his impressive roll call of the faithful, the author reminds his readers that faith is absolutely necessary if we are to understand even the first page of Scripture. No man was present at creation. Mankind is confronted with a universe already existing. The Book of Genesis provides the explanation of how it came about. This explanation must be accepted by faith, for there were no human

---

24. Friedrich Büchsel, "Elenchos," in *Theological Dictionary of the NT,* II, 476.

spectators. **Ages** (*aiōnas*) are the vast eons of time and all that fills them. The term is basically a reference to time, but it may also involve a spatial concept as here. In the author's view, God was responsible not only for the physical universe but also for its temporal progression. Genesis explains that this world was **framed by God's word**. God spoke (*rhēmati*) and it was done. As a result[25] the visible world came into being, **not out of things that appear**, but by the creative fiat of God without previously existing materials. Men may speculate about origins, but no one has firsthand knowledge. If man is ever to know what really happened, he is utterly dependent upon God to reveal it. Then when God does reveal it (and this is precisely what He did in Genesis), man's response must be one of faith if he is to understand. (To reject this revelation leaves him without any certain knowledge of earth or human origins.)

2. The faith of three prepatriarchal men. (11:4-7)

By faith Abel offered to God a superior sacrifice than Cain, through which he was testified to be righteous, God testifying on the basis of his gifts, and through it though having died, he still speaks. (11:4)

The reader should consult Genesis 4:1-15 for the Scriptural background of this reference. Abel's offering consisted of a lamb from his flocks, whereas his brother Cain, who was a farmer, brought an offering of his crops. Although each brought what might be considered appropriate in view of his occupation, the Lord "had respect unto Abel and to his offering, but unto Cain and to his offering he had not respect" (Gen. 4:4, 5). The author of Hebrews describes Abel as offering a superior sacrifice than Cain.[26] In what way was it superior? It was

---

25. This infinitive with *eis to* is best understood as indicating result, although it usually indicates purpose. To insist upon purpose here necessitates inserting the additional idea that creation occurred "that we might know" that visible things came from nonvisible sources. To treat it as result is simpler, and is a well-established use of *eis to*. See A. T. Robertson, *A Grammar of the Greek New Testament in the Light of Historical Research*, pp. 1001-1003.

26. Greek: *pleiona thusian*, "more sacrifice." The sense is not to be construed as more bountiful, but rather as more acceptable because it was accompanied with faith.

hardly a matter of monetary value or of mere quantity. Many point to the fact that Abel's offering was a slain animal and thus was a bloody sacrifice.[27] This accords well with the author's previous statement that "without shedding of blood there occurs no forgiveness" (Heb. 9:22). However, it must be noted that the Genesis account does not specify that the offerings of Cain and Abel were intended to be sin offerings, and thus some have questioned whether Cain was disqualified for using the wrong materials. Furthermore, the author of Hebrews does not state specifically that the superiority of Abel's offering was due to its bloody character. Rather, he says it was accepted because it was offered **by faith.** The statement in Genesis 4:4 that God had respect first "unto Abel" and then "to his offering" may suggest that it was the character of Abel that was primarily in view. With this Matthew, as well as Hebrews, concurs as it emphasizes that Abel was "righteous" (Matt. 23:35). Abel's heart was right in the sight of God, and his offering was a demonstration of his faith. With Cain it was a mere ritual, having no efficacy because it was not offered in faith.

Nevertheless, the offering of Abel is explained as **by faith,** and Biblical faith is always based upon God's revelation. Thus it must be assumed that Abel's response was in direct obedience to the kind of offering God wanted. This fact is reinforced by the statement that God's approving testimony was given **on the basis of his gifts.** This demands that the character of the gift cannot be disassociated from the heart of the offerer. Abel's offering proved something about Abel's heart that was not demonstrated by Cain's gift.

Through which could refer grammatically either to "faith" or to "sacrifice." Because of the emphasis upon faith throughout this passage, it seems most likely that "faith" is the antecedent. Through Abel's faith, which was demonstrated by his offering, he was accepted of God. Although the term **righteous** is not used of Abel in Genesis 4, he was accepted by God (Gen. 4:4) and this implies his righteous character. The testimony to Abel's righteousness was borne **on the basis of his gifts.** God, of course, looks on the heart as well, but in issuing the public verdict, He does so on the basis of the evidence which proves the condition of the heart. At Christ's return He will judge men in the same fashion (Matt. 25:31-46)—in the light of the evidence of their lives. This

---

27. So Pink, *Exposition of Hebrews,* I, 661; Owen, *Exposition of Hebrews,* VII, 24, 25.

does not mean that salvation is by works. It does mean that righteous men will demonstrate their faith by their actions.

And through it (i.e., his faith), **though having died he still speaks.** The language here may have been suggested by Genesis 4:10, where God said that Abel's blood cried out from the ground, but the sense in Hebrews is somewhat different. In Genesis Abel's blood cried out to God for vengeance. Here it is Abel himself (not his blood) that speaks to us (not crying out to God) of the vital importance of faith in God's sight. He may have died prematurely, but he still has something of great value to say to us by way of his life recorded in Scripture.

> *By faith Enoch was translated in order not to see death, and he was not found because God translated him. For before the translation he had been testified to have been well pleasing to God.* (11:5)

The second man in this prepatriarchal period to be mentioned is Enoch, whose brief story is given in Genesis 5:21-24. How was Enoch translated **by faith?** It was faith that made him **well pleasing to God,** and his God-pleasing life brought about his translation. **Translated** (*metatithēmi*) means "removed" or "transferred," and refers here to the circumstance of Enoch's passing into the life beyond without dying. The emphasis upon Enoch as pleasing God calls for special comment inasmuch as the expression does not occur in the Genesis account. **Well-pleasing to God** is the Septuagint rendering of Genesis 5:24, "Enoch walked with God." The Greek translators merely interpreted the anthropomorphic Hebrew idiom into a more readily understood Greek expression. "Walking with God" means pleasing God. This Enoch did in the years prior to his miraculous removal.

> *Now without faith* [it is] *impossible to be well pleasing, for it is necessary for one coming to God to believe that he exists and becomes a rewarder of those who seek him out.* (11:6)

The Old Testament record does not use the word "faith" in reference to Enoch. Nevertheless the author of Hebrews concludes rightly that **without faith** it would have been **impossible** for Enoch to have pleased God, as Genesis asserts. No one can please God in the Biblical sense without faith. To please God is to walk before Him in uprightness and obedience, to respond to His overtures and trust His guidance. Inasmuch as God is unseen and His revelation to men is largely concerned with promises of a spiritual nature, many of which await a future consummation, no meaningful or conscious relationship with God can be established without a willingness to believe that he exists. Likewise, no one comes to God in this way without believing that He keeps His promises. Otherwise there would be no point in seeking to please Him by walking in righteousness before Him. Because God is a rewarder of those who seek him out, it is obvious that faith reposed in Him is not misplaced. Inasmuch as Enoch walked with God in such close harmony that at the end of his earthly life God translated him, it is clear that he had in great depth the sort of faith described here.

By faith Noah, having been divinely instructed concerning the things not yet seen, out of reverent regard constructed an ark for [the] *saving of his house, through which he condemned the world and became heir of the righteousness which is by faith.* (11:7)

The author's third illustration is Noah, whose faith and righteousness were so widely recognized as to be almost proverbial (Ezek. 14:14). Noah had been **divinely instructed**[28] by God concerning the coming flood. **The things not yet seen** implies more than just that the announcement preceded the flood. In all probability Noah had never experienced any rain (Gen. 2:5), and perhaps had never personally seen any sea-going vessel. Certainly he had never witnessed anything like the cataclysm which was about to come upon the earth (Gen. 7:11, 12). [29] Nevertheless, **out of reverent regard** for God, who had been pleased with Noah and had informed him as to the approaching judgment along with instructions on how to escape, Noah **constructed an ark for** [the]

---

28. Greek: *chrēmatistheis.* The term is used regularly in the New Testament in the sense of divine revelation or warning. The lone exceptions occur in Acts 11:26 and Romans 7:3, and these may be entirely different words. So J. H. Moulton and W. F. Howard, *A Grammar of New Testament Greek,* p. 265.

29. For an excellent detailed discussion of the flood and its implications, see H. M. Morris and J. C. Whitcomb, Jr., *The Genesis Flood.*

saving of his house. Even though he had no experience of some of the things God had revealed to him, he believed at once, and set about doing what God required. By his obedience he was able to survive the flood, along with his wife and his three sons and their wives.

Through which he condemned the world. Which may refer either to ark or to faith, although the latter accords best with the emphasis in the passage. How did Noah condemn the world? It is possible that the reference is to Noah's preaching before the flood (II Peter 2:5), in which he must have denounced the wickedness of his contemporaries but won no converts.[30] It is more likely, however, that Noah's faith is regarded as throwing into bold relief the unbelief of those around him.[31] The very fact that Noah believed God made the guilt of his contemporaries all the more inexcusable.

Noah by this remarkable display became heir of the righteousness which is by faith. Through his act of faith Noah, who was already righteous by virtue of his faith (Gen. 6:9; 7:1), gave tangible evidence of his spiritual condition. As James expresses it regarding Abraham, "by the works the faith was made complete" (2:22). Thus the kind of faith which Noah had prompted him to obey God's word, and it is this sort of faith which brings one the righteousness of God. Any other kind of faith is nothing more than intellectual assent, and even demons have this much (James 2:19). To be an heir of this righteousness is to be the recipient of that righteousness which God imputes to those who trust Him, and denotes also the fact that enjoyment of the full inheritance is yet future.

3. The faith of the patriarchs. (11:8-22)

> *By faith Abraham being called obeyed to go out unto a place which he was going to receive for an inheritance, and he went out not knowing where he was going.* (11:8)

When Abraham left Ur he knew nothing as to his destination. He had to entrust himself to God's direction. He not only was unaware of the

---

30. This is the view of R. C. H. Lenski, *Interpretation of the Epistle to the Hebrews,* pp. 388, 389, who regards the statement as a condensed one.

31. So Marcus Dods, "The Epistle to the Hebrews," in *Expositor's Greek Testament,* IV, 355.

place where he was going, but he also had no knowledge of the fact that God would give the land where he was going as an inheritance for his descendants. It was only after Abraham had left Ur and then had subsequently left Haran that God revealed that the land of Canaan was to belong to his descendants (Gen. 12:6, 7). Hence it was clearly by faith in the bare word of God that the patriarch was prompted to make his momentous departure.

> *By faith he lived as a stranger in the land of promise as a foreign* [land] *, dwelling in tents with Isaac and Jacob the coheirs of the same promise. For he was awaiting the city having the foundations, whose architect and builder is God.* (11:9, 10)

Nor was Abraham's faith quickly rewarded with fulfilment. On the contrary, he trusted God in leaving his homeland in Chaldea, but never did find a permanent residence. Even though he did enter Canaan, he lived as a stranger.[32] He never owned any property in Canaan, except for the burial plot he purchased at Machpelah near Hebron when Sarah died (Gen. 23:1-20). Even though it was the land of promise because God had promised it to him (Gen. 12:7), for all practical purposes it was a foreign land to him. He never became a citizen. He never built a house in Canaan. He lived the life of a nomad, moving his tent from place to place.

Dwelling in tents presents an interesting paradox. Dwelling uses a form of *katoikeō*, meaning to settle down or dwell permanently, as compared to the cognate *paroikeō* used earlier in this verse to denote temporary dwelling, or living as a stranger. Tents, however, were the most portable of dwellings. Thus Abraham is said to have dwelled permanently in temporary type residences. In the land of promise he lived variously at Shechem (Gen. 12:6), Bethel (Gen. 12:8), Hebron (Gen. 13:18), and Beersheba (Gen. 22:19). Abraham's son and grandson, Isaac and Jacob, who were coheirs of the same promise that Abraham had received, had to exercise the same faith as Abraham. They too dwelled in tents, awaiting the fulfilment of the promise that did not come in their lifetimes. Their willingness to continue trusting

---

32. Greek: *paroikēsen*, "sojourned," a word used consistently of temporary residency.

God's word without witnessing more than token fulfilment in their own times speaks clearly of the genuineness of their faith, and offers a challenge to every reader, whether of the first century or the twentieth, to emulate the kind of steadfastness which God had so signally approved.

Abraham was willing to live his whole lifetime in the temporary type residence of tents because he was awaiting the city having the foundations. In contrast to the nomad's tent, the city represents permanence, a concept reinforced by the mention of foundations. But it was no earthly or human city on which Abraham's gaze was fixed. It was the city whose architect and builder is God. The term *technitēs* is used in the general sense of craftsman or artisan in Acts 19:24, 38, and Revelation 18:22, but the more restricted meaning of architect is employed here. The word *dēmiourgos* occurs only here in the New Testament. Etymologically it denoted one who pursued public affairs, but came to denote more generally a craftsman, maker, or builder.

Inasmuch as God is the architect and builder of this city, it is clear that the earthly Jerusalem is not meant. Other references in Hebrews to this city are 11:16, where God is said to have prepared it, 12:22, where it is called the "city of the living God, the heavenly Jerusalem," and 13:14, which refers to this city as "the one to come." Galatians 4:26 speaks of "Jerusalem which is above" as the spiritual origin and home of true believers. Revelation 21 describes the new Jerusalem, mentioning also the twelve foundations of its wall inscribed with the names of the twelve apostles (21:12). It should be clear, therefore, that Abraham's faith was centered not only on a city (as something more permanent than a tent) but on a heavenly and eternal goal. It was because his trust was placed in heavenly verities that temporal factors were of small consequence to him. This city, the heavenly Jerusalem, is regarded in Scripture as the final home of God's people.

> *By faith even Sarah herself* [being] *barren received power for the depositing of seed even beyond* [her] *season of age, since she considered him faithful who had promised.* (11:11)

It is by no means inappropriate to mention Sarah at this point, for she too had a vital stake in the promise to Abraham and in the first step of its fulfilment (i.e., the birth of Isaac). **Even Sarah herself** calls special attention to Sarah, not because she was a woman but because at the outset she demonstrated no faith at all. She laughed in unbelief when the announcement was first made (Gen. 18:10-15), but later at the birth of Isaac her laughter was from joy and wonderment (Gen. 21:6, 7). In view of Sarah's initial response, how can our author state that by faith she experienced these momentous events? Although freely admitting Sarah's early laughter, we must not ignore the honored place which the New Testament gives her—not only in Hebrews but also in I Peter 3:6, where she is held up as a model for Christian women. It should not be forgotten also that Isaac was not the product of a virgin birth. Therefore, Sarah's cooperation was required, and this necessitated considerable faith for a woman of ninety years.

A greater problem is posed by the words *katabolēn spermatos*. This expression is the regular one to denote the sexual function of the male, "depositing of seed." Yet here it apparently refers to Sarah. Numerous possibilities may be offered to resolve the question. Aside from those suggestions which regard "even Sarah herself" as an early gloss, or propose some other radical emendation, three interpretations are worthy of mention.

(1) The phrase in question could be translated as "establishing a posterity," and thus could apply equally well to Sarah.[33] Although "establishment" or "foundation" are common uses of the term *katabolē*, the juxtaposition of *spermatos* argues strongly for the regular sense of "begetting" and against this explanation.

(2) The nominative expression "Sarah herself" could be read as a dative "with Sarah herself,"[34] and thus Abraham can be retained as the subject of the verb.[35] Advantages of this explanation are that it refers the depositing of the seed to Abraham, it avoids an embarrassment over attributing faith to Sarah since the faith now becomes descriptive of Abraham, and it retains Abraham as the subject of the whole passage from verse 8 to verse 19 (except for a slight broadening of the reference to include all the patriarchs in verses 13-16). The chief weakness of this

---

33. Arndt and Gingrich, *Greek-English Lexicon,* p. 410.

34. Greek: *autēi Sarrāi* instead of *autē Sarra.* Because iota subscripts were commonly omitted in uncial manuscripts, the forms would appear the same in the oldest Greek texts.

35. Lenski, *Interpretation of Hebrews,* pp. 392-394; F. F. Bruce, *The Epistle to the Hebrews,* pp. 301, 302.

explanation is its absence of any clear manuscript evidence that "Sarah herself" is not nominative.

(3) Sarah may be understood as the subject, and *eis* should be regarded as "in connection with" or "in regard to."[36] Thus the sense would be: Sarah received power with regard to Abraham's depositing of seed, and thus even at her advanced age she was able to do her part in conceiving a child. By this explanation the male function of *katabolē spermatos* is retained, and still Sarah is understood as the subject of the sentence. On the whole, the second or third explanation seems closer to the literal meaning of the phrases, and the third requires less manipulation of the text.

> *Wherefore also from one, and* [he] *being* [as good as] *dead in these things, there were born the innumerable* [descendants] *even as the stars of the heaven in multitude and as the sand which is by the seashore.* (11:12)

From one refers, of course, to Abraham, who was ninety-nine years old when the birth of Isaac was first announced, and one hundred when the child was born (Gen. 17:1, 15-17; 21:5). Thus he was as good as dead in these things, that is, in reference to his powers of natural procreation. Yet by the word of God which not only provided information but also supplied supernatural enabling, Abraham became the progenitor of a vast multitude of descendants, as numerous as the stars of the heaven and the sand which is by the seashore. The language here is drawn from Genesis 22:17 (reinforced in part by Genesis 15:4, 5).

> *In accord with faith these all died, not having received the promises but from afar having seen and greeted them, and having confessed that they were strangers and aliens on the earth.* (11:13)

Rather than the simple dative "by faith," the statement here is introduced by *kata*, in accord with, for those in view did not die by means of faith but in a manner consistent with the faith asserted of them. These all should be understood of the patriarchs only (Abraham, Sarah, Isaac, Jacob), and not inclusive of the earlier names in the passage. This is obvious from the remainder of the sentence (the

---

36. M. Dods, *Expositor's Greek Testament,* IV, 356, 357.

promises began with Abraham), the content of verse 15 (only Abraham had gone out from his country), and also from the fact that Enoch, who did not die, would hardly be referred to in the terms of verse 13.

The patriarchs were mighty examples of the steadfastness that is an integral part of true faith, for they **died not having received the promises, but from afar having seen and greeted them.** The covenant made with Abraham was reiterated to Isaac (Gen. 26:2-5, 24) and Jacob (Gen. 28:10-15; 35:9-12; 46:2-4). Even though their deaths occurred before the promises regarding the land and the great nation to come from them were realized, their lives were characterized by continued trust that God would keep His promises. (The statement in 6:15 that Abraham eventually "obtained the promise" refers only to the birth of Isaac as the opening stage of the fulfilment.) They believed what God said, and they welcomed what they understood, even though that must have involved the recognition that their own participation would necessitate their resurrection.

Mosque of Abraham at Hebron, built over the reputed Cave of Machpelah, in which were buried Abraham, Sarah, Isaac, Rebekah, Leah, and Jacob (Heb. 11:13).

In proof of this assertion that the patriarchs were men of steadfast faith in the promises of God, the author reminds us that they confessed that they were strangers and aliens on the earth. The statement is apparently based upon Genesis 23:4, where Abraham in the process of purchasing the burial site from Ephron said, "I am a stranger and a sojourner with you."[37] At no time did Abraham (or Isaac and Jacob) put down such roots as to cause them to feel that they really belonged to any certain spot on earth.

> For they who say such things are making it clear that they are seeking a homeland. (11:14)

Such a confession as Abraham's is clear indication that he had not found on earth the dwelling place which could provide permanent satisfaction. Homeland is *patrida,* which is literally "fatherland." The term connotes a true homeland from which one has sprung and where he really belongs. When Abraham told Ephron in Hebron that he was a sojourner and an alien, it is clear that even Canaan which was promised by God to his descendants was not regarded as the full import of God's promise.

> And if they were remembering that [country] from which they had gone out, they would have had opportunity to return. But now they aspire to a better one, that is, a heavenly one. Wherefore God is not ashamed of them to be called their God, for he prepared for them a city. (11:15, 16)

Does someone suppose that Abraham did not settle permanently in Canaan because he still regarded himself as from Mesopotamia, and nurtured an inner longing to return? Not so, says the author. Not only Abraham but Isaac and Jacob as well had plenty of opportunity to return, but they did not. When Abraham sought a wife for Isaac, even though he wanted someone from his family rather than a Canaanite, he did not take the opportunity to go himself to Mesopotamia but sent his servant (Gen. 24:1-10). After Jacob had spent twenty years in Mesopotamia, he still did not regard that as his homeland but looked instead to

---

37. The Septuagint has *paroikos* as the first term where Hebrews uses *xenoi,* but the second term is *parepidēmos* in both Septuagint and Hebrews.

Canaan as he requested of Laban: "Send me away, that I may go unto mine own place, and to my country" (Gen. 30:25). When Abraham and his family left Ur of the Chaldees, they did so completely. There was no looking back. Even when Abraham considered himself still an alien in Canaan, it was in Canaan that he purchased a family burial plot, and made no effort to transport Sarah back to Mesopotamia (notice in verse 22 what Joseph directed regarding his own burial).

It should be evident, therefore, that what they really looked to was a **better country, a heavenly one.** This was the true reason why they showed no remorse at Abraham's leaving Mesopotamia. The eternal values involved in the promises of God made them willing to regard their earthly experience as a pilgrimage, and kept them from despair even when it was evident that death would overtake them before fulfilment came. With this sort of steadfast faith, it is understandable why **God is not ashamed of them.** He is pleased to be identified with them and **be called their God.** That this was so is seen in the frequent designation by God of Himself as the God of Abraham and of Isaac and of Jacob (Gen. 28:13; Exod. 3:6). Not only did God show His approval of the faith of the patriarchs by calling Himself their God, but also by what He did for them. **He prepared for them a city.** This is the same city mentioned in 11:10, and referred to again in 12:22; 13:14; and Revelation 21:10-27. It is surely the same as the "better country" mentioned earlier in this passage. Although the city-dweller Abraham left the highly civilized Ur for a wandering life in Canaan, and showed no inclination to return, the reason was that his sights were set on that heavenly abode of God's people which God Himself has prepared. This spiritual goal was shared by all the patriarchs, and their unswerving faith in that eternal habitation makes them models of faith for all believers.

> *By faith Abraham, being tried, has offered Isaac, and he who had received the promises was offering his unique* [son], *regarding whom it was spoken, "In Isaac shall seed be called for you. . . ."* (11:17, 18)

The faith of the patriarchs was no mere creedal tenet, divorced from practical application in life. Instances are here cited which show the heights to which their faith attained. Abraham when **being tried** (*peirazomenos*) by God **offered Isaac.** The Old Testament account is given in Genesis 22:1-19. The word "tried" is sometimes used in the sense of "tempted," but the term itself denotes only a testing. It becomes "tempt" when one is enticed to do evil, and of course God never tempts men in this sense (James 1:13). The use of the perfect tense form has offered (*prosenēnochen*) emphasizes the permanent effect of the act (or perhaps the permanency of the record).

The character of this event as a testing of Abraham's faith from several aspects is obvious to every reader. In addition to the natural revulsion felt by any father at the thought of losing his son (particularly by his own hand), the circumstances of Isaac's birth must have made the prospect especially difficult. Isaac was the child of his old age, and the tie of parental affection must have been particularly strong. Yet the author stresses another factor as being even more important. Abraham was the one who had received the promises. This of course does not contradict verse 13, which referred to the complete fulfilment, but refers to Abraham as the one to whom the promises had been made and who had welcomed them.

By God's direction he was being asked to sacrifice his **unique** son Isaac. The term "unique" (*monogenē*) or "only" is used in the New Testament of children who are the only offspring of their parents (Luke 7:12; 8:42; 9:38), of Christ in His relation to the Father (John 1:14, 18; 3:16, 18; I John 4:9), and of Isaac's relation to Abraham (Heb. 11:17). The translation "only begotten" which is used frequently in the King James Version suggests an emphasis on birth which does not fit in all cases. Isaac was not the only son born to Abraham, for Ishmael had been born to him previously and additional sons were born later by Keturah. Nor will the simple translation "only" serve in every instance (not, at least, without qualification), for others are called "sons" of God in addition to Jesus (angels, Adam, believers). To regard the term as meaning "only" in the sense of "unique" meets the requirements of all the problem passages. Jesus was obviously the unique Son of the Father. Likewise Isaac was Abraham's unique son. He was the one born of the free wife Sarah, not as Ishmael who was born of the slave Hagar and had already been cast out of the family (the sons of Keturah had not yet been born at the time of the incident under discussion). Furthermore, he was the unique heir to whom the promises applied, for God Himself had stated, **In Isaac shall seed be called for you** (Gen. 21:12). Thus we can see Abraham's struggle to keep his faith firm, for the command of God to sacrifice Isaac seemed contradictory to the previous promise God had made.

The verb was offering (*prospheren*) is in the imperfect tense, denoting the action as in process but not completed. The sense is that he was in the process of offering his son.

> ... *having accounted that even from the dead God was able to raise* [him], *from which he received him even in a parable.* (11:19)

Did Abraham actually expect a resurrection, or is the author ascribing a higher element to his faith than Abraham really knew at the time? The facts speak for themselves. God had made a promise to Abraham about a seed for him, and Abraham had believed it. After waiting twenty-five years, long after Sarah had passed her child-bearing years, Abraham experienced the first stage of the fulfilment by the remarkable birth of Isaac. Furthermore, God had confirmed the fact that Isaac was the promised seed. Hence Abraham could not expect some other son to replace Isaac in the event that Isaac would die childless. When God told Abraham to slay his son, Isaac was as yet unmarried and without offspring. Hence Abraham drew the conclusion that since God had definitely related the fulfilment of the covenant to Isaac, if God had ordered his death, then He must intend to resurrect him. This is all the more remarkable when we remember that Abraham had no precedent for any physical resurrection. Yet the author of Hebrews says he accounted that even from the dead God was able to raise him, and the conduct of Abraham recorded in Genesis fully substantiates this statement. He told his servants, "I and the lad will go yonder and worship, and come again to you" (Gen. 22:5).

From which (*hothen*) is an adverb which can denote place, circumstance, or reason, and the choice here must lie between the last two. If the idea of circumstance is meant, the sense is that from the situation just described Abraham was enabled to recover his son. If the sense of *hothen* is cause or reason, the translation should be "therefore" or "hence," indicating that Abraham's faith in God's resurrection power was the reason why he received his son again. On the whole the former understanding commends itself as preferable to this writer, inasmuch as the recovery of Isaac is better regarded as caused not by Abraham's faith but by God's faithfulness to His promise.

From this supreme display of faith in the offering of Isaac, Abraham received him even in a parable. He had given his son unreservedly to God, and got him back again. It was obviously not a literal resurrection but a **parable** of one. It is not at all unlikely that our author has implied by this statement that Isaac's recovery after being given up to God was a prefiguring of the experience of Abraham's ultimate Seed, the Lord Jesus Christ, who experienced a literal resurrection.

> *By faith Isaac blessed Jacob and Esau even concerning things to come.* (11:20)

Moving to Isaac himself, the author cites from the record in Genesis 27:1–28:5. A problem may be posed by the fact that Isaac's pronouncing of the blessing upon Jacob was the result of some chicanery by Jacob and his mother Rebekah and is only with some difficulty seen as **by faith** on Isaac's part. Nevertheless the content of the blessing dealt with **things to come** (Gen. 27:28, 29, 39, 40; 28:3, 4), and thus it must be recognized that Isaac did believe the promises made to Abraham (Gen. 28:4) and wanted them transmitted to his sons. When the deception was discovered, Isaac did not rescind the blessing upon Jacob on the grounds that it had been fraudulently obtained, but confirmed it with these words, "Yea, and he shall be blessed" (Gen. 27:33). Hence even Isaac was also firm in faith regarding the reality of God's promises to the Abrahamic family.

A crucial point was reached with Isaac regarding the covenant blessing, for now a choice had to be made between twin sons, either of whom might conceivably have been the channel for the covenant blessing to be passed on to his posterity.

> *By faith Jacob as he was dying blessed each of the sons of Joseph, and worshipped upon the top of his staff.* (11:21)

The Old Testament background for this illustration is found in Genesis 47:28–49:33. Even in Jacob's dying hours, he did not waver in his belief that the promises of God would be fulfilled to his posterity. Just as Isaac's bestowal of blessing marked a crisis, in that a distinction was made between two equally qualified sons (physically speaking), so Jacob's dying blessing also was a turning point. His blessing did not select one son as the channel for the covenant blessing of Abraham to be transmitted, to the exclusion of the other sons, but regarded them all as equal progenitors of the Abrahamic family.

The Genesis account reveals that Jacob blessed all of his sons. Mention is made in Hebrews, however, of Jacob's blessing only upon the two sons of Joseph, Ephraim and Manasseh. No reason is given why these alone are considered. Perhaps it was partly because they had been born in Egypt to an Egyptian mother,[38] and now Jacob's action fully adopted them into the family. "Thy two sons Ephraim and Manasseh . . . are mine; as Reuben and Simeon, they shall be mine" (Gen. 48:5). A more important reason may be found in the circumstances regarding the blessing of these two sons of Joseph as revealing the faith of Jacob. In spite of Joseph's protestations, Jacob insisted upon bestowing a preferential blessing upon Ephraim, the younger twin. With Jacob it was no question of being deceived (as in the case of Isaac who unwittingly blessed Jacob above Esau), but was his deliberate act. His firm conviction about things to come—far different from the vacillation of his early years—caused him to demonstrate his faith in what God would do, even though it involved a reversal of usual procedures.

The statement that Jacob worshipped upon the top of his staff is drawn from Genesis 47:31, but employs the wording of the Septuagint, rather than the Massoretic Hebrew text which reads "bed" instead of "staff." The problem arose from the fact that the ancient Hebrew Scriptures were written in a consonantal text, and the addition of vowels to indicate pronunciation (i.e., vowel pointing), such as are found in the present text, was not done until by the Massoretic scholars between the sixth and ninth centuries A.D. It so happens that the consonants for the words "bed" and "staff" are exactly the same in Hebrew.[39] The Septuagint translators regarded the term as "staff"; but the Massoretes, who are responsible for our present form of the Hebrew text, pointed it as "bed." The conflict is actually between the Septuagint and the Massoretic pointing, not the Hebrew text as such. The Septuagint rendering, adopted in Hebrews, makes excellent sense as depicting the extreme frailty of Jacob, who nevertheless maintained his faith to the end. There is no warrant, however, for the understanding

---

38. Asenath, Gen. 41:50-52.
39. Hebrew: mṭh. "Bed" would be pointed as miṭṭāh; "staff" as maṭṭeh.

that he "worshipped the top of his staff," as though it were some fetish.

> *By faith Joseph as he was dying remembered concerning the exodus of the sons of Israel, and gave command concerning his bones.* (11:22)

A great many things could have been stated about the faith of Joseph, but the one here mentioned was undoubtedly selected because it showed most clearly his trust that God would fulfil the promises made first to Abraham, Isaac, and his own father Jacob. The Old Testament passage referred to is Genesis 50:22-26. Joseph's prominence in Egypt certainly guaranteed an impressive burial and an imposing tomb. As his death approached, however, these things did not matter to him; and even though he knew he would not live to see the fulfilment of the promise, he wanted to have a share in the promised land. He followed the example of his father Jacob in arranging for his body to be buried in Canaan (see Gen. 49:29—50:13). Hundreds of years later at the Exodus, Moses faithfully carried out Joseph's wishes and took his remains out of Egypt (Exod. 13:19). He was eventually buried at Shechem, after Israel's conquest of the land (Josh. 24:32).

4. The faith of Moses. (11:23-29)

> *By faith Moses when he was born was hidden three months by his parents, because they saw that the child was beautiful, and they feared not the command of the king.* (11:23)

See Exodus 1—2 for the historical background of this reference. Actually it was the faith exhibited by Moses' parents that was involved at this point. The Greek term *paterōn* is usually translated "fathers" but was sometimes used to denote both parents (Eph. 6:4; Col. 3:21). This would seem to be demanded here since it was the mother's role which was emphasized in the Exodus account, the father not even being mentioned. It may be properly assumed that both parents were involved in the plan. The identity of these parents, although apparently named as Amram and Jochebed in Exodus 6:20, is not absolutely certain. The Amram who was the son of Kohath and grandson of Levi

(Exod. 6:16, 18) was probably not the same Amram who was the father of Moses (Exod. 6:20).[40]

The description of the child Moses as beautiful[41] of form is drawn from Exodus 2:2 and is similar to Stephen's words in Acts 7:20.[42] It is strongly suggested that the parents of Moses discerned from his exceptional beauty that God had special plans for him. At any rate, this fact is noted as prompting their efforts to save him, and Hebrews concludes it was by faith. They could have known that the four hundred years of oppression prophesied to Abraham were nearly accomplished. Consequently, they did not obey the command of Pharaoh that called for the execution of all newborn sons (Exod. 1:22). Instead they hid him in their home for three months and then committed him to an ark of bulrushes where he was rescued by a daughter of Pharaoh.

> *By faith Moses when he became grown up refused to be*
> *called a son of a daughter of Pharaoh, having chosen rather*
> *to suffer hardship with the people of God than to have*
> *enjoyment of sin for a season.* . . . (11:24, 25)

According to the chronological data furnished by the Old Testament, the Exodus from Egypt occurred 480 years before the fourth year of Solomon's reign (I Kings 6:1). Inasmuch as Solomon's fourth year is commonly fixed as 966 B.C., the Exodus must have occurred in 1446 or 1445 B.C.[43] Moses was eighty years old at the time of the Exodus (Exod. 7:7), and must have been born around 1525 B.C., when Thutmose I was pharaoh of Egypt. His daughter was the famous Hatshepsut, who married her half-brother Thutmose II; and when he died after a short reign, she took over the rule. At first she acted as regent during the childhood of Thutmose III, a son of Thutmose II by a harem wife; but she soon established herself as pharaoh in her own

---

40. See John J. Davis, *Moses and the Gods of Egypt*, p. 78, for a discussion of this problem.

41. Greek: *asteion.* The Hebrew word in Exodus 2:2 is *tob.*

42. Greek: *asteios tōi theōi,* "beautiful to God," probably a superlative expression, but perhaps implying also acceptability before God.

43. For an excellent résumé of the various views of the date of the Exodus, see Davis, *Moses and the Gods of Egypt,* chap. 1.

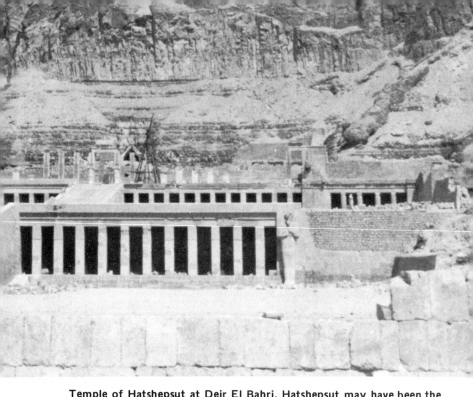

Temple of Hatshepsut at Deir El Bahri. Hatshepsut may have been the pharoah's daughter who adopted Moses (Heb. 11:24).

Model of the Temple of Hatshepsut, reconstructed as it was in 1480 B.C.

right. This condition lasted for about twenty years, until Thutmose III was able to unseat her.[44]

Was Hatshepsut the pharaoh's daughter who rescued Moses? It is tempting to think so, and the dates are agreeable. However, this is not the only possibility. The text merely says a **daughter of pharaoh**, and it is possible that Moses was reared in one of the numerous royal harems that were known to have been kept by pharaohs of the New Kingdom period.[45] If so, he may have been adopted by one of the teen-aged offspring of the king.

In spite of the fact that Moses was reared as the son of pharaoh's daughter (Exod. 2:10), he **refused** to capitalize on his position when he reached mature years. No further information about this refusal has been left to us. It could have been an official rejection of some prominent position in the court which was offered to him. Or it may mean that Moses' identification of himself with his people was unmistakable proof that he intended to be a Hebrew, not an Egyptian.

Verse 25, therefore, is most likely the explanation of Moses' refusal mentioned in the previous verse. By his action Moses displayed his faith that the Israelites were not just slaves of Pharaoh but were a people whose destiny was appointed by God. In casting his lot with them, it was not a display of mere national identification (note that the text does not call them "the people of Israel") but of spiritual affiliation (**the people of God**). At the same time Moses was well aware that his choice would cause him to **suffer hardship**. The alternative would have been to repudiate his national origins and make the most of the opportunities which his fortuitous adoption by Pharaoh's daughter made possible. Surely the life of one in his position provided for enjoyment in stark contrast to Pharaoh's Hebrew slaves. However, for Moses to do this would have been sin; for it would have meant the rejection of his God appointed work as Israel's deliverer (Acts 7:25). This kind of enjoyment resulting from the sin of abandoning God's people Moses refused. (There is no warrant for seeing in this "enjoyment of sin" a reference to the sensual gratification of one's lower

---

44. Lionel Casson, *Ancient Egypt,* pp. 54-56.

45. See Davis, *Moses and the Gods of Egypt,* pp. 52, and the article on "Moses" by K. A. Kitchen in the *New Bible Dictionary,* p. 844. Kitchen describes how children of *Harim* ladies were educated by the overseer of the Harim, and princes were given tutoring by high court officials.

Thutmose III, thought by many to be the pharoah of the oppression.

appetites. What is primarily in view is the high position in Egypt with the satisfactions that such prestige and power could bring.) It must not be inferred that the occupying of high government position is sinful per se. Daniel, for example, served God well under both Babylonian and Medo-Persian rulers, and was not directed by God to abandon his post. Each person needs to be sensitive to God's leading for the special circumstances of his own life.

> . . . having counted the reproach of Christ as greater wealth than the treasures of Egypt; for he was looking away to the reward. (11:26)

The treasures of Egypt were considerable. The wealth and opulence of the Eighteenth Dynasty is well known from the remains of tombs and temples. The fabulous treasures discovered in the tomb of Tutankhamen, a later pharaoh in this dynasty, speak eloquently of the luxuries available to royalty in Egypt. Moses, however, deliberately made a choice that placed such luxuries beyond his reach. Yet our author says that he did so as the result of evaluating the worth of them as compared to the wealth inherent in the reproach of Christ.

What did Moses understand about the reproach of Christ? A similar thought is expressed in 13:13, where believers are exhorted to join Christ "outside the camp, bearing his reproach." Is the meaning only that Moses experienced the same sort of mistreatment from unbelievers as Christ did? The expression seems too bold for that. Or does it mean that Christ was present among God's people even in Old Testament times and suffered along with them?[46] This latter explanation is often expanded to include the idea of Old Testament believers' union with Christ, and thus when they suffered Christ also suffered.[47] One should be careful, however, not to minimize the amount of revelation understood in the Old Testament period. It seems better to recognize that Moses comprehended a great amount of messianic truth, and realized that by identifying himself as a deliverer of God's people (Acts 7:25), he would be inviting the same reproaches that the future Anointed One would endure.[48] Moses was fully aware of a coming divine prophet (Deut. 18:15), and the time when this was first revealed to him has not been made known to us. It could have been much earlier than his announcement to the nation. Even Abraham possessed some awareness of these things. Jesus said, "Abraham rejoiced to see my day" (John 8:56). The language of Hebrews is similar to the thought expressed by the psalmist in Psalm 89:50, 51: "Remember, Lord, the reproach of thy servants; how I do bear in my bosom the reproach of all the mighty people; wherewith thine enemies have reproached,

---

46. Gleason L. Archer, Jr., *The Epistle to the Hebrews,* p. 78.

47. Westcott, *Epistle to the Hebrews,* p. 372.

48. W. F. Moulton, "The Epistle to the Hebrews," in *Ellicott's Commentary on the Whole Bible,* ed. Charles John Ellicott, p. 335; Robert W. Ross, "Hebrews," in *Wycliffe Bible Commentary,* ed. C. F. Pfeiffer and E. F. Harrison, p. 1423.

O Lord; wherewith they have reproached the footsteps of thine anointed.''

Moses' great act of self-renunciation was prompted by his looking **away to the reward.** His gaze was not upon personal satisfaction in Egypt, nor even upon an escape with his people to Canaan, but the ultimate **reward** which would be experienced in the life to come. Verse 27b reinforces this understanding. Thus the faith of Moses was of the same sort as that of Abraham (11:10) and the other patriarchs (11:13-16).

> *By faith he left Egypt, not fearing the wrath of the king,*
> *for he continued steadfast as seeing the Unseen One.*
> (11:27)

Inasmuch as Moses left Egypt on two occasions—the flight to Midian and the Exodus—it may be questioned which incident is meant. In favor of ascribing this statement to the flight to Midian are the following factors: (1) In the order of mention, this leaving of Egypt is placed prior to the passover. This fits the chronological order of the flight to Midian, but not the Exodus. (2) The Exodus occurred at Pharaoh's request, not in his wrath. (3) The singular "he" is more appropriate for the flight to Midian than for the general Exodus from Egypt. This seems to have been the prevailing view among the most ancient interpreters, and is held by many in recent years.[49]

Favoring the identification as the Exodus are the following: (1) "Not fearing the wrath of the king" is difficult to harmonize with Exodus 2:14, 15, which definitely attributes Moses' flight to Midian as resulting from fear of the face of Pharaoh. To say that even though Moses feared, he did not let fear conquer him, hardly conveys the intent of this passage, which states that "by faith Moses left Egypt, not fearing the wrath of the king." It is not easy to see Moses' flight as an act of faith and not of fear. (2) The usual sense of the verb "left" (*katelipen*) indicates an abandonment or permanent forsaking. Although Moses himself may have had no thoughts of returning at the time of the incident, as a matter of fact he did return to Egypt forty

---

49. So Thomas Hewitt, *The Epistle to the Hebrews*, in *Tyndale New Testament Commentaries*, pp. 181, 182; F. F. Bruce, *The Epistle to the Hebrews*, pp. 321-323.

years later, and thus from the standpoint of the writer of Hebrews, *katelipen* is somewhat surprising if Midian was the occasion in view. (3) The wrath of Pharaoh was aroused immediately after Israel's departure, and Moses must certainly have expected it to come (Exod. 14:5). Thus the statement in Hebrews has real point. (4) Even though technically the passover meal preceded the physical departure from Egypt, one may understand that in reality the forsaking of Egypt by Moses began with the events of Exodus 5–11. If one still objects to the violation of strict chronological order, he should note 11:13 where the patriarchs' deaths are recorded although further actions of them are listed later in 11:17-21. This explanation is my preference, especially as it offers a better explanation for the phrase "not fearing the wrath of the king."[50]

The resolute **faith** of Moses caused him to continue **steadfast**, not cowed by the awesome might of the pharaoh of Egypt. Instead, his eye of faith was firmly fixed on **the Unseen One**, and he followed where God led without any visible or earthly means to counteract the obvious human forces arrayed against him. Here was Biblical faith in perfect demonstration.

> *By faith he has instituted the passover and the sprinkling of the blood, in order that the One destroying the firstborn might not touch them.* (11:28)

The use of the perfect tense **has instituted** (*pepoiēken*) suggests a continuing state, and should be understood here in the sense that Moses established the observance of the passover at the Exodus, but it was intended to be a perpetual feast (Exod. 12:14).

Originally **the sprinkling of the blood** was intended to protect the homes of the Israelites from the physical death in the tenth plague to be inflicted by **the One destroying the firstborn.** (See Exod. 12 for the historical account.) Who was this destroyer? The pertinent passages in Exodus are the following:

> And Moses said, Thus saith the Lord, About midnight will I go out into the midst of Egypt (11:4).

> For I will pass through the land of Egypt this night, and will smite

---

50. This is the viewpoint of Westcott, *Epistle to the Hebrews,* p. 373; Owen, *Exposition of Hebrews,* VII, 161; Lenski, *Interpretation of Hebrews,* p. 411.

all the firstborn in the land of Egypt, both man and beast; and against all the gods of Egypt I will execute judgment: I am the Lord (12:12).

And the blood shall be to you for a token upon the houses where ye are: and when I see the blood, I will pass over you, and the plague shall not be upon you to destroy you, when I smite the land of Egypt (12:13).

For the Lord will pass through to smite the Egyptians; and when he seeth the blood upon the lintel, and on the two side posts, the Lord will pass over the door, and will not suffer the destroyer to come in unto your houses to smite you (12:23).

That ye shall say, It is the sacrifice of the Lord's passover, who passed over the houses of the children of Israel in Egypt, when he smote the Egyptians, and delivered our houses (12:27).

And it came to pass, that at midnight the Lord smote all the firstborn in the land of Egypt... (12:29).

It will be noted in the above passages that some of them attribute the smiting of the firstborn to Jehovah Himself, but that Exodus 12:23 mentions an agent called the destroyer. It is common to describe this agent as an angel sent as an agent of God. However, it is very likely that this may be a very particular angel, called elsewhere "the angel of Jehovah," who is regarded by many as the preincarnate Christ. "The angel of Jehovah" was mentioned earlier in Exodus as the one who appeared to Moses at the burning bush, and who identified Himself as God (3:2-6).

> *By faith they passed through the Red Sea as through dry land, in which the Egyptians having made trial of were swallowed up.* (11:29)

The Old Testament account is found in Exodus 14. Israel's passage through the Red Sea is said to be by faith. Inasmuch as the author of Hebrews has made considerable point of the fact that the vast majority of the nation perished in the wilderness because of unbelief (3:12, 18, 19; 4:2, 6, 11), it has been argued that only the faith of Moses, Aaron, Caleb, Joshua, and the believing remnant is in view.[51] More likely is the explanation that the true faith of a portion in Israel is here generalized to cover all the nation.[52] It could also be observed, however, that the

---

51. Pink, *Exposition of Hebrews,* II, 822.
52. Owen, *Exposition of Hebrews,* VII, 170.

faith exercised by Moses in crossing the sea was followed by the rest in Israel (including those whose faith was not enduring), and thus all made it across on dry land. Perhaps it is too restrictive to insist that the author means "saving faith" each time the word appears in this chapter.

The Red Sea translates the Greek expression in Hebrews (*eruthran thalassan*) which in turn reproduced the Septuagint rendering of Exodus 13:18 (et al.). The Hebrew text in Exodus calls it the Sea of Reeds (*yam sûp*). Its precise location has been a problem of long standing.[53] Good reasons exist for placing it in the Bitter Lakes region, north of the Gulf of Suez.

Israel passed through the Red Sea as the result of a great miracle. The Lord instructed Moses to lift his rod over the sea, and this was followed by an east wind that blew all night (Exod. 14:16-22). The waters were made to wall up on both sides of a channel, and the channel itself provided dry land for Israel to walk across. No ordinary wind could have produced all the phenomena described in the Exodus account. By responding positively to God's indicated plan, the entire group made it safely to the other side.

The Egyptians, however, attempted to take the same path through the sea with six hundred chariots (Exod. 14:7), and were destroyed to the last man (Exod. 14:28). It should be obvious from this incident that faith is not mere "daring," for the Egyptians were as daring as the Israelites in attempting to cross between the walls of water. With the Egyptians it was not faith but presumption. Faith is man's response to God's revelation. God had promised safe passage to Israel by these very means, and their action was a genuine display of trust in God. The Egyptians, however, had been given no such instruction by God, and as a result were swallowed up by the engulfing waters.

After the initial faith of Israel evidenced at the crossing of the Red Sea, the author mentions nothing further from the wilderness experience, no doubt because Israel's conduct over the next forty years was characterized in general by unbelief.

5. The faith of Israel since Moses. (11:30-40)

By faith the walls of Jericho fell after being circled for seven days. (11:30)

---

53. A recent brief but excellent discussion may be found in Davis, *Moses and the Gods of Egypt,* chap. 8.

Surely the destruction of the walls of Jericho was a striking display of faith by Israel. (See Josh. 6 for the details.) There was no reason for Israel to imagine that the massive stone walls of Jericho would crumble as a result either of seven days' marching or the blowing of trumpets and the shouts of the people. When nothing resulted from the first six days of this procedure, human logic would have urged that the program be abandoned. Only a firm belief that God would do what He said can explain why the Israelites behaved as they did. Their faith was fully vindicated on the seventh day, when the walls fell flat and Israel then burned the city.

> *By faith Rahab the harlot did not perish with those who were disobedient, because she welcomed the spies with peace.* (11:31)

The experience of **Rahab** was naturally suggested by the immediately preceding mention of Jericho. Her story is described in Joshua 2:1-24 and 6:22-25. To hold up Rahab as exemplary may seem strange. There is no legitimate way to soften the expression **harlot** (*hē pornē*) into something less sordid, such as "hostess" or "innkeeper." The statement remains descriptive of her conduct as a prostitute. Nevertheless, she is also mentioned elsewhere in the New Testament with approval as an example of one whose faith was demonstrated by her works (James 2:25), and as an ancestress of Jesus (Matt. 1:5).[54]

Of course, it is the faith of Rahab which is praised. There is no warrant for supposing that she continued her wicked life subsequent to the encounter with the spies, even though the epithet may have lingered (as epithets often do!). According to the Old Testament account, the two Israelite spies went to Rahab's house for concealment, and soon found that she knew a great deal about Israel's victories beyond Jordan (Josh. 2:9-10). She also indicated her belief in the uniqueness of Israel's God (Josh. 2:11). For this reason she did not betray the spies but

---

54. In the genealogy the name is spelled *Rachab,* rather than *Raab* as in Hebrews.

Site of Old Testament Jericho is the mound in the center of the picture. Here the walls fell down to provide Israel's first victory in Canaan (Heb. 11:30).

joined forces with them. At great personal risk she wanted to be identified with Israel and the Lord, and acted in accordance with her new belief. She accepted by faith the fact that God had given Canaan to this invading nation. For this great faith, found in a most unexpected place, Rahab has been enshrined forever in Hebrews 11. She was also spared along with her family from the destruction that was meted out to the remaining inhabitants of Jericho (Josh. 6:22-25).

> *And what more do I say? For the time will fail me for recounting*[55] *concerning Gideon, Barak, Samson, Jephthah, of David and Samuel and the prophets, . . .* (11:32)

The author cannot continue mentioning every example of faith in Israel's illustrious history. He therefore must content himself with more general statements and a few representative names. The six persons mentioned are not listed in chronological nor Biblical order, for Barak preceded Gideon, Jephthah preceded Samson, and Samuel preceded David (although he was also contemporary). Efforts to explain the arrangement according to some scheme of ascending or descending dignity seem contrived. The important factor in the author's mind was their example of faith, and each one was included for that reason alone. Other persons could have been named, but the reason for narrowing the list has been explained: for the time will fail me.

The first four names come from the period of the judges. **Gideon** (Judg. 6—9) was used of God to free Israel from the Midianites. By following the instructions of the Lord, Gideon and his little band of three hundred men defeated the Midianite coalition of one hundred thirty-five thousand troops (Judg. 8:10). It was obvious that military prowess was not the explanation, but commitment without reserve to the word which God had revealed.

Barak (Judg. 4—5) was the military leader used of God in connection with Deborah, the prophetess and judge, to deliver Israel from the oppression of the northern Canaanites under Jabin of Hazor and his general, Sisera. A casual reading of the Old Testament account might suggest that Barak was not as good an example of faith as was Deborah, since he refused to risk the battle unless she accompanied him.

---

55. The masculine gender of this participle (*diēgoumenon*) indicates that the writer was a male, thus effectively ruling out Priscilla, as a few have suggested.

However, it should be understood that Barak wanted Deborah's presence with him because she was the Lord's spokesman; and when she indicated that victory would come not primarily by military skill but by the Lord's action through a woman, Barak willingly went forth to battle on that basis (Judg. 4:9).

Samson (Judg. 13–16) was God's instrument to defeat Israel's enemies the Philistines on numerous occasions. Certainly there was much in Samson's life that was unworthy of emulation. Nevertheless, there were occasions when he threw himself completely upon the mercy of God; and in dependence upon the Lord he accomplished heroic deeds. One such occasion was the closing episode of his life, when as a blind and wretched prisoner, while being mocked at a pagan Philistine feast, he cried out to God for strength to accomplish his final victory over Israel's enemies. "O Lord God, remember me, I pray thee, and strengthen me, I pray thee," prayed Samson (Judg. 16:28); and he proceeded to demolish the temple of Dagon, killing thousands of Philistines (Judg. 16:27, 30) along with himself.

Jephthah (Judg. 11–12) was the judge of Israel who delivered his people from the threat of Ammonite domination. The son of a harlot, thrust out of his father's house, he became a soldier of fortune and eventually was called back to lead his own people against the Ammonites. In spite of the vexing problems posed by the vow of Jephthah regarding his daughter, it is clear enough that Jephthah believed in God's power and was willing to face the enemy in the faith that God was leading and would give victory (Judg. 11:11, 21-24, 27, 29-32).

Passing from the judges,[56] the author now mentions an illustrious king, and then moves to the prophets. David was the founder of the dynasty from which Messiah had been prophesied to come. It was David who had conquered Jerusalem, and whose exploits made him a truly heroic figure in Israel. In spite of his weakness (and Scripture does not ignore nor excuse the frailties of men), David was a man after God's own heart (I Sam. 13:14; 16:1, 12; Acts 13:22). He displayed his faith in God at his meeting with Goliath (I Sam. 17:37), during his flights from Saul (I Sam. 22:3-5; 23:4-5; 24:12), at the establishment of his

---

56. The use of *te kai* serves to join David and Samuel closely, and thus separates them to some extent from the preceding terms in the listing.

kingdom (II Sam. 5:17-25), in his response to the promises of God about the future of the Davidic throne (II Sam. 7:12-29), and in many other ways.

Samuel was the prophet who anointed David as king (I Sam. 16:13). His faith glowed brightly in a day of much spiritual declension. Even as a child his trust in the Lord was far stronger than that of Eli, the priest who reared him. In later years he anointed Saul at God's bidding, and then showed his faith in God's will at considerable personal risk to anoint David as Saul's successor while Saul was still alive. There had been other prophets before Samuel (e.g., Moses, Deborah), but with Samuel there began a continuing stream of prophets in Israel. It is appropriate, therefore, to speak of **Samuel and the prophets**, naming only the first of a long series.[57]

> *. . . who through faith subdued kingdoms, performed righteousness, obtained promises, shut lions' mouths, . . .*
> (11:33)

The achievements of these heroes of faith stand enshrined in Scripture as evidences of God's power, and also of God's honoring of those who will trust Him and do His will. The judges and David just mentioned are examples of those who by faith in God's leading **subdued kingdoms.** When in the Old Testament period God was working through a particular nation, the overthrow of literal kingdoms which were intended for destruction by God was accomplished by these Israelite men of faith. These heroes also **performed righteousness.** This could be understood of their personal lives as characterized by conduct which was faithful to the light God had revealed (of course, this is not claiming sinlessness for any of them, nor should it be made to contradict the fact of certain notable lapses). More likely, however, is the explanation that sees this as a reference to their official policies as leaders of Israel. An example is found in II Samuel 8:15, where David is said to have executed "justice over all his people" (Septuagint: *dikaiosunēn epi panta ton laon autou*).

Obtained promises could refer to the fact that God made promises to them, or to the actual fulfilment of the things God had promised.

---

57. We should compare the similar terminology of Peter: "Samuel and those that follow after" (Acts 3:24).

Perhaps it is not necessary to restrict it to one or the other. Certainly it is true that God promised various victories to Gideon, Barak, David, and many others; and those promises were fulfilled to them. Of course, this does not contradict the statements of 11:13 and 39, for they did not receive "the promise" (singular) made to Abraham which involved the coming of Messiah for its full consummation.

Shut lions' mouths could conceivably include the experiences of Samson (Judg. 14:5-6) and David (I Sam. 17:34-36), whose exploits were made possible by God. Most probably it was the experience of Daniel that was in the author's mind (Dan. 6:16-23).

> . . . *quenched* [the] *power of fire, escaped* [the] *sword's edge,*[58] *were made powerful from weakness, became strong in war, put to flight* [the] *armies of foreigners.* (11:34)

Quenched [the] **power of fire** refers to the experience of Shadrach, Meshach, and Abednego in Nebuchadnezzar's fiery furnace (Dan. 3:19-30). God honored their faith not only by protecting them from the flames but also by providing a supernatural companion in the furnace (Dan. 3:25). **Escaped** [the] **sword's edge** could refer to victory in battle, as was experienced many times by Israel under the judges, during the kingdom, and in Maccabean times. It may also include individual escapes from execution, such as the cases of Moses (Exod. 18:4), Elijah (I Kings 19:1-3), and Elisha (II Kings 6:31).

Were made powerful from weakness was the experience of Israel, both individually and nationally, on many occasions. Samson, although imprisoned and blinded, was granted strength from God for his final victory (Judg. 16:30). Gideon, by his own admission the least in his father's house (which was itself a poor one), was made by God a deliverer of his people (Judg. 6:14-16). David's experience with Goliath was another instance (I Sam. 17:33, 42, 45, 49-50). Nationally, God took a people enslaved for four hundred years in Egypt and made them conquerors of Canaan.

Became strong in war and **put to flight** [the] **armies of foreigners** describes the frequent occurrence in Israel's glorious past when the

---

58. Greek: *stomata,* mouths (pl.). The plural is sometimes explained as referring to the two edges of a sword. It is more likely a reference to the many instances when the sword was threatening.

nation had truly followed Jehovah. It was loss of her faith in God that brought defeat and oppression. The words armies (*parembolas*) and foreigners (*allotriōn*) are found frequently in I Maccabees to describe the time of revolt under Judas Maccabeus, and it may be that the author of Hebrews was also including that part of Jewish history in his retrospection.

> And he saw the blasphemies that were committed in Judah and in Jerusalem, and he said, Woe is me! wherefore was I born to see the destruction of my people, and the destruction of the holy city, and to dwell there, when it was given into the hand of the enemy, the sanctuary into the hand of aliens [*allotriōn*] ? (2:7).
>
> And there went up with him also a mighty army [*parembolē*] of the ungodly to help him, to take vengeance on the children of Israel (3:15).
>
> But when they saw the army [*tēn parembolēn*] coming to meet them, they said to Judas, What? Shall we be able, being a small company, to fight against so great and strong a multitude? ... And Judas said, It is an easy thing for many to be shut up in the hands of a few; and with heaven it is all one, to save by many or by few: for victory in battle standeth not in the multitude of a host; but strength is from heaven. ... And Seron and his army [*parembolēn*] were discomfited before him. And they pursued them in the going down of Bethhoron unto the plain, and there fell of them about eight hundred men. .. (3:17-24).

Women received their dead in resurrection; but others were tortured, not accepting the release, in order that they might obtain a better resurrection. (11:35)

The Old Testament **women** referred to are the widow of Zarephath, whose son was raised by Elijah (I Kings 17:17-24), and the Shunammite woman, whose son was raised by Elisha (II Kings 4:18-37). At this point the emphasis changes from the achievements resulting from faith to the willingness of others to suffer for their faith. Some of these were tortured (*etumpanisthēsan*). The precise nature of their torture may be indicated by the cognate noun *tumpanon,* meaning "drum," which was used of the drumlike or wheellike rack upon which victims were stretched and then savagely beaten, usually to death (II Macc. 6:19, 28). Not accepting the release and the mention of resurrection make it likely that several incidents from Maccabean times were in the author's mind. It should be remembered that the author has been citing passages from the Septuagint, and the books of Maccabees were a part of that version and must have been familiar to the readers.

In II Maccabees the following account is given of Eleazar, a ninety-year-old scribe who was threatened with death at the time of Antiochus Epiphanes.

> Eleazar, one of the principal scribes, a man already well-stricken in years, and of a noble countenance, was compelled to open his mouth to eat swine's flesh. But he, welcoming death with renown rather than life with pollution, advanced of his own accord to the instrument of torture [*to tumpanon*], but first spat forth the flesh. . . (6:18-19).

In the very next chapter the account is given of a mother and her seven sons. The sons declared their willingness to die rather than apostatize, and stated their hope in an eternal resurrection.

> And when he was at the last gasp, he said, Thou miscreant, dost release us out of this present life, but the King of the world shall raise up us, who have died for his laws, unto an eternal renewal of life (7:9).
>
> And after him was the third made a mocking-stock. And when he was required, he quickly put out his tongue, and stretched forth his hands courageously, and nobly said, From heaven I possess these, and for his laws' sake I contemn these; and from him I hope to receive these back again (7:10-11).
>
> And being come near unto death he said thus: It is good to die at the hands of men and look for the hopes which are given by God, that we shall be raised up again by him; for as for thee, thou shalt have no resurrection unto life (7:14).

These and others like them could have had a release from their tortures if they had been willing to give up their faith. This they would not do, preferring to put their trust in a better resurrection. By dying for their faith, they had the confidence that the resurrection to come would be even better than that return to mere mortal life referred to in the early part of the verse. Elijah and Elisha raised the women's sons to temporal life, only to have them die again. These martyrs, however, were looking to the final resurrection which would clothe their bodies with immortality.

> *And others received* [the] *trial of mockings and scourgings, and in addition, of bonds and prison.* (11:36)

Instances of such treatment are far too numerous to give any sort of exhaustive list. Mockings were the common experiences of Old Testament prophets and in intertestamental times. Elisha faced this (II

Kings 2:23), as did others (II Chron. 36:16). Scourgings were lashings with brutal whips, undergone by such faithful men as Jeremiah (Jer. 20:2). Bonds and prison were the lot of Joseph (Gen. 39:20), Micaiah (I Kings 22:27), Hanani (II Chron. 16:10), and Jeremiah (Jer. 20:2; 37:15; 38:6).

> They were stoned, they were sawn in two, they were tempted, they died by murder of [the] sword, they went around in sheepskins, in goatskins, being destitute, afflicted, ill-treated, of whom the world was not worthy, wandering in deserts and mountains and caves and holes of the earth. (11:37, 38)

An instance of an Old Testament man of faith who was stoned was Zechariah, son of Jehoiada, whose martyrdom was accomplished within the temple court (II Chron. 24:20-22). No instance of anyone sawn in two (*epristhēsan*) is recorded in the Old Testament. However, a well-known tradition coming from pre-Christian times states that this was the experience of Isaiah during the reign of Manasseh. In the early writing *Ascension of Isaiah,* several of its sections were by Christian authors, but the first part, "The Martyrdom of Isaiah," was of Jewish origin. It is probably to be dated in the first century A.D.[59] In it the prophet is described as in the presence of King Hezekiah and his son Manasseh. Isaiah is recorded as saying to the king:

> All these commands and these words shall be made of none effect by Manasseh thy son, and through the agency of his hands I shall depart mid the torture of my body. . . . And many in Jerusalem and in Judea he shall cause to abandon the true faith, and Beliar shall dwell in Manasseh, and by his hands I shall be sawn asunder (1:7-9).[60]

That this prediction came to pass is stated in the same work:

> And he sawed him asunder with a wood-saw. And when Isaiah was being sawn in sunder Balchîrâ stood up, accusing him, and all the false prophets stood up, laughing and rejoicing because of Isaiah (5:1).

> And they seized and sawed in sunder Isaiah, the son of Amoz, with a wood-saw. And Manasseh and Balchîrâ and the false prophets and

---

59. R. H. Charles (ed.), *The Apocrypha and Pseudepigrapha of the Old Testament in English,* II, 155.

60. Charles, p. 159.

the princes and the people [and] all stood looking on. . . . And when Isaiah was being sawn in sunder, he neither cried aloud nor wept, but his lips spake with the Holy Spirit until he was sawn in twain (5:11-14).[61]

The same tradition is mentioned by the second century Christian writer Justin Martyr:

For if your teachers had understood them [i.e., prophecies of certain prophets], they would most assuredly have expunged them from the text, as they did the words describing the death of Isaias, whom you Jews sawed in half with a wooden saw.[62]

They were tempted translates a reading which has raised considerable question. The reading (*epeirasthēsan*) is included in Nestle,[63] but not in the United Bible Societies text. If the reading is genuine, the reference must be to the temptation to apostatize, which went hand in hand with many of the sufferings enumerated, particularly those incurred during Maccabean times. However, it must be admitted that the inclusion of this word at this point is a bit puzzling, occurring as it does in a list of violent experiences. The documentary support for the text is conflicting. Some manuscripts transpose *epristhēsan* ("were sawn in two") and *epeirasthēsan* ("were tempted"); some give one or the other but not both; some replace *epeirasthēsan* with another word. Papyrus 46, a third century papyrus and our oldest manuscript of Hebrews, omits it. Some who favor its omission explain it as an instance of "false dittography,"[64] in which the first term was inadvertently repeated, and misspelled in the process. Among the more recent versions, "tempted" has been omitted by the Revised Standard Version and New English Bible, but included in the American Standard Version, New American Standard Bible, and Phillips.

Of the many who **died by murder of** [the] **sword**, the prophets slain by Israel at the time of Ahab and Jezebel (I Kings 19:10) and the prophet Urijah during the reign of Jehoiakim (Jer. 26:23) are ones who

---

61. Charles, p. 162.

62. Justin Martyr, "Dialogue with Trypho," in *The Fathers of the Church*, ed. Thomas B. Falls, VI, 334.

63. Both in Nestle-Aland (25th ed.) and in the British and Foreign Bible Society edition (1954).

64. F. F. Bruce's term, *The Epistle to the Hebrews*, p. 330, fn. 239.

could be mentioned. Sheepskins (*mēlōtais*) and goatskins (*aigeiois*) were the strange dress of some Jewish prophets. Elijah's "mantle" was a sheepskin,[65] and his girdle also was made of leather (II Kings 1:8). Romantic notions that this unusual apparel was a sort of uniform should be discarded. The author of Hebrews obviously understood it as indicative of their lack of anything else to wear. They dressed this way because they were destitute,[66] lacking even what most would regard as the barest necessities of life. They were continually afflicted and ill-treated by their fellow countrymen, the very ones for whose benefit they ministered.

No wonder the author poignantly observes, of whom the world was not worthy. By and large the contemporaries of these men of faith rejected them as being unworthy of respect and in many cases as deserving of death. The truth of the matter was exactly the opposite. The world was not worthy of them. It was the grace of God that had granted such stalwarts to Israel as a testimony to them, but Israel's persecution of God's faithful servants showed their own woeful state.

The previous statement was somewhat parenthetical. The description of the hardships of God's faithful ones now resumes. Because of the rejection of God's servants by a world that was hostile to God and hence opposed to His emissaries, these men of faith were driven to a life of wandering in deserts and mountains and caves and holes of the earth. The Old Testament recounts how caves were utilized by such persons as Obadiah, who hid a hundred prophets from the wrath of Jezebel (I Kings 18:4, 13). Elijah fled for his life and took refuge in a cave (I Kings 19:9). In more recent Jewish history, deserts and mountains were hiding places for Mattathias and his sons and followers during the great Maccabean revolt (I Macc. 2:28, 29). The land of Palestine is pockmarked with holes in the earth; and these natural openings were used for many purposes, including shelter for soldiers (I Sam. 22:1; 24:3) and repositories for valuables (e.g., Qumran scrolls, Bar Cochba letters). Here, however, they are indicative of the meagerness of the circumstances in which God's faithful servants often had to exist. A

---

65. I Kings 19:13 (Septuagint, *mēlōtēi*, III Kings 19:13); II Kings 2:8 (Septuagint, *mēlōtēn*, IV Kings 2:8).

66. The same term, *hustereō*, was used by Jesus in questioning His disciples: "When I sent you without purse, and scrip, and shoes, lacked ye any thing?" (Luke 22:35).

similar description occurs in "The Martyrdom of Isaiah," where it is said:

> And there also there was much lawlessness, and withdrawing from Bethlehem he [Isaiah] settled on a mountain in a desert place. . . . They were all clothed with garments of hair, and they were all prophets. And they had nothing with them but were naked, and they all lamented with a great lamentation because of the going astray of Israel. And these eat nothing save wild herbs which they gathered on the mountains, and having cooked them, they lived thereon together with Isaiah the prophet. And they spent two years of days on the mountains and hills (2:8-11).[67]

And these all having been testified to through their faith received not the promise, God having provided something better for us, that not without us should they be brought to completeness. (11:39, 40)

These all refer to the entire list of examples enumerated previously in this chapter, who of course are representative of an even larger number of godly persons in the Old Testament era. The author has demonstrated in instance after instance how their faith had been testified to by God's treatment of them (e.g., 11:4, 5-6, 7, et al.), as well as by their inclusion in the written Scriptures. The strength of their faith is seen in the fact that during their lifetime they still received not the promise. Hence their need to persist in faith even to death was amply demonstrated. They did receive "promises" (plural), as 6:15 and 11:33 state, but not the promise. They experienced the answers to many prayers and saw God fulfil His word on numerous occasions. But the promise required the coming of Messiah in order for the blessings indicated to Abraham to occur.

It must be remembered that Christians also must look forward in faith to certain fulfilments still future. (That is why the author has been urging his readers to keep firm in their faith without wavering.) It was stated in 10:36 that "the promise" must be preceded by patience before it will be received. In one sense the promise has been fulfilled inasmuch as Christ has come and has made the once-for-all sacrifice. But there are future realities that still await consummation (the "better resurrection" [11:35] being among them).

---

67. Charles (ed.), *Apocrypha and Pseudepigrapha of the OT,* II, 160.

The reason given why the Old Testament saints did not fully realize the fulfilment of the promise during their lifetime was that God had a plan to include the New Testament economy in His grand scheme of salvation. **They** in verse 40 refers to Old Testament believers, and **us** denotes New Testament believers. The Old Testament saints were not **brought to completeness** during their lifetime because the once-for-all sacrifice of Christ had not yet occurred. This did not mean that they had no spiritual experience, for true believers in the Old Testament period obviously had a genuine knowledge of God; and this occurs only by the operation of the Holy Spirit upon the heart. But the only truly efficacious sacrifice for sin was as yet unoffered during their lifetime. Comparison should be made with 12:23, which speaks of Old Testament saints now dead whose "spirits" have been brought to completeness. Being presently in heaven, they now know that Christ's sacrifice has been made, and their spirits rest in perfect fulfilment, awaiting only the resurrection of their bodies.

In the meantime **something better for us** has been **provided.** Christian believers are the recipients of certain blessings unavailable in the Old Testament period. The sacrifice of Christ is an accomplished fact for them, not a future hope. Many of the blessings of the new covenant are already being enjoyed (see 8:6-13). Thus by delaying the fulfilment beyond the Old Testament saints' lifetime, God has brought in the better revelation in Christ, and has secured salvation for New Testament believers also. Both groups will find their salvation fully consummated when Christ returns and physical resurrection as well as the other provisions of the Abrahamic promise and of the new covenant will be brought to pass.

D. AN EXHORTATION TO ENDURE SUFFERING AND CHASTENING. (12:1-29)

1. Some examples of suffering. (12:1-3)

Therefore we also, having so great a cloud of witnesses surrounding us, after putting off every weight and the sin which so easily besets, let us run with endurance the contest that lies before us, . . . (12:1)

Just as it was needful for Old Testament saints to remain firm in faith through the sufferings they faced, **we also** (i.e., we Christians) must **run with endurance.** To provide incentives, the author points first to the Old Testament personages who have finished the course, and to Christ Himself. The **cloud of witnesses** refers to the noble list just given in chapter 11 (**cloud** being a metaphor for a large mass). In this context it is difficult not to inject the idea of "spectators" as the sense of *marturōn,* although this is not the basic meaning of the term.[68] A *martus* was one who bore testimony to what he personally knew about. The use of the cognate participle in 11:39 must influence our understanding of 12:1. The point is that these Old Testament heroes were approved for their faith by the testimony of God, and their experience now stands as a testimony to us as to what pleases God. If we insist on understanding them as the audience in the stadium (in the light of the figure of the contest), we should view them as the cheering bloc rather than as mere spectators. To draw from this the notion that the dead are presently viewing the activities of believers on earth is not supported by other Scripture, and is to press the illustration in 12:1 beyond its necessary limits. The point of the statement is that the experience of these Old Testament saints testifies to us of the importance of persistent faith.

Under the figure of an athletic contest (*agōna*), each believer is likened to a participant in a footrace. **Putting off every weight** depicts the runner as removing all encumbrances in order to run efficiently. In classical Greek *ogkos* meant "mass," "weight," and it also came to mean "burden."[69] Whether the meaning in this passage could be restricted to the runner's excess bodily weight (i.e., obesity), or should be understood more generally of anything that might hamper his progress (such as loose clothing) is uncertain. In application the author probably has in mind those hindrances which may not be sinful in themselves (as distinguished from the next phrase) but which would prevent the progress that ought to occur. In the case of these readers

---

68. It is probably asserting too much to insist that it never denotes spectators, for that idea seems involved in II Timothy 2:2.

69. Heinrich Seesemann, "Ogkos," in *Theological Dictionary of the New Testament,* V, 41.

perhaps a too-great emphasis upon their ancestral traditions may have been one of the "weights."

The sin which so easily besets is difficult because *euperistaton* occurs nowhere else in the New Testament. The root of the adjective is *periistēmi*, "to stand around," "surround." The reference is probably not to some specific sin, but to the peculiar characteristic of all sin as continually surrounding men and so easily getting hold of them. The article with sin should then be understood as the generic use. As believers pursue the course of their Christian life, they must always be sensitive to the fact that sin constitutes an ever-present threat to their best efforts. Whether sin takes the form of sensual gratification or temptation to draw back in unbelief, each believer needs to run with endurance, mindful that it was this trait which characterized the Old Testament witnesses to whom God's testimony was given (11:39).

> . . . *looking away to Jesus, the Leader and Completer of the faith, who for* [the] *joy lying before him endured a cross, having despised* [the] *shame, and has sat down at the right hand of the throne of God.* (12:2)

The second incentive to encourage faithful persistence in suffering is a reminder of the experience of Jesus. As the Leader (*archēgon*) and Completer (*teleiōtēn*) of the faith, Christ has blazed the trail for us and has completed the course. Thus He appears in the Father's presence today, not only as our high priest to represent us, but also as our forerunner to open the way for us to follow (6:20). The term *archēgos* occurs four times in the New Testament (Acts 3:15; 5:31; Heb. 2:10; 12:2) and may have the sense of "originator" or of "leader" and "pioneer." Sometimes these meanings appear to coalesce. Here it is difficult to rule out either emphasis, inasmuch as "originator" agrees well with Completer as describing the full import of Christ's work, and Leader or pioneer also fits the context easily. On the whole it is best to understand the concept as a broad one, with the emphasis here being particularly upon the sense of pioneer or trailblazer to whom believers should look as they run in the contest of the Christian life.

Christ is also the Completer of the faith. As indicated in 2:10, He was "made complete" as our Savior, and has now entered heaven after accomplishing our eternal redemption. He was not only a perfect exemplar of faith Himself (by His perfect trust in the Father), but brought objective completion to the facts of the Christian faith (on which our subjective faith reposes) by His death, resurrection, and exaltation.

Christ provides us an incentive for faithful persistence through suffering by His own performance. He endured a cross, the most cruel and disgraceful of deaths, having despised [the] shame of it; that is, not allowing its shame to dissuade Him or cause Him to waver. He did it for [the] joy lying before him. The preposition *anti* (for) is used here in its developed meaning of "for the sake of," "because of."[70] The author does not refer to the prior bliss which our Lord enjoyed before His incarnation, but to His prospect of final victory when His redemptive work would be completed. This has now been accomplished, as evidenced by the fact that He has sat down at the right hand of the throne of God.

> *For consider him who has endured such hostility by sinners against himself, in order that you do not grow weary by becoming slack in your souls.* (12:3)

The readers should consider Christ, examining minutely and from all angles His example in relation to the hostility shown to Him by sinners. The term *antilogian* should not be restricted to opposition expressed in words (as the etymology might suggest), but should be understood as denoting all kinds of hostility of word and deed. The same term was used in the sense of "rebellion" to describe the case of Korah (Jude 11).

In place of the words against himself (*eis heauton*), several alternate readings give the phrase as a plural, either "against themselves" (*eis heautous*), or "against them" (*eis autous*). These plural forms are supported by impressive manuscript authority, including Sinaiticus, Beza, Papyrus 13, and Papyrus 46. In spite of this, the singular has been adopted by Erwin Nestle and Kurt Aland in the Greek New Testament edited by them (1963, 25th ed.) and the United Bible Societies text, and by the King James Version, American Standard Version (the plural appears in the margin), Revised Standard Version, and New American Standard Bible among English versions. It yields the best sense and avoids the difficulties of the alternate. However, if the plural is

---

70. Büchsel, "Anti," in *Theological Dictionary of the NT,* I, 372.

adopted, the meaning may have been suggested by the Scripture regarding Korah in Numbers 16:38 as "sinners against their own souls."

The purpose of considering the case of Jesus was to draw strength and encouragement that the readers may not grow weary (*kamēte* is probably a culminative aorist here, pointing to the consequence of becoming slack). The verb describes weariness and fatigue, sometimes even to the point of illness (see James 5:15). Becoming slack (*ekluomenoi*) utilizes a present participle, describing the process which may eventually produce this wearied condition. What is needed is a fresh commitment to Christ and a nurturing of faith so that testing and suffering do not defeat.

2. The explanation of suffering. (12:4-11)

Not yet have ye resisted unto blood striving against sin.
(12:4)

Although some regard this reference to resisting unto blood as perhaps a part of a continuing athletic metaphor, and interpret it to mean strenuously or to the utmost,[71] it is more likely a reference to martyrdom. Even though these readers had suffered much (10:32), none of them had paid with their lives. This would appear to rule out Jerusalem as the home of the original readers, for they had lost Stephen (Acts 7:60), James (Acts 12:2), and perhaps others by this time (Acts 26:10). Inasmuch as Jesus Himself had challenged His followers to take up their cross and follow Him (Luke 14:27), and none of these readers had yet endured as much physical suffering as Jesus had, the challenge was still pertinent.

And ye have forgotten the exhortation which is spoken to
you as to sons:
  "My son, do not treat lightly the Lord's discipline,
    Neither faint while being reproved by him.
  For he whom the Lord loves, he disciplines,
    And he scourges every son whom he receives."
  (12:5, 6)

---

71. Henry Alford, *The New Testament for English Readers,* p. 1570.

The exhortation is from Proverbs 3:11-12. Our author is explaining the sufferings which befall Christians as a part of the larger context of God's dealings with His sons. He, of course, is not suggesting that God is responsible for the evil which wicked men bring upon believers. He is, however, saying that God has incorporated even these circumstances as instruments to accomplish His will. Hence to treat lightly or to despise these circumstances that come into the believer's life is to display ignorance of God's means of ministering to His children.

The Lord's discipline refers to that instructive and correctional training which God administers. The term *paideia* was used in the Greek world to denote the upbringing and handling of a minor child, and included such aspects as direction, teaching, and chastisement.[72] The Septuagint has used this Greek term as best representing the concept of God as man's educator in Proverbs 3:11. In times of affliction caused by opponents to their faith, God's people are to realize that persecution is actually overruled by God and used for the training of believers. They must not faint while being reproved by him. Recognizing that God is in ultimate control of all conditions, and that He is using even adverse situations as part of the "all things" that work together for good to His children (Rom. 8:28), the believer is thus encouraged not to despair, compromise, or apostatize in the face of persecution.

Whom the Lord loves he disciplines is a much needed reminder in times of adversity. Instead of causing a believer to become disillusioned, adversity should be regarded as an indication that God loves him, and an evidence that He regards him as His son. It is all too common to conclude that sufferings are always sent by God as punishment for sin. It must be remembered that Christ, God's unique Son, learned through His suffering (2:10), and believers should adopt His mind on this matter.

The term scourges (*mastigoi*) refers literally to the act of flogging with a whip or lash. It is used here figuratively of God's chastising of His children. This clause, although an instance of Hebrew poetic parallelism in the quotation, seems to add the idea of corrective discipline to the more general reference to child training. The point is that proper training must include correction of faulty behavior. This

---

72. See the thorough treatment of this term by Georg Bertram in *Theological Dictionary of the NT,* V, 596-625.

should bring no discouragement, however, but realization that God is concerned about the healthy spiritual development of His children.

> *For discipline ye are enduring. As with sons God is dealing with you. For what son* [is there] *whom a father does not discipline? But if ye are without discipline, of which all have become partakers, then ye are bastards and not sons.* (12:7, 8)

Although the King James Version follows an alternate reading, *ei* ("if"), the better textual authorities support *eis* (for) as the first word of the verse. This yields a simple statement of purpose, rather than a conditional sentence. The sense is that it is for the purpose of training that you are asked of God to undergo suffering. Discipline (*paideian*) is used here in a sense slightly different from verse 5. There it referred to the process of disciplining; here it refers to the end or object in view. When believers are confronted with the prospect of enduring hardships, they must understand that it is not as punishment coming from God's wrath, but is a part of the heavenly Father's program of educating His sons. Even when that disciplining must involve correction for waywardness, the purpose is not the venting of God's anger, but the positive one of fostering spiritual maturity and preventing further sinfulness. The illustration from human practice is pertinent: what son [is there] whom a father does not discipline? Because the correctness of this principle is accepted by humans generally, God's children can reflect upon the analogy in the spiritual realm. The same thought is expressed in Deuteronomy 8:5 and II Samuel 7:14. By regarding suffering as God's means of training His sons, it can be more easily accepted and temptations to escape by compromise or apostasy can be avoided.

The common reaction is to be envious of the person who escapes suffering (or at least seems to). It involves the old problem of why the righteous suffer and the wicked prosper. The author reminds us that to be without discipline is to reveal something significant about one's father. Bastards are those who are born out of wedlock and have no legal father. They have no one who is responsible to train them properly. To the immature this may seem like a happy arrangement. What normal lad has not been secretly envious of the boy who never had to give any accounting for his actions to a sometimes stern father? There comes a time, however, when the wisdom of a disciplined life is clearly apparent, and the folly of an unchastened boyhood becomes tragically obvious. All of God's true children are called upon to be partakers of suffering at some time or other. To be otherwise is to demonstrate that such are not properly God's acknowledged sons.

> *Furthermore, we had the fathers of our flesh as discipliners, and we were respecting* [them]. *Shall we not much more be subject to the Father of our spirits and live? For they were disciplining us for a few days according to what seemed good to them, but he* [disciplines] *for what is profitable that we may partake of his holiness.* (12:9, 10)

Fathers of our flesh are our human fathers who have the responsibility of being discipliners during our childhood years. (See Proverbs 13:24. Mothers may discipline as well, but fathers are the head of the home and God holds them ultimately responsible.) And we were respecting [them]. Even when undergoing discipline which may involve chastising, never a pleasant experience, it is normal for children to continue respecting their parents. It is not usual for a spanking to cause a child to abandon his home.

The argument is *a fortiori.* How much greater reason do we have for being subject to the authority and training of the Father of our spirits. Although this statement has been used in the interests of creationism as opposed to traducianism,[73] such hardly seems to be in view here. The expression is contrasted to "the fathers of our flesh," and the contrast intended is between our human fathers and our spiritual Father. Father of our spirits reminds us that it is only through our spirits that we have come into an intelligent relationship with God and can understand and profit from His dealings with us. And live. This living must be interpreted in the light of the previous context, in which it is made clear that one is either a son of the Father and thus a sharer of His life and nature, or else is spiritually a bastard without God as his father. It has also been asserted that all who are true sons of God are partakers of His disciplining. Only those who are born of God by His Spirit (John 3:5, 6) and are thereby obedient to God (Rom. 15:18) are spiritually

---

73. Creationism holds that God creates each human spirit directly; only the body is procreated by the parents. Traducianism holds that the entire person is descended from Adam and thus procreated by the parents.

alive. If we are truly God's sons, then we have acknowledged Him as our Father, together with His right to our obedience.

There is also a difference both in the scope and in the quality of the discipline meted out by human fathers and by God. **They** [our human fathers] **were disciplining us for a few days.** The comparatively short time of childhood is in view, when as children still at home, the offspring were subject to parental supervision. The discipline exercised by fathers was **according to what seemed good to them.** Sometimes these fatherly efforts at securing proper conduct from their children are carried out intelligently, sometimes not. Yet in all cases we understand their prerogative and recognize that respect is due them. Even in the cases where human discipline is not wisely performed, the principle of parental authority is still accepted.

With God, however, no allowances are necessary. He always disciplines in accord with **what is profitable,** and His methods are always wise. God's goal is that we may **partake of his holiness.** Holiness is the basic characteristic of God's nature, and because He has shared His nature with us by regeneration, it is incumbent upon believers to reflect increasingly His holiness in their lives (I Peter 1:15, 16). The particular aspect of holiness in view here is probably "the goal for which God is preparing His people—that entire sanctification which is consummated in their manifestation with Christ in glory."[74]

Now all discipline for the present seems to be not [a matter] *of joy but of grief, but afterward it yields peaceable fruit to those who have been exercised by it—*[the fruit] *of righteousness.* (12:11)

All discipline, whether inflicted by human fathers or by God, is unpleasant while it is in process. Scripture does not require believers to enjoy the experience of trial—only its outcome. It is afterward that its values are clearly seen. The product is here called **peaceable fruit,** perhaps in contrast to the violence experienced during the chastening. It may also suggest the spiritual quality of peace which the believer experiences when he knows that all is right between him and God. **Righteousness** is appositional to **fruit,** and refers to that righteousness

---

74. F. F. Bruce, *The Epistle to the Hebrews,* p. 359.

of life which is encouraged by God's disciplining. Another reference to "the fruit of righteousness" occurs in James 3:18, where peacemakers (in contrast to strife causers) are said to be planting a crop which will issue in the fruit of righteousness. Jesus spoke of the Father's purging work that enables His branches to bear more fruit (John 15:2). God's discipline is purifying in its aim. Of course, this aim is accomplished only if there is an appropriate response in the sufferer. Those who have been exercised by the disciplining are those who have regarded it rightly, and have been sensitive to God's purposes instead of reacting with bitterness and complaint. Exercised (*gegumnasmenois*) again reflects the athletic metaphor with which the author began the chapter.

3. The Christian's response to suffering. (12:12-17)

Wherefore, straighten out the slack hands and the paralyzed knees, and make straight paths for your feet, in order that what is lame not be turned out of the way, but rather be cured. (12:12, 13)

The Christian needs to prepare himself so as to profit from God's disciplining when it comes. In order to be properly "exercised" (v. 11), he must not be spiritually "out of condition." The language is drawn from Isaiah 35:3, and describes the slack hands and paralyzed knees of one who is spiritually in danger of collapse. The exhortation calls for a strengthening of their inner resolve so that they may face their challenges bravely.

Make straight paths for your feet. Here the allusion is to Proverbs 4:26. The reference is to one's course of conduct. If one's feet are lame, special care must be taken that the path on which they walk has no dangerous obstacles. Spiritually speaking, the one whose faith is weak must not venture into areas where his spiritual strength is insufficient. Otherwise the weak believer may be turned out of the way in which he ought to go (or to render by a medical metaphor, the lame believer may aggravate his lameness into a dislocation of his limbs[75]). Instead the aim should be that the lame be cured. God's disciplining will do this if

---

75. It is possible that *ektrepō* is used in the medical sense of a dislocated limb. See Arndt and Gingrich, *Greek-English Lexicon*, p. 245.

it is received properly. (Some view verse 13 as describing the danger of offending weaker brethren who may be turned aside by the example of those who are "slack" and "paralyzed,"[76] but the above explanation meets the demands of the language without the necessity of seeing two groups of people.)

> *Pursue peace with all, and the sanctification without which no one shall see the Lord, seeing to it lest anyone be excluded from the grace of God, lest any root of bitterness springing up cause trouble, and through it many be defiled, . . .* (12:14, 15)

The believer should respond to all of God's dealings with him by continually endeavoring to pursue peace with all. All can be understood generally to include believers and persecutors as the objects of our peaceable intentions. It is more likely, however, that the main thrust of the admonition here is toward fellow believers, inasmuch as the local church seems to be primarily the sphere of the author's reference in verses 13 and 16. Now peace must not be promoted at the expense of holiness. Therefore it must be coupled with the sanctification whose importance is such that without it no one shall see the Lord.

The definite article (*ton*) with sanctification (*hagiasmon*) is probably intended to recall the mention in verse 10 of God's "holiness" (*hagiotētos*), of which believers partake. The Biblical doctrine of sanctification teaches that all believers have obtained God's holiness judicially (i.e., past sanctification). However, Scripture is also clear that there is a present sanctification which is to be demonstrated, as well as a future sanctification to be consummated. It is obviously the present aspect which is emphasized here, for this sanctification is something to be pursued. The believer's present life is to become progressively more Christ-like, and should increasingly conform to the perfect standing which is already possessed in Christ.

No one shall see the Lord without possessing this sanctification. Of course, the author is not talking about any sort of righteousness produced by mere human works. Sanctification itself is made possible only by the Word of God acting upon the life of the believer who submits to the Spirit's control. Scripture makes it clear that the process

---

76. Pink, *Exposition of Hebrews*, p. 990.

is completed only when we see Christ and are finally changed into His perfect likeness. Nevertheless, the process must go on now in the life of each believer, for every Christian is a "new creature" (II Cor. 5:17). If this is not evidenced by his life, there is grave reason to doubt his claim.

At verse 15 the writer begins his transition to the warning passage which actually starts at 12:18. It is the Christian reader's responsibility to be concerned about the spiritual welfare of the whole congregation, seeing to it[77] that no one be excluded from the grace of God. The reference is to those who may have made a beginning in the Christian community, but may through fear of persecution or faintheartedness in suffering be tempted to defect and thus fall short of true salvation. They would be shut out of the blessings provided by God's saving grace, and demonstrate to all that they really had never been made new creatures in Christ. To illustrate their situation the author borrows some terminology from Deuteronomy 29:18 describing apostate Israel in the wilderness: "Lest there should be among you man, or woman, or family, or tribe, whose heart turneth away this day from the Lord our God, to go and serve the gods of these nations; lest there should be among you a root that beareth gall and wormwood." A root of bitterness embodied in someone who was not really born again might start growing in their midst and become a source of infection to others. The result could be that many would be spiritually defiled by the unbelief of one or a few. Apostasy in doctrine or in conduct is usually contagious. A leader always manages to get some followers.

> . . . lest [there be] *any fornicator or profane one like Esau,*
> *who for one meal gave away his birthright. For you know*
> *that even afterward when wishing to inherit the blessing, he*
> *was rejected, for he found no place of repentance, although*
> *he sought it with tears.* (12:16, 17)

Was Esau intended to be illustrative of both a fornicator and a profane one, or only of the latter? The sense of fornicator (*pornos*) is also debated. Its consistent New Testament usage is with the literal sense, as also in 13:4. Some would point to a metaphorical sense of

---

77. The participle is from *episkopeō*, used elsewhere in the sense of to oversee, care for, or serve as a bishop.

idolatry, as in Judges 2:17,[78] or suggest that profane one (*bebēlos*) was intended to explain the sense of this spiritual fornication.[79] To me it seems preferable to take fornicator in its literal sense, but to explain **Esau** as illustrative only of the profane one. Certainly the explanation of the birthright incident illustrates only Esau's profaneness, and there is no Old Testament evidence of Esau as a fornicator, unless the term is considerably stretched to include his unfortunate marriages to two Hittite women (Gen. 26:34, 35).

Esau demonstrated his nonsacred interests when he traded away his **birthright** for a single meal (Gen. 25:29-34). To be **profane** meant to be completely concerned with temporal and material matters, with no thought for spiritual values. It describes those whose response to God was nonexistent. Esau was so involved in the immediate satisfaction of his momentary hunger that he treated as of negligible value his rights as a firstborn son, and his responsibility as the heir to receive the blessing of the Abrahamic covenant. He preferred immediate material possessions over the sacred rights that were more deeply meaningful.

Esau **afterward** came to regret his bargain but was unable to change it (Gen. 27:30-40). Even though Jacob had tricked his father and had secured the **blessing** (Gen. 27:6-29) that had been intended by Isaac for his brother, Esau found no place of repentance. There was repentance on his part, for he obviously had changed his mind about his relinquished birthright and desired to have the blessing that it provided; but he found no opportunity or place (*topon*) for his remorseful tears to change the situation. Some decisions, once they are made, are irrevocable. It has been suggested that the "repentance" here refers to a change of mind in his father Isaac, but this is not quite as obvious as the above explanation, inasmuch as Isaac is not mentioned in the passage. It could hardly be understood as Esau's rejection by God in spite of repentance, for the matter of salvation is not the point here.

FIFTH WARNING PASSAGE (12:18-29)

The fifth and final warning passage now urges the readers to think seriously about the importance of heeding what God has spoken, in

---

78. F. F. Bruce, *The Epistle to the Hebrews,* p. 366, fn. 109 (although Bruce himself does not adopt this view).

79. Lenski, *Interpretation of Hebrews,* pp. 446-447.

view of their immeasurably better position in comparison to believers of former years. Their present spiritual privileges, in addition to the lesson provided by the awesome scene at Sinai, should combine to emphasize the importance of absolute compliance with every word from God.

a. The scene at Sinai. (12:18-21)

For ye have not come to what is touched and to fire that is set aflame and to darkness and gloom and storm and a noise of a trumpet and a sound of words, which those who heard begged that there not be added a word to them. (12:18, 19)

Although the word "mountain" does not appear in our oldest and most reliable texts,[80] it is clear that the incident at Sinai recorded in Exodus 19:10-25; 20:18-21; and Deuteronomy 4:10-24 is in view. That was a day unequaled in Jewish history, when God demonstrated His awesome power in conjunction with His giving of the law. The rugged heights of Sinai rocked with thunder and crackled with lightning which set the mount aflame. God's presence descended upon the mountain in fire and smoke accompanied by an earthquake. The smoke doubtless produced the darkness (Exod. 20:21) and gloom, and the mighty flames would cause strong air currents that would produce a most frightening storm.

The sound of a trumpet, possibly blown by an angel, grew louder and louder (Exod. 19:19); and when Moses spoke, God answered him with a sound of words (Deut. 4:12). These words were so terrifying that the Israelites begged Moses henceforth to act as God's spokesman rather than have God address them directly (Exod. 20:19).

For they could not bear what was being commanded: "And if a beast should touch the mountain, it shall be stoned." And—so frightful was the spectacle—Moses said, "I am terrified and trembling." (12:20, 21)

What was being commanded refers to the regulations regarding the people's conduct at the mount (Exod. 19:9-13), rather than to the Ten

---

80. Although missing from P[46], Aleph, A, and C, *orei* (mountain) does occur in the Byzantine and Western families.

Mount Sinai, probable site of an awesome display of God's power at the giving of the law (Heb. 12:18-21).

Commandments (Deut. 4:12, 13). This is made clear by the remainder of the statement, which includes a citation of one of the commands having to do with the people's preparations at Sinai. These preparations included restrictions against sexual relations immediately prior to the divine visitation (Exod. 19:15), and against anyone's approaching the mount too closely (Exod. 19:12, 13). The people were also required to wash their clothes and sanctify themselves (Exod. 19:10). The fearsomeness of what was about to happen was emphasized by the warning regarding animals. **If a beast should touch the mountain, it shall be stoned.** The gap which separates the majestic and holy God from sinful men was also pictured by this commandment. The straying **beast** itself was not to be touched by men, but was to be **stoned** to death. Perhaps this was also a safeguard against any person's trespassing beyond the boundary to retrieve his animal. The Exodus account specifies either stoning or shooting with a dart, neither of which required physical touching by the slayer (Exod. 19:13).

Even **Moses,** in spite of his being taken into God's confidence, was not unmoved by the frightful nature of this spectacle. Our author quotes him as saying, **I am terrified and trembling.** This exact statement is not found in the Old Testament record of these Sinai events. Several solutions suggest themselves. (1) The statement could have been drawn from traditional records (not as yet identified), which were nevertheless trustworthy, at least on this point. This would be paralleled by numerous other New Testament instances where such data are mentioned. (2) The author may have used language drawn from several experiences of Moses which are here telescoped. Part of the statement is similar to Moses' response when he saw the people's idolatry with the golden calf (Deut. 9:19). Stephen said that Moses "trembled" at the burning bush (Acts 7:32), although that precise feature is not mentioned in the Old Testament account (Exod. 3:6). (3) Exodus 19:16 states that when the stupendous phenomena occurred at Sinai, "all the people that was in the camp trembled"; and this would have included Moses also.

This awesome and frightening scene which accompanied the giving of the law at Sinai was not the situation of these Christian readers. They had not come to "what is touched," that is, to the physical and material matters which characterized the Mosaic system. Their better position is next explained, and then shown to involve even greater responsibility to God.

b. The position of Christians. (12:22-24)

But ye have come to Mount Zion, and [the] *city of* [the] *living God,* [the] *heavenly Jerusalem, and to myriads of angels in festal gathering, . . .* (12:22)

As Mount Sinai symbolized God's dealings with men under the Mosaic covenant, and particularly its fearsome, earthly, and temporal aspects, so **Mount Zion** symbolizes the final grace and blessing in salvation, the accomplished realities in contrast to types and shadows. Geographically, **Zion** is one of the hills on which Jerusalem is built. It was the site of the citadel which David and his men captured in order to make the city his capital (II Sam. 5:6-9). In Hebrews, however, it is used symbolically of [the] city of [the] living God, [the] heavenly Jerusalem. (In the Greek text no articles are used in the paragraph [vv. 22-24] except with the name "Abel," a feature emphasizing the rich qualitative import of all these terms.) This symbolic use is similar to that of Paul in Galatians 4:24-26, in which "Jerusalem which is above" is described as the "mother" of all present believers who are not under the bondage of Sinai. Even the differences in the symbols do much to emphasize the different character of the old economy and the new, for there could have been no city on craggy Sinai; but Zion was the location of Jerusalem whose "beautiful situation" was extolled frequently in the Old Testament (cf. Ps. 48:2).

This city of [the] **living God** was that to which Abraham and the patriarchs looked (11:10, 16). Christian believers are here said to have come to it, but there is a sense in which its full enjoyment is future for them also, as 13:14 indicates. In Revelation 21:2 it is referred to as the "new Jerusalem." This **city** is the habitation of the **living God** (Rev. 21:22, 23), but is also the final home of the saints of all ages, as the following context in Hebrews reveals. Walvoord writes:

> The subsequent description of the new Jerusalem in this chapter [Rev. 21] makes plain that saints of all ages are involved and that what we have here is not the church per se but a city or dwelling place having the freshness and beauty of a bride adorned for marriage to her husband.[81]

Pentecost states, "The city is to be inhabited by God, by the church, by the redeemed of Israel, and by the redeemed of all ages, together with the unfallen angels."[82]

Myriads of angels begins the listing of the inhabitants of the heavenly Jerusalem. Difference of opinion centers on whether *panēgurei*

---

81. J. F. Walvoord, *The Revelation of Jesus Christ,* p. 313.
82. J. Dwight Pentecost, *Things to Come,* p. 576.

should go with "angels" or with "church." Conclusive criteria are not available, but on the whole the construing of the term with "angels" seems preferable. The sense then is **myriads of angels in festal gathering.** This is somewhat similar to the presence of angels at Sinai (see comments on 2:2), although here the emphasis is on festive celebration rather than awesome majesty.

> ... *and to* [the] *church of firstborn ones registered in heaven, and to* [the] *Judge,* [the] *God of all, and to* [the] *spirits of righteous men made perfect,* ... (12:23)

The **church** appears to be a reference to living New Testament believers. They are viewed as still on earth, but their names are registered in heaven (cf. Luke 10:20); and thus they will also inhabit the heavenly Jerusalem. This is in harmony with 13:14, where it is stated the present believers still await certain aspects of the city which is "to come." They are **firstborn ones,** enjoying the rights of firstborn sons, because of their union with Christ, the Firstborn (Col. 1:15). These Jewish Christian readers were a part of this church.

Through faith in Christ, they had come to the one who is the **Judge,** [the] **God of all.** There is no other God, and hence all are responsible to Him. The readers should think soberly about the consequences of forsaking the new covenant for the old. One cannot abandon this Judge and escape His judgment.

The **spirits of righteous men made perfect** is a reference to Old Testament saints with whom we share salvation. They are called **spirits** because they have not yet been united with their bodies in resurrection. They are **made perfect** in their spirits, however, because Christ's sacrifice for sins has actually accomplished the removal of their sin (see comments on 11:40).

> ... *and to* [the] *mediator of a new covenant, Jesus, and to* [the] *blood of sprinkling speaking a better thing than Abel.* (12:24)

By becoming Christians the readers had come into relationship with Jesus, the **mediator** of the **new covenant.** This is the only time in the New Testament that *neos* is used instead of *kainos* to describe this covenant. The usual distinction between these terms is that *neos* denotes what is recent or new in time, while *kainos* describes what is new in quality or nature.[83] The choice of *neos* here emphasizes the fresh and recent character of the revelation in Jesus Christ. His blood, which validated the new covenant for all those who by faith have qualified for its cleansing effects, is speaking a message far better than the blood of Abel, which also spoke. Abel's martyr blood testified of his faith (11:4), but in this reference seems undoubtedly to refer to its mute cry for vengeance. "The voice of thy brother's blood crieth unto me from the ground" (Gen. 4:10). Abel's blood cried out for vengeance, but Christ's blood promises pardon and cleansing.

c. The consequent duties of Christians. (12:25-29)

See that ye refuse not him who is speaking. For if those did not escape when they refused him who was giving divine instruction on earth, much more we [shall not escape] *who turn aside from him* [who gives divine instruction] *from heaven.* (12:25)

The person who is speaking is certainly God (not Moses or Christ). This seems assured from a comparison with verse 19, where it was God's speaking, not Moses' mediatorship that Israel refused (Exod. 20:19). The word refuse (*paraitēsesthe*) is the same as used of Israel in verse 19 (*pareitēsanto*, "begged off"). There is also an undoubted play on the "speaking" in verse 24, where the blood of Jesus is said to be still speaking to men.

Those who did not escape refers to the Israelites who experienced various temporal judgments because they refused him who was giving divine instruction. Perhaps it should not be limited to the experiences of Mount Sinai (11:18-21), but understood as including the numerous subsequent incidents in the wilderness and beyond (golden calf, strange fire, etc.). On earth has a somewhat unstable position in the manuscripts. It appears immediately following "did not escape" in many ancient texts, thus suggesting the sense to be "they did not escape on earth." However, our oldest manuscript of Hebrews (Papyrus 46), and the Textus Receptus construe it with "giving divine instruction." The

---

83. Johannes Behm, "Kainos," in *Theological Dictionary of the NT,* III, 447.

latter construction is more in harmony with what appears to be the obvious parallelism with **from heaven** in the next clause.

If God is the speaker in both instances, how can we explain **on earth** in the case of the Old Testament incident? The answer seems to be that the author regards God as descending upon Sinai (see Exod. 19:11, 18, 20), and His speaking of the law was from a geographical locale. Christians, however, have responded to God who speaks to men in Christ (1:2); and Christ has ascended into heaven itself (4:14; 6:20; 7:26; 9:24). The gospel message goes out empowered by the heaven-sent Holy Spirit (I Peter 1:12). The argument is similar to that in 2:2, 3, where the admitted gravity of obedience to the Mosaic law was shown to argue for an even greater obligation to heed the revelation of God in Christ.

> *Whose voice then shook the earth, but now he has promised saying, "Yet once I will shake not only the earth but also the heaven." Now this "yet once" indicates the removing of the things being shaken as things that have been made, in order that the things which are not shaken may remain.* (12:26, 27)

The author is still developing his argument from the events of Sinai, and particularly the physical phenomena that occurred. **Whose voice then shook the earth** refers to the literal earthquake which shook the whole mountain (Exod. 19:18), a feature corroborated by other Old Testament passages (Judg. 5:4, 5; Pss. 68:8, 9; 77:18; 114:7). **Now** refers to the passage in Haggai 2:6 which is here cited. The citation speaks of a far more thorough shaking in judgment, affecting not just one mountain but the **heaven** (atmospheric, astral) as well. Although some[84] interpret the prophecy metaphorically as referring to the up-heavals accomplished by Christ's first coming in its effect upon Jewish worship and politics, the parallelism with the former shaking makes this view unlikely. The first shaking was physical and geographical at Sinai. There is no good reason to take this second shaking of the earth and the heavens above it in any less literal sense. The reference then is to the second coming of Christ, which will involve great physical judgments as

---

84. So Owen, *Exposition of Hebrews,* VII, 364-366.

foretold by the prophets in both the Old Testament and the New Testament. The employment of now (*nun*) is in contrast to then (*tote*), and may infer that the author already regards the last days as upon them.[85]

The author picks up the yet once from his quotation of Haggai 2:6, and uses it to stress the fact that the new shaking mentioned by the prophet will be the final one. In this coming judgment there will be a removing of all that does not survive this experience of being divinely shaken. The language reminds one of what happens when a tree with many dead leaves and branches is buffeted by a high wind, or when an animal shakes itself to remove water or loose hair from its fur.

As things that have been made is somewhat parenthetical, but almost certainly goes with what precedes (removing) rather than with the purpose clause which follows. By interpreting this eschatologically as explained above, the particular reference is found to be to the divine judgments to come upon the material universe and all that it contains. To speak of the material creation as transitory is in agreement with the author's argument in 1:10-12, "They will perish, but thou remainest." It is not dissimilar to his comment in 9:11 regarding heaven as "the greater and more perfect tabernacle not made with hands, that is, not of this creation." This created physical universe will be the focus of God's final shaking depicted by the prophet.

> *Wherefore, inasmuch as we are receiving an unshakable kingdom, let us be grateful, by which we may offer service well pleasing to God with reverence and awe. For indeed our God is a consuming fire.* (12:28, 29)

What will survive this shaking? The answer is the unshakable kingdom which believers are receiving (*paralambanontes*). The present tense of the participle suggests that Christians are even now receiving it, but also that its full reception is not as yet complete. They are presently heirs and citizens, but the final experiencing of the full inheritance is still awaiting.

Let us be grateful is a legitimate way of rendering *echōmen charin*, which the King James Version has translated "let us have grace." Of the

---

85. This attitude regarding the "last days" was shared by Peter (Acts 2:17), John (I John 2:18), and Paul (I Tim. 4:1; II Tim. 3:1-5).

six other New Testament occurrences of this phrase, four are clearly with the sense of "be grateful" (Luke 17:9; I Tim. 1:12; II Tim. 1:3; III John 4), and two with the meaning of "receive grace, favor, or benefaction" (Acts 2:47; II Cor. 1:15). Either meaning is agreeable to the context in Hebrews. In 4:16 the readers have been urged to come to the throne where grace is dispensed, and thus be enabled to serve God acceptably. On the other hand, 13:15 speaks of serving God through praising Him. Our communion with Him, while a happy and blessed privilege, must always be accompanied with reverence and awe, for we must never forget who He is. **Our God is a consuming fire,** just as was revealed at Sinai. He is the same God, who still regards with utmost seriousness the response of His children. The statement is a quotation of Deuteronomy 4:24, drawn from the same passage utilized earlier in the discussion of the awesome events of Sinai. God's fiery holiness was demonstrated to Israel at Sinai, was reiterated in New Testament times (Luke 3:16, 17), and must not be forgotten by Christians. Believers need not be filled with terror at God's coming judgment, but its prospect should instill in them a healthy respect for His absolute holiness. Surely any temptation to refuse God's final revelation in Christ should be most soberly weighed in the light of this warning.

E. AN EXHORTATION TO PERFORM CHRISTIAN DUTIES. (13:1-17)

1. Social duties. (13:1-6)

> *Let the brotherly love continue. Do not be forgetful of the friendliness to strangers, for by this some have entertained angels unawares. Keep remembering the prisoners, as having been bound with* [them]; [and] *those being ill-treated as also yourselves being in a body.* (13:1-3)

The first of these admonitions concerns the display of love and sympathy. The passage may reflect the tendency of some in times of persecution to show indifference to their persecuted brethren, and thus escape suffering themselves. This would be especially tempting to Jewish Christians who were toying with the idea of reverting to Judaism. They would then avoid persecution from Gentiles for pursuing an unrecognized religion, as well as from their Jewish kinsmen who despised their Christian commitment.

Brotherly love (*philadelphia*) denotes the display of kindness, sympathy, and helpfulness. The concept is presented frequently in the New Testament as expected among all Christians (Rom. 12:10; I Thess. 4:9; I Peter 1:22; II Peter 1:7). The reality of the spiritual brotherhood among those who are born of God makes such an admonition eminently reasonable. This love must not grow slack, even when its exercise proves dangerous. To urge that it continue does not suggest that it has ceased, but does caution against any such eventuality.

Two areas for special application of this injunction are mentioned. **Friendliness to strangers** broadens the reference to include not only the local Christian brotherhood, but also traveling believers. In the empire travel was not as uncommon as might be supposed. (For instance, Aquila and Priscilla are seen in the New Testament as moving about from Rome to Corinth [Acts 18:2], to Ephesus [Acts 18:18, 19], back to Rome [Rom. 16:3], and then to Ephesus again [II Tim. 4:19].) Public accommodations were not always safe and often were morally offensive to Christians. To encourage such hospitality, reference is made to the fact that by courteous welcoming of visitors some have entertained angels unawares.[86] Biblical examples are the cases of Abraham (Gen. 18:1-3), Lot (Gen. 19:1-2), Gideon (Judg. 6:11-24), and Manoah (Judg. 13:6-20). The author does not mean that Christians should entertain strangers chiefly with the hope of being honored with supernatural visitors, but he has mentioned this feature to show how God is pleased when this sort of love is displayed.

Another opportunity to exhibit real brotherly love was provided when any of their number were taken as **prisoners.** These readers were to continue giving whatever assistance they could to their persecuted and imprisoned brethren. In earlier days their conduct in this regard had been exemplary (10:32-34). They must not let threats of personal danger cause them to withhold their love now. **As having been bound with** [them] does not mean that they had once been prisoners themselves (certainly that would not have been true of all the readers), but is

---

86. Greek: *elathon tines xenisantes angelous.* This utilizes a classical idiom in which the main idea is found in the participle "entertained" rather than in the verb.

a reminder that they were really in union with the prisoners, so that when "one member suffereth, all the members suffer with it" (I Cor. 12:26). As also yourselves being in a body. Those who thus far had escaped imprisonment might be stimulated to be sympathetic by the sober reminder that they possessed no inherent immunity to suffering, for they were still in a physical body and thus susceptible to similar treatment. There is no warrant for understanding *en sōmati* as though it meant "the body of Christ," as that idea is not as clear in this passage as the explanation above.

> [Let] *marriage* [be] *honorable among all, and the bed undefiled, for fornicators and adulterers God will judge.* (13:4)

No verb appears in the first clause, although some form of the copula "to be" seems warranted. Should the statement be regarded as declaration or exhortation? If the indicative "is" is supplied ("marriage is honorable in all," KJV), the statement becomes a refutation of asceticism by asserting that there is nothing unwholesome or tainted about the marriage relation. If the imperative "let . . . be" is supplied (see translation above, also ASV), the statement is understood as a command to purity. The latter seems considerably more suited to the context. The whole section is hortatory in nature. Furthermore, the next clause is introduced by for (*gar*), indicating a logical connection (not "but," as KJV). Hence we should regard fornicators and adulterers as examples of offenders against the author's injunction. It was against those sins which defiled marriage before it was established (fornicators, *pornous*), or after it had been consummated (adulterers, *moichous*) that this injunction was aimed, rather than against ascetics who had no use for marriage at all. It should be observed, however, that the order to keep marriage honorable and the marriage bed undefiled by any act of unfaithfulness implies that marriage is inherently pure unless sin sullies it. Thus ascetic views which impugn the sanctity of marriage are also ruled out by this passage, even though that was probably not the chief purpose of the writer at this juncture.

God will judge these defilers of marriage. They often escape detection on earth, but they do not avoid God's notice nor His eventual judgment.

[Let] *your way of life* [be] *without money-love;* [be]
*content with the things at hand; for he himself has said, "I
will never desert you, nor ever abandon you." So that being
of good courage we say, "The Lord is a helper to me, and I
will not fear. What shall man do to me?"* (13:5, 6)

Passing from faithfulness in marriage, the author now moves to the
need for contentment in the lives of his readers. Perhaps the monetary
losses of these Christians (10:34) had discouraged their liberality, and
had caused them to concentrate unduly on replacing their lost wealth.
Certainly the poverty of many early Christians, coupled with the
not-unlikely taunts of their richer enemies, must have made this a
frequent problem. **Money-love** (*aphilarguros*) is not confined to a by-
gone era. Modern society, with its almost total emphasis upon material
benefits, has had its influence upon believers as well as others. In
contrast, the believer is to find his satisfaction not in some hoped-for
wealth, but is to be **content with the things at hand.** By estimating
properly the relative importance of material wealth and spiritual realities, he is able to find contentment in whatever goods God may have
provided him in this life (Phil. 4:19); for these things are of limited
significance when viewed with a truly spiritual eye.

Encouragement is found in the promise of God made to Joshua, and
recorded in Deuteronomy 31:6, 8: **I will never desert you, nor ever
abandon you.**[87] The same promise was cited by David to his son
Solomon (I Chron. 28:20). The assurance of God's personal presence
and care should prevent materialistic notions that wealth alone can
solve our problems.

We should be able to make the words of the psalmist our own: **The
Lord is a helper to me and I will not fear. What shall man do to me?**
(Ps. 118:6). Fainthearted Jewish converts who were tempted to forsake
Christ and return to Judaism through fear of persecution should take
note that such an act would be to turn away from the attitude of the
Old Testament psalmist also.

---

87. The quotation is given in Hebrews in a slightly different form, although
it is exactly the same as found in Philo. Rather than suppose the author to have
utilized Philo, it is more likely that this saying from the Old Testament had
acquired popular usage as a proverb, and both Philo and Hebrews employ this
prevalent form.

2. Religious duties. (13:7-17)

Remember your leaders, who spoke to you the word of God, whose faith continue imitating while considering the outcome of their manner of life. (13:7)

The discussion now turns from the practical and personal duties of individual Christians to a consideration of those matters pertaining to the religious aspect of their lives. In view are the various relationships they bear within the Christian society.

First, they need to remember their former leaders, and draw encouragement from their faithful example. The King James Version leaves the impression that these leaders are still living. However, a number of factors argue for the view that these have now died. (1) The readers are urged to **remember** them. (2) Present leaders are referred to in verse 17. (3) **Outcome** (*ekbasis*) is used elsewhere in the sense of "death" (Wisdom 2:17), and that meaning is readily understandable here. (4) The present participle (*tōn hēgoumenōn*) is often used as a substantive: "leaders."

It was their first **leaders** who had brought to these readers the **word of God.** They needed to remember the results of those early days, how a real work of God's grace had been accomplished through the ministry of their faithful leaders. Eventually these leaders had passed from the scene. It need not be inferred that they had all died martyrs' deaths, although some may have. The real importance was that all had been faithful to the end. None had wavered and given up faith in Christ. Let these readers **continue imitating** that steadfast example. May not even one fail to arrive at the goal. May each one "hold fast the beginning of the confidence firm until the end" (3:14). As their leaders and as the patriarchs of old (11:13), they should take courage that they too might "die in faith."

Jesus Christ, yesterday and today the same, and forever. Be not carried aside by various and strange teachings. For it is good for the heart to be made firm by grace, not by meats, in which those who were walking were not profited. (13:8, 9)

There is an easy transition from the former teachers to the true doctrine which they taught. Perhaps some had a tendency to feel that times had changed since their first encounter with the Christian faith, and that their former leaders' faith was no longer relevant to them. If so, they are here reminded that Jesus Christ, the very one who was proclaimed by the leaders of yesterday, has not changed. His person, and consequently the doctrine about Him, remains the same even today. And because He is the eternal Son of God, He remains the same forever. Faith reposed in Him needs no basic alterations; it merely needs to grow continually firmer.

The problem was that false teaching had appeared. It was various and strange because it came in great variety and was in essence foreign to the gospel of the grace of God in Christ. Because it centered on meats (*brōmasin*), it seems clear that at its heart was an attempt to elevate Judaism at the expense of true Christianity. It appears certain that some sort of ceremonial distinctives are in view rather than asceticism, particularly in view of verse 10. However, this might be merely one aspect of an even larger movement. Paul wrote to the Colossians about those who made unwarranted judgments about meat and drink (Col. 2:16). He told the Corinthians that meat per se has no spiritual value either positive or negative (I Cor. 8:8). Those who were walking were the Old Testament Jews who blindly followed the ritual. They were not profited, for ceremonialism alone did not bring them salvation. It is not by observing distinctions about meats that men grow strong spiritually. It is by grace—God's favor bestowed upon believers in Christ—that Christians are brought to maturity. The readers needed greater stability in doctrine.

We have an altar from which they who serve the tabernacle have no authority to eat. For of which animals the blood is brought for sins into the sanctuary by the high priest, of these the bodies are burned outside the camp. (13:10, 11)

The author now calls upon his readers to recognize their need for separation to Christ. *We have an altar* is a clause posing considerable hermeneutical difficulty. *We* is commonly regarded as meaning "we Christians" as distinguished from Jews, and then *altar* is interpreted in several ways. Many Roman Catholics[88] and Greek Orthodox[89] writers explain it as the communion table, although the author's consistent purpose throughout the letter has been to show that Christians possess the spiritual realities in sharp contrast to physical types and shadows. How strange it would be for the author now to say that the reality is merely another physical ceremony. Another explanation regards the altar as either the cross[90] (i.e., the place of sacrifice) or as Christ[91] (the sacrifice itself), or perhaps as a combination of both ideas. These views regard they who serve the tabernacle as adherents to the Levitical system who are thereby cut off from participation in the benefits of Christ's sacrifice. Verse 10 is thus seen as contrasting Christians with Jews.

Another possibility notes that verse 11 is introduced by the explanatory conjunction for (gar), and regards it as providing the interpretation for verse 10. The statement is then understood to be a reference to a particular Old Testament ritual which serves as an illustration of the author's point.[92] We is understood to mean "we Jews in our national heritage and practice."[93] Reference is made to the sin offering on the annual Day of Atonement. In contrast to the sin offerings made by rulers and by common people at other times of the year which were eaten by the priests (Lev. 4:22-35; 6:25-26), there were certain specific sin offerings which were not to be eaten at all. These included the sin offering of the priest himself (Lev. 4:3-7, 12), the sin offering for the whole congregation (Lev. 4:13-21), and the sin offering for the high priest and congregation combined on the Day of Atonement (Lev. 16:27). The author's particular interest in the Day of Atonement ritual (see 7:27; 9:7, 25; 10:1-3) makes it likely that it was this which he had

---

88. James Cardinal Gibbons, *The Faith of Our Fathers,* p. 358; Dom Aelred Cody, "Hebrews," in *A New Catholic Commentary on Holy Scripture,* ed. Reginald C. Fuller, p. 1238.

89. Apostolos Makrakis, *Interpretation of the Entire New Testament,* II, 1890.

90. E.g., Alford, *NT for English Readers,* pp. 1584-1585.

91. E.g., F. F. Bruce, *The Epistle to the Hebrews,* pp. 399-400.

92. So A. C. Downer, *The Principle of Interpretation of the Epistle to the Hebrews,* pp. 133-146; Newell, *Hebrews Verse by Verse,* pp. 448-450.

93. W. H. Griffith Thomas, however, regards "we have" as merely a literary alternative to "there is." *Hebrews, A Devotional Commentary,* p. 176.

in mind in verses 10-11. On that annual Day, the slain animals (the bullock for the priest, the goat for the people), whose **blood** was taken into the **sanctuary** (here particularly the holy of holies), were carried **outside the camp** of Israel and burned in entirety (Lev. 16:27). It was this ritual which was fulfilled so dramatically by Jesus Christ, the true Sin Offering. The author is building to the point that Christ fulfilled the type by suffering "outside the gate," and believers must be willing also to accompany Him "outside the camp."

> *Wherefore Jesus also, that he might sanctify the people through his own blood, suffered outside the gate.* (13:12)

As the animal carcasses were burned outside the camp of Israel (Lev. 16:27), Jesus also experienced something quite similar. He suffered outside the gate of Jerusalem. The analogy was not meant to be

The hill called Golgotha outside the Second Wall is encircled in this picture of the model of ancient Jerusalem, Holyland Hotel, Jerusalem.

pressed, and that may be why the author used the word **suffered** (*epathen*) rather than "died." The Old Testament sin offering was actually slain *within* the tabernacle precincts, and only after its blood was sprinkled on the altar was the carcass carried outside the camp for burning. In the case of Jesus, of course, His death occurred outside the city. The main point in view is the disgrace involved. The burning of the animal carcass outside the camp was not part of a burnt offering ritual, for that would have occurred on the brazen altar. It was rather to picture the removal of sin from Israel, and also the disgraceful character of sin and its repudiation. In the instance of Christ, the author is using the analogy to demonstrate the ignominy of His death.

The mention of Christ's death as occurring **outside the gate** is not stated specifically in any other New Testament passage, although it is certainly a valid inference. Furthermore, the fact was doubtless common knowledge to the author through his contacts with eyewitnesses (2:3). Matthew describes the crucifixion as taking place at Golgotha, a spot reached after "coming out" (*exerchomenoi*), presumably "out" of the city (Matt. 27:32-33). Mark says they were "leading him out" (*exagousin*) to crucify Him, again presumably "out" of the city (Mark 15:20). This conclusion appears warranted from the mention in John that the place of crucifixion was "near the city" (*engus . . . tēs poleōs*), an expression that would not be used if the spot were within the city (John 19:20).

The purpose of Christ's suffering was the fulfilment of the sin offering ritual. It was that **he might sanctify the people.** His purpose was to set them apart to God by removing their guilt, and thus to enable them to have continuing access to God on the basis of forgiveness by expiation. This was accomplished by our Lord through the shedding of **his own blood,** being a means incomparably superior to any animal sacrifice in ancient or contemporary Judaism.

> *Hence let us go out to him outside the camp, bearing his reproach. For we do not have here a continuing city, but we are seeking the one to come.* (13:13, 14)

The author now reverts to the word **camp** rather than "gate," because he wants to emphasize Judaism rather than just Jerusalem. Christ's death outside the city gate was the death of a common criminal, a **reproach** in the eyes of those who observed the scene without any spiritual comprehension. Those who have professed Christ to be their Lord have obligated themselves to follow Him. For Hebrew Christians, that posed some momentous decisions. Jesus had been rejected by Judaism, both literally by crucifixion at the demand of Jewish leaders and symbolically by suffering outside the gate analogous to the sin offering repudiated and burned outside the camp. Were these Jewish Christian readers actually willing to join Jesus outside the camp? Were they willing to accept his reproach as they faced rejection from family, friends, and their religious traditions? The stirring challenge let us go out left them no alternative. The old system had been superseded in the program of God. They must leave the camp of Judaism and come wholeheartedly to an identification of themselves with Christ.

Doubtless the chief culprit in the struggle faced by the readers was the attractiveness of the earthly system which they had known all their lives. Judaism had its physical worship center, its visible priests, its tangible sacrifices, and its ancestral traditions which were not easily cast aside. They must be reminded that all Christians (whether Jewish or Gentile) are strangers and aliens on earth (11:13), and have no continuing city—that is, no permanent associations with organizations that are only earthly. Rather we must be like Abraham and have our gaze fixed on the one to come (11:10, 16). Eternal and spiritual verities must occupy our thoughts and constitute our goal in place of earthly institutions, however honorable may have been their function. The truth enunciated here should be carefully considered by everyone, for whether his background is Judaism or some Gentile religious or cultural system, the call still comes with equal urgency, "Let us go out to him outside the camp."

Through him, therefore, let us offer up a sacrifice of praise continually to God, that is, [the] fruit of lips confessing his name. (13:15)

Through him occupies the emphatic position in this statement, stressing that it is through Christ alone, not through any Levitical mediation, that worshipers truly come to God. No longer are animal sacrifices necessary, but this does not mean that Christians offer no sacrifices at all. On the contrary, the Christian is not limited to a few annual festivals, nor to those times when he may be present at Jerusalem. He may offer to God a sacrifice of praise continually. The sacrifice of praise (*thusian aineseōs*) employs the vocabulary of the Septuagint at Leviticus 7:12, which describes the Old Testament peace offering which was offered when special thanks were to be rendered to God. On such occasions certain items made from meal were added to the animal sacrifice. The author makes it clear, however, that he does not refer to material sacrifices at all, but to spiritual ones. It was the fruit of lips confessing his name that form the kind of sacrifice God was ultimately concerned about. The words proceeding from our lips should be the overflow of what is in our hearts (Matt. 12:34).

This figure fruit of lips is drawn from the Septuagint rendering of Hosea 14:3.[94] The Hebrew Massoretic text, however, has the expression "calves of our lips." The difference is caused apparently by two different ways of dividing the consonants in the Hebrew text, which would yield the two words in question.[95] The Massoretic text we now possess has done it one way. The Septuagint may be based upon a Hebrew text which did it differently. It is also possible that the Septuagint was intended to be a paraphrase interpreting the Hebrew "calves." Whatever may have caused the Septuagint to translate as "fruit," the point of the passage is clear. God is primarily interested not in calves slain upon material altars, but in "calves of our lips"; that is, the spiritual sacrifice of lips devoted to the acknowledgment of God and the praise of Him. And of course, the words of praise spoken by human lips are the product or fruit of the heart.

> *But do not forget the doing of good and sharing, for with such sacrifices God is well pleased.* (13:16)

Believers are also held accountable to God for showing benevolence to others. The doing of good translates a Greek term used only here in the New Testament (*eupoiias*). Sharing is the rendering of *koinōnias*, a word used frequently in various senses drawn from the basic idea of participation or community. The meaning can be the general one of "fellowship" or the more restricted sense of "sharing," "contribution," or "gift." In this instance some sort of practical sharing of goods seems warranted. Hence three kinds of Christian sacrifices have been mentioned: praise to God (v. 15), doing good, and sharing with others. The

---

94. In the English Bible it appears as Hosea 14:2.
95. See F. F. Bruce, *The Epistle to the Hebrews,* p. 405, n. 90.

exhortation is that every Christian should be continually offering all such sacrifices. No one can legitimately conclude that God is well served if praises alone are offered. As John stated it, "But whoso hath this world's good, and seeth his brother have need, and shutteth up his bowels of compassion from him, how dwelleth the love of God in him?" (I John 3:17). It may be unduly restrictive, however, to limit *koinōnia* to the sharing of material goods. There are many ways in which Christians fellowship with one another. Sharing of experiences, encouraging one another in suffering or discouragement or temptation—all of these and countless other situations are opportunities for the Christian virtue of sharing to be exercised.

God is well pleased with such displays of spiritual vitality. No believer must feel that the absence of the Levitical ritual (or any other kind) renders spiritual sacrifices inadequate. True worship proceeds from the human spirit, made alive by the regenerating work of God (John 4:23, 24).

> *Be obedient to your leaders and submit, for they are watching over your souls as ones who will give account, that they may do this with joy and not while groaning, for this is unprofitable for you.* (13:17)

The last of the author's exhortations regarding religious duties reminded the readers of their need to obey their spiritual leaders. As verse 7 spoke of remembering former leaders, this passage commands obedience to present ones. Sometimes the former is easier than the latter. Be obedient (*peithesthe*) denotes assenting to another's direction. Submit (*hupeikete*) involves yielding one's contrary opinions in favor of someone else's. It is apparent that the author has confidence that their leaders are fully reliable and are in no sense responsible for the wavering attitude among some of the readers. It was their official task to be watching over the souls of the Christians in the congregation. Watching (*agrupnousin*) denotes wakefulness and alertness. As shepherds must remain awake and alert to care for their feeblest sheep, so these pastors were likewise exercising great care. Their task was actually a stewardship for which they must someday give account at the judgment seat of Christ. These words serve also as a solemn reminder to the leaders of the awesome responsibility which is theirs.

The purpose clause that they may do this with joy and not while groaning should probably be construed with "watching over your souls" rather than with "give account." The present tense of the subjunctive form *poiōsin* (**may do**) emphasizes continuing activity, and this is more appropriate for the leaders' performance of their ministries than of their appearance at the judgment. The response of a congregation can make a great difference in the enjoyment of the pastor. Parishioners who are spiritually sluggish, or rebellious, or who lack the vision to move forward in the exercise of their Christian privileges, or who become enamored with every doctrinal innovation promoted by some spellbinding advocate, cause much heartache to those charged with their spiritual care.

For this is unprofitable for you. Recalcitrant church members may cause their pastors to groan over their rebellion, but the rebels themselves will finally do more than groan. **Unprofitable** (*alusiteles*) is an example of litotes or understatement, a rhetorical device which often heightens the effect of the point being made. There will not only be the absence of any spiritual profit when they stand before Christ, but there may be actual loss (I Cor. 3:13-15; II Cor. 5:10). Of course, if some show by subsequent apostasy that they had never been saved at all, their unprofitableness will be an eternal perishing.

PART III

Personal Instructions

13:18-25

The final portion of the epistle consists of a series of personal requests, admonitions, and information, along with a concluding greeting and benediction.

A. A REQUEST FOR PRAYER. (13:18, 19)

Pray for us, for we are persuaded that we have a good conscience, in all things wishing to conduct ourselves well. And I beseech [you] *much more to do this, that I may be restored to you more quickly.* (13:18, 19)

Is the us a true plural referring to the author and his associates, or the author and their leaders, or is it a literary plural that refers only to the author? It seems most unlikely that the author would mix the plurals "us" and "we" with the singular "I" in adjacent sentences if he really meant himself alone in all of these references. Thus a true plural is in order. Inasmuch as the leaders of the church being addressed are mentioned in the third person in verse 17, it is not so likely that they are to be understood as included in the first person us in verse 18. It is best, therefore, to regard us as meaning the author and whatever associates were with him.

This request for prayer makes it clear that the identity of the author was no secret to the readers, though his name is not known with certainty to us. The basis for their praying was the integrity of the author and his companions. They have a **good conscience**, one which operated in the light of God's truth and was not accusing because of false conduct. Their activity had always been honorable, and their motives—wishing to conduct ourselves well—were also above reproach. The statement may reflect some false accusations in circulation, although we cannot be sure of their nature. Perhaps the author is thinking of some of his severe statements in the epistle (with which his associates concurred), but is convinced that truth was being served by them.

Prayer for the author—I—is especially needed that he may be restored to the readers' presence more quickly. This implies a former presence with them; but whether his absence was due to imprisonment, illness, or something else is unknown to us.

B. A PRAYER FOR THE READERS. (13:20, 21)

Now the God of peace, who brought up from the dead the great Shepherd of the sheep, our Lord Jesus, through the blood of an eternal covenant, may he equip you in every good thing to do his will, doing in us what is well pleasing in his sight through Jesus Christ, to whom [belongs] *the glory forever and ever. Amen.* (13:20, 21)

The God of peace is an expression used six[1] other times in the New Testament, always by Paul (Rom. 15:33; 16:20; I Cor. 14:33; II Cor. 13:11; Phil. 4:9; I Thess. 5:23). It is tempting to imagine that the author is thinking particularly of the discord among his readers, and utilizes this title somewhat pointedly, especially since all the other New Testament occurrences appear in contexts where some sort of difficulty existed among the readers. It is true, however, that this designation of God connotes a blessed truth relevant to everyone, not just those engaged in strife. He is the God of peace who ministers to every sin troubled heart that turns to Him in faith.

---

1. A similar expression, "the Lord of peace," occurs in II Thess. 3:16.

In this prayer occurs the only explicit mention of Christ's resurrection in the epistle, although it may be implied in 5:7 and in the passages that mention His present exaltation. Delitzsch comments:

> In other places his glance, passing over all the intervening stages, turns forthwith from the depth of our Lord's humiliation to the highest pinnacle of His exaltation. He is here induced to make mention of the event intermediate between Golgotha and God's throne, between the altar of the cross and the holiest of holies—the resurrection of Him who died as a sin-offering for us.[2]

The language and figure may have been suggested to the author by Isaiah 63:11, "Where is he that brought them up out of the sea with the shepherd of his flock?" This was rendered in the Septuagint, "And he who brought up out of the earth the shepherd of the sheep remembered the days of old."[3] In the context Moses appears to be the shepherd. In Hebrews the author regards Moses' being brought up by God out of the sea (or earth) as illustrative of God's raising up Jesus in resurrection. Jesus, however, is the great Shepherd, far superior to Moses (see 3:1-6). This figure of Messiah as the shepherd of God's sheep is frequent in both Old Testament and New Testament (Ps. 23; Isa. 40:11; Ezek. 34:23; John 10:11; I Peter 2:25; 5:4).

Through the blood of an eternal covenant is connected in thought with who brought up. It was the efficacy of Christ's blood sacrificed for sin at the cross that made possible the resurrection. God's justice was fully satisfied because the penalty (death) was paid in full. The resurrection clearly demonstrated this blessed fact. This covenant is, of course, the new covenant discussed in 8:6-13 and 9:15—10:18. It is eternal in the sense that it secures eternal life for its beneficiaries and will never be invalidated nor superseded.

May he equip you is a reminder that the successful Christian life is the result of God's action upon us. Equip (*katartisai*) denotes putting in order, mending, restoring, or preparing. Only when God equips believers are they really qualified to perform every good thing which their Christian commitment requires. The doing of God's will, the highest ideal of human life and the duty of every person, is made possible by

---

2. Franz Delitzsch, *Commentary on the Epistle to the Hebrews,* II, 399.
3. This translation is based upon Alfred Rahlfs' edition of the Septuagint, 1950. A variant replaces "earth" with "sea" in the Vaticanus manuscript, thus conforming to the Massoretic text.

God's doing in us what is required. He does not require the impossible. God has made full provision for victorious living for every person who will submit himself to God's control. The life which is **well-pleasing in his sight** must utilize the mediatorship of Jesus Christ, however, for it is not through the ceremonies of the Old Testament system that men may establish a true relationship with God.

The doxology **to whom** [belongs] **the glory forever and ever** can be understood either of the Father (the subject of the sentence) or Christ (the nearest antecedent). The emphasis in the epistle upon Christ's perfect mediation makes the ascription of this praise to Him especially appropriate.

C. AN EXHORTATION TO HEED THE EPISTLE. (13:22)

Now I exhort you, brethren, bear with the word of exhortation, for indeed I have written to you briefly. (13:22)

The author is well aware of the forceful way he has dealt with certain issues, and that not all of the readers will immediately respond approvingly. Therefore he urges that his **word of exhortation** to remain unwavering in their faith not be set aside. His reference is not restricted to the words immediately preceding, but includes the entire epistle which has taken the form of an appeal or exhortation to stand firm in their commitment to Christ, and to sever their ties with Jewish ceremonialism. He wants them to **bear with** (*anechesthe*) his message, and not be like those who refused to "bear with" healthful doctrine (II Tim. 4:3, same word). Even though an unconvinced reader might think the treatise was long, the author had really written **briefly** in view of the momentous issues under discussion.

D. INFORMATION ABOUT TIMOTHY. (13:23)

Know ye that our brother Timothy has been released, with whom if he comes soon, I will see you. (13:23)

Ginōskete can be either indicative ("ye know") or imperative ("know ye"). It is more likely imperative here, presenting new information about **Timothy**. If it were indicative, it is difficult to understand why the statement would be made at all, inasmuch as it would be adding nothing to what they already knew. Released implies a release from some imprisonment, although the circumstances are completely unknown to us. On the assumption that Timothy is the well-known associate of Paul (and it is doubtful whether anyone else would be referred to without additional identification), he would have been a prominent figure in the early church, known at Rome (where he was present when Paul wrote Philippians) as well as in Greece, Asia Minor, and Palestine. Timothy's release had already occurred, but he was not now with the author. It was hoped that the two could make a joint visit to these readers. The implication is also clear that the author himself was not a prisoner at this time, inasmuch as his visit hinges on Timothy's coming, not on his own release from custody.

E. FINAL GREETINGS AND BENEDICTION. (13:24, 25)

Greet all your leaders and all the saints. Those from Italy
greet you. The grace [be] *with you all.* (13:24, 25)

The epistle would be delivered to one or a few of the leaders, and they in turn are asked to **greet all your leaders**, as well as **all the saints**—that is, the rest of the Christians making up the Hebrew Christian readership of this letter. Greetings are also sent by the author from some of his associates who are described as **those from Italy** (*hoi apo tēs Italias*). This has been utilized in the interests of determining the author's location at the time of writing. It can be explained as meaning those in Italy where the author was. Or one might interpret it as meaning those of Italian descent who were away from Italy with the author, and who send their greetings back home. The fact is that this phrase is not determinative for either position. It is used in Acts 10:23 (*apo Ioppēs*) to name those from Joppa who were still in Joppa, and in Acts 17:13 (*apo tēs Thessalonikēs*) to describe residents of Thessalonica who were still there. On the other hand, the phrase appears in Acts 21:27 (*apo tēs Asias*) to denote those from Asia who were visiting in Jerusalem. It should be clear that the phrase itself indicates nothing about present residence; it merely identifies their origin. **Those from Italy** means "Italians." Where they happened to be at this moment cannot be ascertained, except to say that they were with the author. They probably were acquainted with at least some of the readers or else had been informed about them sufficiently to have developed a sincere Christian interest in their spiritual welfare.

The epistle closes with the simple benediction the grace [be] with you all. The definite article with grace particularizes the reference as denoting the grace of God given to men in Christ. It was this grace which really covered all that the writer was trying to say. When the readers came to appreciate fully what matchless grace had been provided in Christ, the attractions of types and shadows would fade away. Let us hope that the epistle succeeded with its first readers. And let us make certain that its purpose has been accomplished in us.

Bibliography

Aland, Kurt; Black, Matthew; Metzger, Bruce M; and Wikgren, Allen, eds. *The Greek New Testament.* London: United Bible Societies, 1966.

Alford, Henry. *The New Testament for English Readers.* Reprint. Chicago: Moody Press, n.d.

Allis, Oswald T. *Prophecy and the Church.* Philadelphia: Presbyterian and Reformed Publishing Co., 1945.

Archer, Gleason L., Jr. *The Epistle to the Hebrews,* in the Shield Bible Study Series. Grand Rapids: Baker Book House, 1957.

Arndt, William F., and Gingrich, F. Wilbur. *A Greek-English Lexicon of the New Testament.* Chicago: University of Chicago Press, 1957.

Barker, Glenn W.; Lane, William L.; and Michaels, J. Ramsey. *The New Testament Speaks.* New York: Harper & Row, Publishers, 1969.

Barmby, James. "Hebrews," in *The Pulpit Commentary.* New York: Funk & Wagnalls Co., n.d.

Bartlet, J. Vernon. "Barnabas and His Genuine Epistle," in *The Expositor,* Sixth Series, Vol. 5. Edited by W. Robertson Nicoll. London: Hodder & Stoughton, 1902.

Brooks, Walter Edward. "The Perpetuity of Christ's Sacrifice in the Epistle to the Hebrews," *Journal of Biblical Literature,* Vol. 89, Part 2 (June 1970).

Bruce, Alexander Balmain. *The Epistle to the Hebrews.* Edinburgh: T. & T. Clark, 1908.

Bruce, F. F. *"The Epistle to the Hebrews,"* in The New International Commentary on the New Testament. Grand Rapids: Wm. B. Eerdmans Publishing Co., 1964.

———. "The Kerugma of Hebrews," *Interpretation,* Vol. 23, No. 1 (January 1969).

———. " 'To the Hebrews' or 'To the Essenes'?", *New Testament Studies,* Vol. 9, No. 3 (April 1963).

Calvin, John. *Commentaries on the Epistle of Paul the Apostle to the Hebrews.* Translated by John Owen. Reprint. Grand Rapids: Wm. B. Eerdmans Publishing Co., 1948.

Carlston, Charles Edwin. "Eschatology and Repentance in the Epistle to the Hebrews," *Journal of Biblical Literature,* Vol. 78, Part 4 (December 1959).

Casson, Lionel. *Ancient Egypt.* New York: Time, Inc., 1965.

Chadwick, G. A. *The Epistle to the Hebrews.* London: The Religious Tract Society, n.d.

Chafer, Lewis Sperry. *Systematic Theology.* Dallas: Dallas Seminary Press, 1948.

Charles, R. H., ed. *The Apocrypha and Pseudepigrapha of the Old Testament in English.* Oxford: Clarendon Press, 1913.

Cody, Dom Aelred. "Hebrews," in *A New Catholic Commentary on Holy Scripture.* Edited by Reginald C. Fuller. London: Thomas Nelson and Sons, Ltd., 1969.

Dale, R. W. *The Jewish Temple and the Christian Church.* London: Hodder and Stoughton, 1872.

Daniel-Rops, Henri. *Daily Life in Palestine at the Time of Christ.* Translated by Patrick O'Brian. London: Weidenfeld and Nicolson, 1962.

Darby, J. N. *Synopsis of the Books of the Bible,* Volume 5. Revised ed. New York: Loizeaux Brothers, Publishers, 1942.

Davidson, A. B. *The Epistle to the Hebrews.* Edinburgh: T. & T. Clark, n.d.

Davidson, F., ed. *New Bible Commentary.* Grand Rapids: Wm. B. Eerdmans Publishing Co., 1958.

Davis, John J. *Conquest and Crisis.* Grand Rapids: Baker Book House, 1969.

———. *The Birth of a Kingdom.* Grand Rapids: Baker Book House, 1970.

———. *Moses and the Gods of Egypt.* Grand Rapids: Baker Book House, 1972.

DeArmey, Richard Paul. "We Have an Altar, Whereof They Have No Right to Eat Which Serve the Tabernacle." Unpublished monograph, Grace Theological Seminary, 1953.

Delitzsch, Franz. *Commentary on the Epistle to the Hebrews.* Edinburgh: T. & T. Clark, 1870.

Dods, Marcus. "The Epistle to the Hebrews," in *The Expositor's Greek Testament.* Vol. 4. Edited by W. Robertson Nicoll. Reprint. Grand Rapids: Wm. B. Eerdmans Publishing Co., n.d.

Downer, A. C. *The Principle of Interpretation of the Epistle to the Hebrews.* London: Charles Murray, n.d.

Eusebius Pamphili *Ecclesiastical History.* Translated by Roy J. Deferrari in *The Fathers of the Church.* Washington, D.C.: The Catholic University of America Press, 1953. Reprinted 1969.

Farrar, F. W. *The Epistle of Paul the Apostle to the Hebrews,* in The Cambridge Bible for Schools and Colleges. Cambridge: University Press, 1883.

Feine, Paul; Behm, Johannes; and Kümmel, Werner G. *Introduction to the New Testament.* Translated by A. J. Mattill, Jr. Nashville: Abingdon Press, 1966.

Freeman, Hobart E. "The Problem of the Efficacy of Old Testament Sacrifices," *Bulletin of the Evangelical Theological Society,* Vol. 5, No. 3 (Summer 1962).

Gibbons, James Cardinal. *The Faith of Our Fathers.* Baltimore: John Murphy Company, 1905.

Gregory, Caspar René. *Canon and Text of the New Testament.* Edinburgh: T. & T. Clark, 1907.

Griffith, Thomas, W. H. *Hebrews, A Devotional Commentary.* Reprint. Grand Rapids: Wm. B. Eerdmans Publishing Co., n.d.

Guthrie, Donald. *New Testament Introduction: Hebrews to Revelation.* Chicago: Inter-Varsity Press, 1962.

Harrison, Everett F. *Introduction to the New Testament.* Grand Rapids: Wm. B. Eerdmans Publishing Co., 1964.

————. "The Theology of the Epistle to the Hebrews," *Bibliotheca Sacra.* Vol. 121, No. 484 (October 1964).

Hefele, Charles Joseph. *A History of the Councils of the Church.* Edinburgh: T. & T. Clark, 1876.

Hewitt, Thomas. *The Epistle to the Hebrews,* in The Tyndale New Testament Commentaries. Grand Rapids: Wm. B. Eerdmans Publishing Co., 1960.

Howard, W. F. "The Epistle to the Hebrews," *Interpretation,* Vol. 5, No. 1 (January 1951).

Hoyt, Herman A. "The Epistle to the Hebrews." Unpublished course notes, Grace Theological Seminary, 1949.

————. *The Epistle to the Hebrews.* Winona Lake, Ind.: BMH Books, n.d.

Johnson, S. Lewis. "Some Important Mistranslations in Hebrews," *Bibliotheca Sacra.* Vol. 110, No. 437 (January 1953).

Jones, Alexander, ed. The Jerusalem Bible. New York: Doubleday & Co., Inc., 1966.

Josephus *Jewish Antiquities.* Translated by H. St. J. Thackeray, in The Loeb Classical Library. Cambridge: Harvard University Press, 1957.

Justin Martyr "Dialogue with Trypho," in *The Fathers of the Church.* Edited by Thomas B. Falls. Reprinted 1948. Washington, D.C.: The Catholic University of America Press, 1965.

———— "First Apology," in *The Fathers of the Church.* Washington, D.C.: The Catholic University of America Press, 1965.

Kelly, William. *An Exposition of the Epistle to the Hebrews.* London: T. Weston, 1905.

Kilpatrick, G. D., ed. *Hē Kainē Diathēkē.* 2d ed. London: The British and Foreign Bible Society, 1958.

Lake, Kirsopp A., trans. *The Apostolic Fathers,* in The Loeb Classical Library. London: William Heinemann, Ltd., 1912. Reprinted, 1959.

Kitchen, K. A. "Moses," in *New Bible Dictionary.* Edited by J. D. Douglas. Grand Rapids: Wm. B. Eerdmans Publishing Co., 1962.

Kittel, Gerhard, ed. *Theological Dictionary of the New Testament.* Translated by Geoffrey W. Bromiley. Grand Rapids: Wm. B. Eerdmans Publishing Co., 1964-1968.

Lenski, R. C. H. *Interpretation of the Epistle to the Hebrews.* Columbus: The Wartburg Press, 1937.

————. *The Epistle to the Hebrews and The Epistle of James.* Columbus: The Wartburg Press, 1946.

Leonard, William. *The Authorship of the Epistle to the Hebrews.* Vatican Polyglot Press, 1939.

Lindsay, William. *Lectures on the Epistle to the Hebrews.* Philadelphia: Smith, English, and Co., 1867.

Makrakis, Apostolos. *Interpretation of the Entire New Testament.* Chicago: Orthodox Christian Educational Society, 1950.

Manson, William. *The Epistle to the Hebrews*. London: Hodder & Stoughton, Ltd., 1951.

Marchant, G. J. C. "Sacrifice in the Epistle to the Hebrews," *The Evangelical Quarterly,* Vol. 20, No. 3 (July 1948).

Mickelsen, A. Berkeley. "Hebrews," in *The Biblical Expositor*, Vol. 3. Philadelphia: A. J. Holman Co., 1960.

Moffatt, James. *Epistle to the Hebrews,* in The International Critical Commentary Series. New York: Charles Scribner's Sons, 1924.

Moll, Carl Bernhard. "The Epistle to the Hebrews," in *Commentary on the Holy Scriptures*. Edited by John Peter Lange, translated by A. C. Kendrick. Reprint. Grand Rapids: Zondervan Publishing House, n.d.

Morris, H. M., and Whitcomb, J. C. *The Genesis Flood*. Philadelphia: The Presbyterian and Reformed Publishing Co., 1961.

Moulton, James H., and Milligan, George. *The Vocabulary of the Greek Testament*. Grand Rapids: Wm. B. Eerdmans Publishing Co., 1949.

Moulton, James H., and Howard, W. F. *A Grammar of New Testament Greek*. Vol. 2. Edinburgh: T. & T. Clark, 1929.

Moulton, W. F. "The Epistle to the Hebrews," in *Ellicott's Commentary on the Whole Bible*. Edited by Charles John Ellicott. Vol. 8. Grand Rapids: Zondervan Publishing House, n.d.

Moulton, W. F., and Geden, A. S. *A Concordance to the Greek Testament*. Edinburgh: T. & T. Clark, 1950.

Nestle, Eberhard; Nestle, Erwin; and Aland, Kurt, eds. *Novum Testament Graece*. 25th ed. Stuttgart: Wurttembergische Bibelanstalt, 1963.

Newell, William R. *Hebrews Verse by Verse*. Chicago: Moody Press, 1947.

Oehler, Gustav F. *Theology of the Old Testament*. Translated by George E. Day. New York: Funk & Wagnalls, Publishers, 1884.

Orr, James, ed. *International Standard Bible Encyclopedia*. Grand Rapids: Wm. B. Eerdmans Publishing Co., 1939, 1946.

Owen, John. *Exposition of the Epistle to the Hebrews*. London, 1840.

Pentecost, J. Dwight. *Things to Come*. Findlay, Ohio: Dunham Publishing Co., 1958.

Pink, Arthur W. *An Exposition of Hebrews*. Grand Rapids: Baker Book House, 1963.

Price, James L. *Interpreting the New Testament.* New York: Holt, Rinehart, and Winston, 1961.

Purdy, Alexander C., and Cotton, J. Harry. "The Epistle to the Hebrews," in *The Interpreter's Bible.* Edited by George A. Buttrick. New York: Abingdon Press, 1955.

Rahlfs, Alfred, ed. *Septuaginta.* Stuttgart: Privileg. Wurtt. Bibelanstalt, 1950.

Rendell, Robert. "Old Testament Quotations in Hebrews," *The Evangelical Quarterly,* Vol. 27, No. 4 (October 1955).

Roberts, Alexander, and Donaldson, James, eds. *Ante-Nicene Fathers.* Reprint. Wm. B. Eerdmans Publishing Co., 1951.

Robertson, Archibald, and Fremantle, W. H., eds. *Nicene and Post-Nicene Fathers.* Second series. Reprint. Grand Rapids: Wm. B. Eerdmans Publishing Co., 1951.

Robertson, A. T. *A Grammar of the Greek New Testament in the Light of Historical Research.* Nashville: Broadman Press, 1934.

Ross, Robert W. "Hebrews," in *Wycliffe Bible Commentary.* Edited by Charles F. Pfeiffer and Everett F. Harrison. Chicago: Moody Press, 1962.

Rowell, J. B. "Exposition of Hebrews Six," *Bibliotheca Sacra,* Vol. 94, No. 375 (July 1937).

Ryrie, Charles C. *The Basis of the Premillennial Faith.* New York: Loizeaux Brothers, 1953.

————. *Biblical Theology of the New Testament.* Chicago: Moody Press, 1959.

Sandren, C. "The Addressees of the Epistle to the Hebrews," *The Evangelical Quarterly,* Vol. 27, No. 4 (October 1955).

Saphir, Adolph. *The Epistle to the Hebrews.* 7th ed. Grand Rapids: Zondervan Publishing House, 1943.

Schaff, Philip, ed. *Nicene and Post-Nicene Fathers.* First series, Vol. 2. Buffalo, 1887.

Scofield, C. I., ed. *New Scofield Reference Bible.* New York: Oxford University Press, 1967.

Scofield, C. I., ed. *Scofield Reference Bible.* New York: Oxford University Press, 1917.

Selwyn, Edward Gordon. *The First Epistle of St. Peter.* London: Macmillan & Co., Ltd., 1964.

Spicq, C. *L'Épître aux Hebreux.* Paris: J. Gabalda et Cie, Editeurs, 1952.

Stott, Wilfrid. "The Conception of 'Offering' in the Epistle to the Hebrews," *New Testament Studies,* Vol. 9, No. 1 (October 1962).

Suetonius *The Twelve Caesars.* Translated by Robert Graves (Penguin Books). London: Whitefriars Press, Ltd., 1957.

Tenney, Merrill C. "A New Approach to the Book of Hebrews," *Bibliotheca Sacra,* Vol. 123, No. 491 (July 1966).

Thiessen, Henry C. *Introduction to the New Testament.* Grand Rapids: Wm. B. Eerdmans Publishing Co., 1943.

Thomas, Kenneth J. "The Old Testament Citations in Hebrews," *New Testament Studies,* Vol. 11, No. 4 (July 1965).

Walvoord, John F. *The Millennial Kingdom.* Findlay, Ohio: Dunham Publishing Co., 1959.

―――. *The Revelation of Jesus Christ.* Chicago: Moody Press, 1966.

Westcott, Brooke Foss. *The Epistle to the Hebrews.* Reprint. Grand Rapids: Wm. B. Eerdmans Publishing Co., n.d.

―――. *A General Survey of the History of the Canon of the New Testament.* Cambridge: Macmillan & Co., 1855. London, 1875.

Westcott, B. F., and Hort, F. J. A. *The New Testament in the Original Greek.* New York: The Macmillan Co., 1947.

Wilson, Geoffrey B. *Hebrews.* London: The Banner of Truth Trust, 1970.

Wuest, Kenneth S. "Hebrews Six in the Greek New Testament," *Bibliotheca Sacra,* Vol. 119, No. 473 (January 1962).

Young, Robert. *Analytical Concordance to the Bible.* New York: Funk & Wagnalls Company, n.d.

Zahn, Theodor. *Introduction to the New Testament.* Reprint. Grand Rapids: Kregel Publications, 1953.